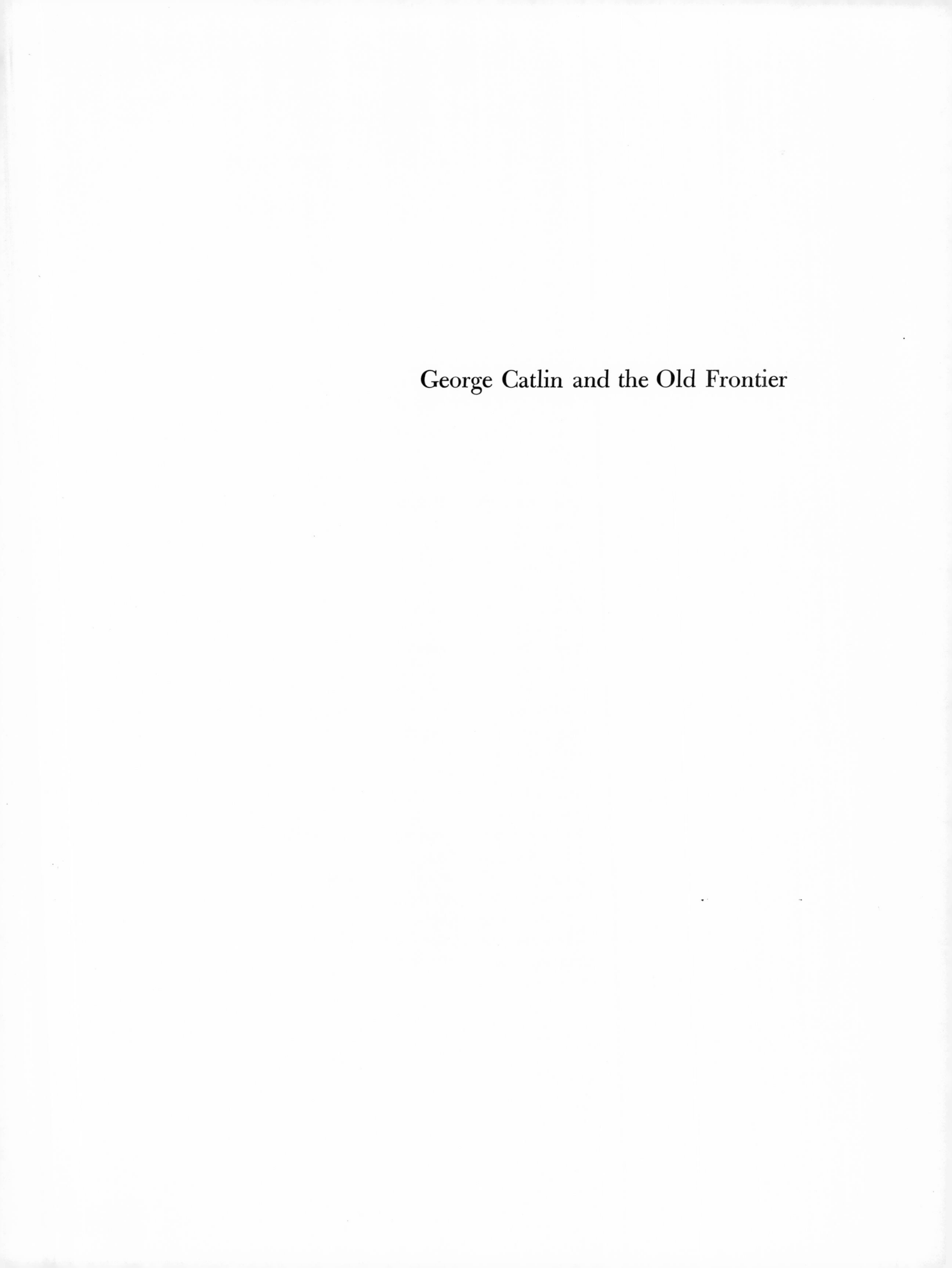

George Catlin and the Old Frontier

Books by Harold McCracken, LITT.D.

IGLAOME
GOD'S FROZEN CHILDREN
PERSHING — THE STORY OF A GREAT SOLDIER
ALASKA BEAR TRAILS
BEYOND THE FROZEN FRONTIER
THE LAST OF THE SEA OTTERS
THE BIGGEST BEAR ON EARTH
SON OF THE WALRUS KING
SENTINEL OF THE SNOW PEAKS
THE GREAT WHITE BUFFALO
FREDERIC REMINGTON — ARTIST OF THE OLD WEST
TRAPPING — THE CRAFT OF CATCHING FUR-BEARING ANIMALS
TOUGHY — BULLDOG IN THE ARCTIC
CARIBOU TRAVELER
THE FLAMING BEAR
PORTRAIT OF THE OLD WEST
PIRATE OF THE NORTH
THE FREDERIC REMINGTON MEMORIAL COLLECTION
WINNING OF THE WEST
THE BEAST THAT WALKS LIKE MAN
HUNTERS OF THE STORMY SEAS
THE STORY OF ALASKA
THE CHARLES M. RUSSELL BOOK
HOOFS, CLAWS AND ANTLERS

National Collection of Fine Arts, Washington, D.C.

GEORGE CATLIN (1796–1872)
by William H. Fisk—1849

George Catlin and the Old Frontier

by Harold McCracken

BONANZA BOOKS · NEW YORK

Library of Congress Catalog Card Number: 59-9434
Manufactured in the U.S.A.
This edition published by Bonanza Books
a division of Crown Publishers, Inc.,
by arrangement with The Dial Press, Inc.
g h i j k l m n o
This book was designed by William R. Meinhardt.

To all the documentary artists
who left to us a realistic portrayal of
the story of the Old West —
and especially to the pioneer
and dean of them all,
George Catlin.

Acknowledgments

It is with deep gratitude that acknowledgment is made to those who in many ways have helped to make this book possible. Particularly to those at the Smithsonian Institution, who have so valuably cooperated and assisted in the obtaining of color and black-and-white photographs of their original collection of the Catlin paintings, and who have otherwise so generously aided and guided this writer in the whole project. F. M. Setzler, John C. Ewers, Robert A. Elder, Jr., S. H. Riesenberg, and Thomas M. Beggs. To Stephen Sears and *American Heritage*, for giving me the benefit and use of their entire file on George Catlin; The American Museum of Natural History, for permission to reproduce selections from their collection of paintings; Brenda R. Gieseker, Librarian, Missouri Historical Society; Bertha L. Heilbron, Editor, *Minnesota History;* Stanley Pargellis, The Newberry Library, Chicago; R. W. G. Vail, Director, New York Historical Society; The New York Public Library, Rare Book Division; E. K. Burnett, Director, Museum of the American Indian; Rudolf Wunderlich, Kennedy Galleries, N.Y.; William Davidson, Knoedler Galleries, N.Y.; John Fleming, The Rosenbach Company; Yale University Library; Peter Decker; George I. Quimby, Chicago Natural History Museum; M. J. Walsh, Goodspeed's Book Shop, Boston; Richard W. Norton, Jr.; The Thomas Gilcrease Institute; The Library of Congress; John Harton, Green-Wood Cemetery; and to the numerous other historical societies, libraries and museums which have so graciously searched and answered my inquiries. Also to Clarkson Potter, my editor; and to Irma and Larry Larom, on whose Valley Ranch, deep in the Rocky Mountains of Wyoming, a large part of this book was written after the long toil of research was completed.

Harold McCracken

Contents

Color Illustrations

Black-and-White Illustrations

Thomas Gilcrease Institute

GEORGE CATLIN, SELF-PORTRAIT, 1824

1

Documentarian of a Primitive Race

Newberry Library, Chicago

CROW CHIEF

GEORGE CATLIN was the first artist of stature to travel our Western Plains for the purpose of making a documentary record of the primitive Indian tribes. Between 1830 and 1836 he visited and became well acquainted with almost all the important tribes, scattered over the vast and still little-known area from the Upper Missouri and the headwaters of the Mississippi to the Mexican Territory in the far Southwest. He made the most comprehensive pictorial record we have of these people in their natural state — portraits of the most notable of their chieftains, warriors, medicine-men and women, as well as pictures of their religious and other tribal ceremonies and dances, pursuits of warfare and hunting, games, amusements, and various other activities. At the same time Catlin compiled a detailed and comprehensive written record to supplement his pictures, which covered nearly every aspect of the Indians' daily lives and ethos. He also gathered together an extensive collection of the finest of their decorated skin garments, ceremonial paraphernalia, weapons, and other ethnological materials.

To accomplish all this he wandered from tribe to tribe, alone and unaided by outside financial assistance — and George Catlin lived and died a poor man. He was received by the Indians with the greatest friendship and their dignitaries posed for their portraits and permitted him access to their most sacred religious ceremonies. Those first six years of travel were, however, only the beginning of the long career which entitles George Catlin to a place of distinction among the most extraordinary men of the nineteenth century.

In reading the Catlin story one should keep in mind that in the 1830's, when he was wandering about with canvas, paints and note books, the region that spread far to the west of the Mississippi River was *terra incognita*. It was then not so many years after the Lewis & Clark Expedition had made its historic journey across the Northwest to the Pacific Coast and the great fur companies were barely beginning to harvest their rich plunder of furs and buffalo hides. Travel was extremely difficult and hazardous, and even the best informed persons knew little about the Plains Indians. The vanguard of traders and trappers were familiar only with their own areas, caring little about anything except how cheaply they could get the largest possible quantity of fur. And, fortunately for Catlin, the Indians knew little or nothing about the white man and what his coming was to mean to their future.

In his own day Catlin was accused of being a sentimentalist, because of the way he felt about the Indians and because of the life-long crusade which he carried on in their behalf.

There are those who even today hold a low opinion of the Indian, for it is only recently that we have broken away from the old popular idea that "the only good Indian is a dead Indian," or, as General Sherman said, as late as August 1882, in trying to justify the military campaigns of subjugation and destruction against the red men, "They are . . . wasteful and hostile occupants of millions of acres of valuable agricultural, pasture and mineral lands."[1] It is now, however, particularly ironic that we Americans, as champions of freedom and democracy for all peoples, should persist in adhering to the ideas of our conquering ancestors. Nearly a hundred years ago we fought a bloody civil war to provide freedom for the negroes — who are as much alien to America as ourselves — and yet the Indians from whom we took the whole vast land which is ours today, have continued to remain the pawns of their invaders. The whole history of the struggle of our race to make this land our own, from the earliest colonial days to the last of the Indian wars in the Dakotas, has usually been written from our own viewpoint or even as a salve to our conscience. What George Catlin wrote in his day was an extremely unpopular viewpoint — truthful though it was:

"I love a people who have always made me welcome to the best they had . . . who are honest without laws, who have no jails and no poor-house . . . who never take the name of God in vain . . . who worship God without a Bible, and I believe that God loves them also . . . who are free from religious animosities . . . who have never raised a hand against me, or stolen my property, where there was no law to punish either . . . who never fought a battle with white men except on their own ground . . . and oh! how I love a people who don't live for the love of money."[2]

New York Historical Society

CATLIN PAINTING MANDAN CHIEF

New York Historical Society

INDIANS ATTACKING GRIZZLY BEARS

Thus did George Catlin declare his opinion of the Indians of the Great Plains of the West, after wandering and living alone among approximately forty-eight tribes, in the days when they were still living in the primitive elegance of their original culture, before the white man's *civilization* had been imposed upon them.

"I have viewed man in the innocent simplicity of nature," he continues, "in the full enjoyment of the luxuries which God has bestowed upon him . . . happier than kings and princes can be, with his pipe and little ones about him . . . I have seen him shrinking from civilized approach, which came with all its vices, like the dead of night, upon him . . . seen him gaze and then retreat like the frightened deer . . . I have seen him shrinking from the soil and haunts of his boyhood, bursting the strongest ties which bound him to the earth and its pleasures. I have seen him set fire to his wigwam and smooth over the graves of his fathers . . . clap his hand in silence over his mouth, and take the last look over his fair hunting ground, and turn his face in sadness to the setting sun. All this I have seen performed in nature's silent dignity . . . and I have seen as often the approach of the bustling, busy, talking, elated, and exultant white man, with the first dip of the plough share, making sacrilegious trespass on the bones of the dead . . . I have seen the grand and irresistible march of civilization . . . this splendid juggernaut rolling on and beheld its sweeping desolation. And I have held converse with the happy thousands, living as yet beyond its influence, who had not been crushed, nor have yet dreamed of its approach. I have stood amidst these unsophisticated people, and contemplated with feelings of deepest regret the certain approach of this overwhelming system which will inevitably march on and prosper; reluctant tears shall have watered every rod of this fair land; and from the towering cliffs of the Rocky Mountains, the luckless savage will turn back his swollen eyes on the illimitable hunting-grounds from which he has fled, and there contemplate, like Caius Marius on the ruins of Carthage, their splendid desolation . . . All this is certain . . . and if he could rise from his grave and speak, or would speak from the life some half century from this, they would proclaim my prophecy true and fulfilled."[3]

The art of George Catlin has for generations been the subject of as strong a controversy as his feelings about the Indians. His paintings have been enthusiastically praised and severely condemned. To some critics his work has seemed romantic; to others it is that of a realist, while still others call it American primitive. The reason for the confusion is that there are many who lose track of the fact that documentary art is an area of art in itself. They overlook the fundamental idea of those artists who devoted their talents to preserving for posterity, in as truthful and meticulous a manner as they could, the important scenes and likenesses of the era and field in which they worked. George Catlin's field was the primitive Indians as they were in their original state, and the truthfulness and accuracy of these portrayals is not only their most important reason for being, but it far outweighs any of their other qualities.

Criticized as Catlin was, he was not without supporters and praise in his own day, and some of the most ardent of these sat in high places. The Hon. Henry Clay said of him, in a letter of introduction to Lord Selkirk, dated July 7, 1838, when the artist took his "Indian Gallery" to London: "Mr. George Catlin . . . has been engaged many years among the various Indian tribes who inhabit this continent, and collected a mass of valuable information touching the habits, usages, and laws, and the state of society among them, surpassing that which was probably ever possessed by any man, or what is to be found in any books." The Hon. Daniel Webster, speaking in the United States Senate in 1849, paid this tribute to Catlin's work: "Their (the Indians) likenesses, manners and customs are portrayed with more accuracy and truth in this collection by Catlin than in all the other drawings and representations on the face of the earth . . . I look upon it as a thing more important to us than the ascertaining of the South Pole, or anything that can be discovered in the Dead Sea, or the River Jordan."

Catlin's work received equal praise from his contemporaries who knew most about the tribes and individual Indians he portrayed. Among these was General Lewis Cass, who for eighteen years was Superintendent of Indian Affairs in the Northwest Territories, had personally negotiated seventeen treaties for peace and the purchase of lands with the same tribes, and who was for more than five years United States Secretary of War. In a letter to the artist dated December 8, 1841, on stationery of the American Embassy in Paris, he wrote: "Your collection (of paintings of the Indians) will preserve them as far as Indian art can do, and will form the most perfect monument of an extinguished race that the world has ever seen." Joseph Henry, Director of the Smithsonian Institution, on December 13, 1873, said about Catlin's paintings: "They will grow in importance with advancing years, and when the race of which they are the representation shall have entirely disappeared, their value will be inestimable."

George Catlin's career was an extraordinary one. The life that he led among so many of the primitive tribes of the Great Plains is unique. Following his period of travel he carried his thesis to the whole civilized world. He took his "Indian Gallery" to New York, Washington and other cities of the East, where he held exhibitions and lectured extensively. Then he went to Europe, where similar exhibitions and lectures were given in London, Paris and elsewhere. Among his European patrons were Queen Victoria, the King and Queen of Belgium and the Czar of Russia. By command of King Louis Philippe, he displayed his entire gallery in the Louvre, Paris. But his personal life and his ultimate hopes were plagued by tragedy and mis-

Smithsonian Institution

WUN-NEE-TOW, The White Buffalo
Blackfoot Medicine Man

fortune. He sacrificed everything to his singular purpose and when nearest to success, he lost everything that he owned and held dearest to his heart.

George Catlin was a thin, wiry man, about 5′8″ in height and weighing in the neighborhood of 135 pounds. He was of dark complexion, and with his black hair, this gave him the appearance of having Indian blood in his veins, although his eyes were blue. A long scar ran down his left cheek, the result of a blow from an Indian tomahawk that glanced off a tree when thrown by a boyhood playmate, while "playing Indians" at ten years of age. In his daily habits he was extremely abstemious, even in the use of tobacco; he was as moral as he was religious; and he had a particularly warm and charming personality. He was repeatedly the victim of malice because of his outspokenness about the treatment of the Indians which put him far in advance of his contemporaries. Although the truthfulness of his most important observations were publicly challenged by scientists who were themselves unfamiliar with the real facts, he patiently restrained his pen and his tongue. Modesty, charity, understatement and complete divorcement from all matters which might be personal stand out most clearly in the story of his career. He became deaf at fifty, and died at the venerable age of 77, destitute and completely frustrated in all the aims to which he had devoted his life.

No individual who has made so great a contribution, and who has been so great an influence on Western art, literature and history has waited so long for recognition as has George Catlin.

New York Public Library

A CROW CHIEF ON HORSEBACK

Smithsonian Institution

KEE-O-KUK On Horseback

American Museum of Natural History

KONZA WARRIORS, WOMAN AND CHILD

Smithsonian Institution

KEE-O-KUK, The Running Fox
Chief of the Sauk and Foxes

Newberry Library, Chicago

RED JACKET

2

Destiny Beyond the Mississippi

GEORGE CATLIN'S family background was deeply rooted in the earliest traditions of frontier life and Indian lore. He was born at Wilkes-Barre, Pennsylvania, July 26, 1796. Two brothers and two sisters had come before him, and nine more were to follow. His father, Putnam Catlin, was born at Litchfield, Connecticut, April 5, 1764. At the age of thirteen, Putnam enlisted in the Revolutionary Army and became the regimental fife-major of the Second Connecticut Regiment, in which his own father, Eli Catlin, began his service on the same day as a lieutenant. That was in January, 1777. Both served eight years. The youthful fife-major received a "badge of merit" and his discharge papers were signed twice by Washington. Long before all this, George's great-great-great-grandfather, Thomas Catlin, had come to America and in 1644 was a resident of Hartford.

George's mother was Polly Sutton, born in Luzerne County, Pennsylvania, September 30, 1770, the daughter of early settlers in the Wyoming Valley. Her father fought against Indians during the famous "Wyoming Massacre" of July, 1778, and was one of the very few who escaped alive. Polly was seven years old at the time, and with her mother was captured by the Indians. She was subsequently released.

After the Revolutionary War, Putnam Catlin returned to Litchfield and studied law. In 1789, when twenty-five years old, he went to Wilkes-Barre to establish himself in his profession. That same year he met and married Polly Sutton. They had five children in the first six years and he was as successful at law as he was in raising a family. An extremely cultured man, he was well-read in the classics, sciences and arts. Poor health caused him to quit his profession, and in 1797 Putnam Catlin moved his family to a farm about forty miles from town. His wife carried the infant George in her arms as she rode a horse over an Indian trail through the wooded hills to their new home on the bank of the Susquehanna River.

In later life George Catlin had this to say about his parents: "My mother was a Methodist, and a devoted Christian, and my father was a philosopher, professing no particular creed but keeping and teaching the Commandments."

Making a home and providing for a large family from a farm in the forest was no small struggle for a man and his wife around 1800. Nevertheless, the Catlin home was one in which the reading of good books went along with the evening prayers. As George grew up, the surrounding forest with its variety of game and the streams with their abundance of fish provided a happy hunting ground for a boy with such strong interests in nature; and, too, the lore and legend of the country fired his fertile imagination. Not only did his mother spend long hours reading to him, but her stories of the Wyoming Massacre and her capture by the Indians established in the boy an everlasting interest in the primitive red man. Then too, the Susquehanna Valley was a much used trail to the West, and Putnam Catlin's hospitality made their modest house a frequent stopping place for other Revolutionary veterans, Indian fighters, trappers, hunters and explorers, bound for or returning from enchanting scenes of adventure far out on the Ohio and the magic Mississippi. As George grew old enough to rig a simple fishing pole and carry a gun he became far more interested in emulating Daniel Boone than in the digesting of dry school books, and he dreamed of the day when he too would follow the trails into the West. As he put it (in later life): "The early part of my life was whiled away, apparently somewhat in vain, with books reluctantly held in one hand, and a rifle or fishing pole firmly and affectionately grasped in the other."

Putnam Catlin and his wife had their own ideas of what George's future should be. As he had a keen memory they felt he should become a lawyer as his father had been. To this end they saved money and in 1817, when George was twenty-one, they sent him to study in the law school of Reeves and Gould at his father's birthplace in Litchfield, Connecticut. Although he disliked the routine curriculum, he had a penchant for reading about subjects which particularly interested him — Indians, natural history, science and the arts — not unlike his father, who was apparently a walking encyclopedia on the most notable of 15th and 16th century European artists. This may have been one of the most important influences in young George Catlin's life, for while art was merely a side-line, he had taken to it with growing seriousness and had begun dabbling in drawing and sketching. By the time he arrived at a school he was well-read and had developed a natural proficiency in drawing and painting which had already gained considerable attention among his friends.

He returned to Pennsylvania in less than two years and began practicing law in the courts of Luzerne County. The mediocre success he made was not caused by inefficiency. Later in life he gave his own explanation: "During this time [while practicing law from 1820 to 1823], another and stronger passion was getting the advantage of me, that of painting, to which all my pleading soon gave way; and after having covered nearly every inch of the lawyer's table (and even encroached upon the judge's bench) with penknife, pen and ink, and pencil sketches of judges, jurors, and culprits, I very deliberately resolved to convert my law library into paint pots and brushes, and to pursue painting as my future, and apparently more agreeable profession."[5]

There is a considerable amount of contradictory information about George Catlin and his work. As Thomas Donaldson points out at the beginning of his voluminous and annotated catalogue of *The George Catlin Gallery* (Smithsonian . . . 1886): "Surely no man who has done so much ever left so little personal data behind him; he seemed to have entirely sunk self in his work." Possibly this is a worthy example of modesty in a man of great accomplishment. Whether Catlin quit the practice of law in 1821, as the evidence produced by other researchers has indicated, or in 1823 as he himself states, is relatively unimportant—as are many of the other contradictions in the record.

By 1821 he had gained something of a local reputation as an amateur portrait painter. On March 26th of that year his father wrote him the following letter addressed from the family farm: "My dear George . . . I am pleased that you have at length resolved to attempt portraits, though you had convinced me last fall that miniatures were as valuable. Most painters of eminence have worked at portraits and history . . . To convince you that I sometimes think of you and your art, I have set down the names of the Artists in your line . . .

Smithsonian Institution

CLARA GREGORY CATLIN
Wife of the Artist
Miniature on Ivory, by George Catlin

of whose works you will read, they were chiefly of the 15th and 16th centuries . . ." Thereafter follows a remarkably concise and comprehensive catalogue of the most important of the early European artists, covering four large pages and set down in minute and fine handwriting, listing the best names from Michelangelo to Giorgio Vasari and Leonardo da Vinci. The long and very painstakingly prepared letter ends with the salutation, "God bless you and preserve you. Your P. Catlin."[6]

Although George had had no formal training in art, and very meagre funds, he went to Philadelphia in 1823 with the determination to make painting his life's profession. What he lacked in formal training was more than over-balanced by his natural talent and by a magnetic personality which always won him warm friendships among the most intellectual and prominent persons with whom he came in contact. Almost immediately he was admitted to the comradeship of such distinguished Philadelphia artists as Thomas Sully, John Neagle, Charles Willson and Rembrandt Peale and others. He was not only fortunate in making friendships with the right people, but in keeping them with mutual devotion and respect. Throughout his life, he was counted a most stimulating friend by many of the most notable statesmen and scientists of the period. When he went to Europe he was received into the company of Queen Victoria, King Philippe of France and the King and Queen of Belgium. His normal state of financial insecurity made little difference to his intimates.

It is apparent, and quite naturally so, that he had submitted miniature paintings on ivory for the consideration of the Philadelphia Academy of Art some time before he went to that city to give art his undivided attention. He worked with intense determination. That his progress was remarkably rapid is confirmed by a formal letter which he received shortly after abandoning the courtrooms of Wilkes-Barre. The letter was dated Philadelphia,

February 18th, 1824, and is given here in full: "At a Special Meeting of the President and Directors of the Pennsylvania Academy, which was held this Evening, The Election of Mr. G. Catlin as a Pennsylvania Academician was submitted to the Board for Confirmation and the same was duly approved and confirmed. [Signed] Francis Hopkinson, Sec'y."[7]

This acknowledgement seemed to assure him a profitable future as a portrait painter of the elite and wealthy. George Catlin was not content with such a prosaic future. There is no better way to tell how he found the inspiration for his life's work than in his own words: "My mind was continually reaching for some branch or enterprise of the arts, on which to devote a whole life-time of enthusiasm; when a delegation of some ten or fifteen noble and dignified-looking Indians, from the wilds of the 'Far West,' suddenly arrived in the city, arrayed in all their classic beauty—with shield and helmet—with tunic and manteau—tinted and tassled off, exactly for the painter's palette! In silent and stoic dignity, these lords of the forest strutted about the city for a few days, wrapped in their pictorial robes, with their brows plumed with the quills of the war-eagle, attracting the attention of all who beheld them. After this they took their leave for Washington City, and I was left to reflect and regret, which I did long and deeply, until I came to the following deductions and conclusions . . . Man, in the simplicity and loftiness of his nature, unrestrained and unfettered by the disguises of art, is surely the most beautiful model for the painter—and the country from which he hails is unquestionably the best study or school of the arts in the world . . . And the history and customs of such a people, preserved by pictorial illustrations, are themes worthy the life-time of one man, and nothing short of the loss of my life shall prevent me from visiting their country, and becoming their historian . . . I set out on my arduous and perilous undertaking with the determination of reaching, ultimately, every tribe of Indians on the Continent of North America, and of bringing home faithful portraits of their principal personages, and full notes of their character and history. I designed, also, to procure their costumes, and a complete collection of their manufactures and weapons, and to perpetuate them in a *gallery unique*, for the use and instruction of future ages."[8]

George Catlin fulfilled that self-determined goal, though he little realized, at the time he chose it, what a high price he would pay in pain, sorrow and ultimate disappointment.

Financially unable to undertake an expedition into the little-known regions of the West beyond the Mississippi, he continued to do portrait work. In December, 1824—the same year he was made an Academician — he was in Albany, New York, painting a miniature portrait on ivory of His Excellency, Governor De Witt Clinton.[9] This was the first of at least three portraits which Catlin painted of the Governor (see page 26) who became perhaps the most important friend in the artist's early career. De Witt Clinton was a very influential person. He was at the time beginning a second term as Governor of the State of New York (1817–'22 and 1824–'27). He was leader of the Republican Party in New York and in 1812 had been chosen as the candidate for President of the United States, but was defeated by James Madison who was running for re-election. He was a founder and the first president of the Literary and Philosophical Society of New York and a dominant figure in the American Academy of Fine Arts. He was involved in the construction of the Erie Canal. One of Catlin's very remunerative commissions of this period was a series of pictures commemorating the building of the Erie Canal.[10] Through the same patronage Catlin also met William Leete Stone (1792–1844), the influential editor of the *New York Commercial Advertiser*, in which Catlin's "Letters from the Upper Missouri" were later published. Stone was a kindred spirit — deeply interested in Indian lore and later the author of such books as *Life of Joseph Brandt* (1838) and *Life and Times of Red Jacket* (1841).

On May 3, 1826, Catlin was elected an Academician of the National Academy,[11] which was at that time known as the Academy of Fine Arts. Now his future seemed doubly assured. But he had not lost his determination to become the pictorial historian of the Indians of the West. In spite of the rapidly increasing number of commissions for portraits by distinguished and wealthy men, he began making trips to the Indian reservations of Western New York. This was something of a compromise, but it fired his desire to see the more primitive tribes beyond the Mississippi. Probably his earliest known Indian subject is a presumably unfinished portrait of the famous Seneca orator, Red Jacket, signed and dated at Buffalo, 1826. This picture is today in the museum of the Thomas Gilcrease Foundation in Tulsa, Oklahoma.

R. W. Norton Foundation

GENERAL SAM HOUSTON
Miniature on Ivory

For George Catlin it now became a struggle between the desire to fulfill a great inspiration which urged him toward a unique and creative career which would be full of difficulties, dangers and very slight rewards, and a career of ease, luxury and rich rewards in painting the portraits of urbane gentlemen.

George's brother Julius, eight years younger than himself, had been very close to him and shared the dream of painting Indians in the West. Together they had enlarged the plan to include the collecting of all sorts of ethnological materials and specimens of natural history and geology. They hoped to create a great museum which George Catlin would head. Julius had gone to West Point and George frequently visited him there. Two of George's earliest published prints were made from scenes he painted of the Military Academy on the Hudson.[12] The brother was graduated in 1824 as a second lieutenant and assigned to the First U.S. Infantry to be stationed at Cantonment Gibson, on the western frontier in Arkansas. Being in the West, Julius fully realized the possibilities of George's ideas, and resigned on September 8, 1826, in order to go to New York and encourage George in the Western project.[13] But the young artist had accepted so many commitments for portraits that he could not readily get away. In a letter from Utica, January 7, 1827, addressed to Wm. L. Stone, Editor of the *New York Commercial Advertiser*, the artist wrote: "I have had within the last year more orders [for portraits] than I could handle, but I have refused all of them, as I have more of my own orders than I can attend to for a long time to come . . . [Signed] Geo. Catlin."[14]

The busy painter traveled from city to city, for his portraits were invariably painted from life; but he managed to spend considerable time in Albany, where he was frequently a guest at the Governor's mansion. At one of the elegant parties there he had met a beautiful

The New York Historical Society

DeWITT CLINTON
Governor of New York

James Graham & Sons

OLIVER WOLCOTT
U.S. Secretary of the Treasury

young lady, Miss Clara Bartlett Gregory, (page 23) sister of the wealthy and prominent Hon. Dudley S. Gregory of Jersey City, New Jersey. She completely captivated his heart, and the courtship which followed led to their marriage on the evening of Saturday, May 10, 1828, in Albany's St. Peter's Episcopal Church.[15] He was thirty-two and Clara was only twenty. This union was destined to have its wonderful interludes of happiness and children, although it was also doomed to tragedy that haunted George Catlin to the end of his days.

After the marriage George spent more time in Albany. The Franklin Institute of Rochester, New York, had ordered a copy of one of his portraits of Governor Clinton. When it was finished, in September of the year George was married, he sent his brother Julius to make the delivery. While in Rochester Julius joined a group for a swim in the river north of the city, and was drowned. This first of a series of bitter tragedies in the life of George only increased his drive to fulfill the dreams which he and Julius had built together.

He made more trips to paint nearby reservation Indians — the Senecas, Oneidas, and Tuscaroras, and also the Ottawas and Mohegans. At Red Jacket's request, Catlin did a full-length, life-sized picture of the aged Indian standing on the brink of Niagara Falls. The whereabouts of this important picture is now unknown. In the meantime he had watched other artists go out to the Western frontier. James Otto Lewis had been commissioned by the Government to paint portraits of notable tribal chieftains attending the Indian Council Meetings along the Mississippi. Peter Rindisbacher, the young Swiss immigrant to the ill-fated Red River Colony on the Canadian border, was gaining some prominence for his *genre* paintings of that area. He had come down to St. Louis and established a studio there. Before this, Samuel Seymour, a landscape painter of Philadelphia, had accompanied the expedition of Major Stephen H. Long across the Great Plains to the Rocky Mountains.

While none of these had seriously approached the broad plan which George Catlin had in mind, they were encroaching upon it. To go on now, however, meant leaving Clara behind, and neglecting family obligations. His planning for the future became a desperate struggle between devotion and desire.

In spite of all the outdoor activities of his youth and the tremendous stamina and energy he possessed, George Catlin was handicapped by periodic ill health. It may have been that he burned himself out physically by the intensity he put into everything he did. In the early winter of 1829–30 his health failed, probably in part due to the inner conflict over his two great desires. As Clara was also in poor health, the couple went from Albany to the warmer climate of Richmond, Virginia. The Virginia Constitutional Convention of 1829–30 was then in session at Richmond and Catlin was commissioned to make a composite picture of this august body. What he did was a miniature portrait of each of the individuals. The accompanying "key", which he also made, lists 101 persons, including James Madison, James Monroe, and John Marshall[16] (see illustration below). Some of the other portraits included in this remarkable painting are the only ones that now exist of these gentlemen. He also painted a miniature on ivory of Dolly Madison.

By this time, George Catlin had definitely decided on his future. Satisfied that his destiny lay not among the urbane sophisticates of the big cities, but among the primitive Indians beyond the Mississippi, he made plans to leave for the West. He went to Washington, D.C., and obtained letters of introduction to people in Saint Louis. With Clara safely and comfortably settled in Albany for a long, slow convalescence, he set out in the early spring of 1830 to devote the rest of his life to the singular plan which he had set for himself. The personal sacrifice this meant for him cannot be over-emphasized, nor can the fact that his devoted wife was a full partner in that sacrifice. George Catlin never deviated from his plan, and to the end of her days Clara faithfully supported him in the great purpose of his life.

The New York Historical Society

VIRGINIA CONSTITUTIONAL CONVENTION OF 1829–30
Watercolor, by George Catlin

Kennedy Galleries, New York

GENERAL WILLIAM CLARK
Co-leader of Lewis and Clark Expedition
Portrait in Oil, by George Catlin

3

On the Western Frontier

Newberry Library, Chicago

KONZA WARRIOR

WHEN GEORGE CATLIN went to St. Louis in 1830, a great deal depended upon the reception he received from General William Clark. Probably no government official was better informed, from personal experience, about the Indian tribes of the West, and certainly no one wielded a greater influence in the country beyond the Mississippi River. As co-leader of the Lewis and Clark Expedition, he had gone up the Missouri at the beginning of May 1804; wintered at the big Mandan Village; crossed the Rocky Mountains to the Pacific Coast in the summer of 1805, and returned to St. Louis on September 23, 1806, after an absence of almost two and a half years. This expedition of exploration and investigation had furnished the first reliable information of the vast region between the Mississippi and the Pacific—and that had been only twenty-four years before Catlin's arrival in St. Louis. William Clark had been chosen as a leader of the great expedition because of the knowledge and experience he already had of the Indians along the American frontier. (Afterward he was commissioned a Brigadier-General, and served as Governor of the Missouri Territory and Indian Agent of the Territory of the Upper Louisiana, and as Superintendent of Indian Affairs, at St. Louis, from 1813 to the time of his death on September 1, 1838.) There was hardly a tribe in the whole vast area with which he had not had some contact. He had represented the United States Government in the most important of the land acquisition and treaty meetings in the West, and representatives of most of the distant tribes had traveled to St. Louis to meet and consult with him. There was no one better qualified to introduce George Catlin to the Indians of the West, or to facilitate his plans.

St. Louis was the gateway to the West, both north and south. It was the headquarters of the big and small fur companies, and of the individual traders, trappers, hunters and adventurers who were pushing the frontier trade and conquest of the West. It was also the official headquarters for the Army of the West and the Northwest. General Clark exercised dominant control over practically every aspect of the white man's activities in the new land. He literally ruled the whole West.

General Clark was quite naturally a very busy man. He was then sixty years old and had dealt with rough frontiersmen and Indian warriors for so many years that he had developed a blunt and brusque manner in dealing with all matters that were not strictly personal. Representatives of the powerful fur companies had to patiently wait their turn to see him, as did the tribal chiefs, who may have traveled two thousand miles through the wilderness.

In preparation for his meeting with Clark, Catlin not only took along the most impressive letters of introduction he could obtain, but he also carried with him a selection of sketches and finished pictures of some of the Eastern Indians he had painted. When he finally entered the governor's office he promptly displayed his paintings. Clark had seen the somewhat crude portraits that J. O. Lewis had painted of the tribal dignitaries at the council meetings over which Clark had presided, and he had seen the paintings of others who had done similar work. Catlin had had many weeks to anticipate this important moment and he had repeatedly rehearsed what he would say. While the general sat stolidly and let his sharp eyes move critically from picture to picture, he listened. His formality began to relax. Here was a young man who could really paint portraits and dreamed of a plan that was worth listening to. All this was also something very close to the general's heart. Furthermore, this artist was not seeking any government or other subsidy for the comfortable promotion of his scheme, and there was no doubt about his sincerity and his determination to go out into the wild back country, to paint the Indians as they were in their native villages and homes, whether he received official cooperation or not. What General Clark said to Catlin during that first meeting is not known, but it was the beginning of a friendship which may have been even more important to the artist's life and career than the one with De Witt Clinton.

There was plenty of material immediately at hand and General Clark saw to it that Catlin could take full advantage of every opportunity. Indian dignitaries of various tribes were coming regularly to the governor, to tell him their grievances over treaty violations with white men or with other tribes. These red patriarchs were accustomed to making prolonged, histrionic speeches and these speeches had to be carefully translated. The meetings generally took hours, during which the visitors stood in the most pompous attitudes, bedecked in their finest regalia. The general invited Catlin to bring his easel and paints into the office and pursue his work. Conceivably this could have been to see how Catlin behaved and how the red men reacted, as well as to obtain further evidence of his artistic abilities. It was much to Catlin's advantage that one of his greatest skills was for putting a faithful portrait on canvas in a remarkably brief time. In addition, he had an unusual photographic memory which he relied on for finishing the picture later. Besides that, the Indians instinctively liked Catlin. Primitive peoples always seem to have an instinctive understanding of the human attitudes and motives, and General Clark was undoubtedly well aware of this. The young artist not only became well launched on his mission, but also gained the general's complete approval and friendship.

Catlin painted Governor Clark's portrait (see page 28) and that of General Winfield Scott. He was introduced to the most prominent and prosperous persons in St. Louis, with the suggestion that they commission the artist to put their own likenesses on canvas — and for the general to make such a suggestion was virtually a demand. This provided a substantial boost to Catlin's dwindling finances — for there was no remuneration for the Indian portraits.

Catlin acquired a great deal of general information about the Western Indians during those first weeks in St. Louis. He learned that, with very few exceptions, every tribesman was a military man and always ready to go to war, either by necessity or spontaneous impulse; that "warriors" were those who had taken one or more scalps, and that "braves" were those who had gone to war but had taken no scalp nor killed an enemy. He became aware of the importance and power of the chieftains and the medicine-men in the tribal society. Being a meticulous documentarian, he tried to establish a basis for recording the names of tribes and individuals, about which there had always been much confusion among white men.

Smithsonian Institution

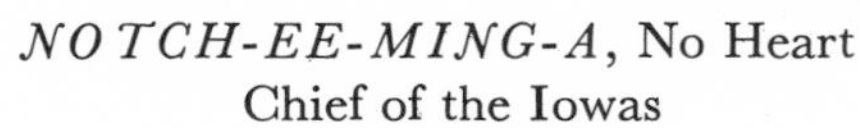

NOTCH-EE-MING-A, No Heart
Chief of the Iowas

Smithsonian Institution

LAY-LAW-SHE-KAW
He Who Goes Up The River
Chief of the Shawnees

From earliest times many of the tribes had become known by the names other tribes called them, but this was often quite different from what they called themselves. Some of the names had come down from designations of the earliest fur traders — such as the French appellation of "Sioux" for the "Dakota" tribes. When the United States government began to regulate the Indians the confederations, tribes and branches were given names in the more or less competent published reports, and this added more confusion. Then too, the western movement of the white men which forced the Indians to move periodically, and the occasional merger of small tribes for mutual protection, led to even further complications. Later on, Catlin tried to correct some of these errors and misapprehensions, although his spelling was generally phonetic and is frequently different from that which is accepted today.

The individual native names of the Indians were even more confusing. The red men generally had no Christian names. (A boy might be named after his father or grandfather, but neither his brother nor sister would bear a similar name.) To these names they usually attached significations which are wrongly supposed to be their translations, such as "*Kee-o-kuk*, the Running Fox," or "*Mi-neek-e-sunk-te-ka*, the Mink." A great proportion of Indian names (like Jones, Brown, Roberts, etc. in English) admit to no translation, but they might have joined to them qualifications for which the individuals were best known, just as we might refer to Jones the shoemaker, or Brown the butcher, or Robert the tailor. Still another difficulty among the tribesmen was the fact that most of their celebrated individuals had several names.[17] Personal names were sometimes given at birth and sometimes changed at critical times of life, such as puberty, the first war expedition, some notable feat, elevation to chieftainship, or retirement from active life. Names were often loaned, pawned, given or thrown away — although jealously guarded — and it was considered discourteous to address a man directly by his proper name.[18] For example, the famous "Black Hawk," leader of the Black Hawk war, was correctly known by a number of Indian names. He signed himself in several ways. To the treaty of June 30, 1831, he signed *Mucatatullhi-eatah*. Prior to this, in 1827, his name was written *Kara-Zhonsept;* when he surrendered to General Street, he called himself *Mucatamish-kakaekq;* and he also had a number of other names.[19] Catlin used the name *Muk-a-tah-mish-o-kah-kiak*, which was evidently the correct one at the time he painted his portrait from life, although the artist also referred to Black Hawk as *Ma-ka-tai-ne-she-kia-kiah*. As the Indians, of course, had no written language of their own, it can readily be understood how *this* confounded the situation.

In July, after Catlin's arrival in St. Louis, he accompanied General Clark to Prairie du Chien and Fort Crawford on the upper Mississippi River, to attend treaty-making council meetings with the Iowas, Missouris, Sioux, Omahas, and the Sauk and Foxes. Representatives of these tribes gathered to negotiate the sale of land to the United States Government and to settle their various problems and disputes in a sort of supreme court over which the general presided with dictatorial authority. A good many of the controversies involved frontier infringements by white men upon the Indians' designated lands and rights. It is significant that the terms of settlement were generally more faithfully respected by the red men than the whites, in spite of the fact that some of the tribesmen had been betrayed in their agreements on more than one occasion. Among them were The Black Hawk, who was then called the "Old Chief," and *Kee-o-kuk*, the Running Fox, both powerful leaders of the Sauk and Foxes. The latter, with representatives of his tribe, on July 15th, 1830, signed a treaty of sale of the Sauk and Fox lands, by which they agreed to move farther west. But Black Hawk steadfastly refused to be a party to any further sale of lands and within less than two years his determination led to the Black Hawk War.

Here was the real beginning of George Catlin's painting of the Western Indians in their native element, although the painting of portraits at a council meeting with the white men had been done before. Catlin was still a long way from the goal he had set himself. He was finding more to think about. Even around Prairie du Chien there were very few white men living in the lodges or villages of the Indians, except the lowly French-Canadians and other squaw-men. Certainly he must have speculated seriously what such a life would be like, when he finally realized his dream in the wilderness a thousand or more miles to the West.

In the fall he made two trips from St. Louis. He went up the Missouri River to Cantonment Leavenworth, in the northeastern corner of Kansas. This was a frequent gathering place for members of a number of tribes — the Iowa, Delaware, Potawatomie, Shawnee, Kickapoo, and others. Some of these were peaceful tribesmen who had previously been removed by the government from the Eastern Woodlands, but as Leavenworth was on the outer fringe of the Western frontier it was occasionally visited by some of the wild and untamed red riders of the *terra incognita*. Among the latter, Catlin painted *Notch-ee-ming-a*, No Heart, also known as White Cloud, the principal chief of the Iowa (Ioway) tribe (page 31). This celebrated warrior was all bedecked in his war-path regalia with a necklace of grizzly claws and many strings of wampum as he sat for his portrait.

Catlin also painted two very notable Shawnees. *Ten-squat-a-way*, the Open Door, called the "Shawnee Prophet" (page 33), was a brother of the famous *Tecumseh*, who had played an important role in the earlier Indian wars east of the Mississippi and, as a Brigadier-General in the British Army, had aided in the capture of Detroit. This younger brother, blind in one eye, had almost succeeded in forming a broad confederacy of the Western tribes to rise up together and drive the Americans out of their territory. Catlin's journal includes a vivid account of the efforts and exploits of this Indian patriot.[20] The artist also painted the head

Smithsonian Institution

TEN-SQUAT-A-WAY, The Open Door or "Shawnee Prophet"

New York Public Library

KONZA (KANSAS) WARRIORS, WOMAN AND CHILD

chief of the Shawnees, *Lay-law-she-kaw*, He Who Goes Up the River (page 31). This veteran of many wars is shown as having a fine and intelligent face, his hair white with age and his ears slit and greatly elongated from the weights which had been hung in them according to a custom of the tribe.

Later that same fall Catlin accompanied General Clark to the villages of the Konza (Kansa or Kansas) tribe, then situated on the Kansas River about seventy miles west of the Missouri in the present state of Kansas. A group of these Indians is shown in the color plate on page 19, and one of the artist's rather ornate drawings of the same subject is reproduced on page 34. Both of these were done subsequent to his visit and combine four of the original portraits he painted from life. From left to right they show: *Sho-me-kos-see*, The Wolf, head chief; *Wa-hon-ga-she*, No Fool; *Chesh-oo-honga-ha*, The Man of Good Sense and *Mesch-o-shin-ga*, The Little White Bear. Sitting in front are the chief's wife and child.

Returning to St. Louis Catlin did some studio refining of the pictures he had made in the field, painted a few commercial portraits to replenish his depleted finances, and returned East to rejoin his wife and show her what he had accomplished. His stay in St. Louis had seen the beginning of his Western painting and of his acquaintance with the Western Indians, although it was merely a modest prelude to far more important and exciting experiences.

Early the following spring George Catlin was off again for St. Louis, leaving Clara behind. He had made arrangements to accompany Major John Dougherty on a trip up the Platte River, to the primitive villages of the Grand Pawnee, Oto, Omaha and Missouri tribes which were under the major's jurisdiction as Indian Agent. This was the trail to what in 1834 became the famous Fort Laramie, in the present state of Wyoming — the trail followed by Major Long on his expedition to the Rockies, and which a good many years later became the "Oregon Trail" of the California gold rush days. Dougherty's agency headquarters were at Bellevue, a short distance above Leavenworth on the Missouri River, from where the two adventurers rode up the Platte, traveling from one village to another.

There is a considerable amount of mystery and lack of documentary information regarding this trip. Just how far the two travelers went is a subject of doubt. Catlin very briefly states that at one time he traveled through the Pawnee country to Fort Laramie and on through the passes of the Rocky Mountains to Great Salt Lake. He indicates that this was in 1833. Some historians have disputed that he made that trip at all, because Catlin recorded no positive proof in pictures or notes. Loyd Haberly, who has done a considerable amount of research on the subject, is inclined to believe that Catlin made the trip to Great Salt Lake in 1831,[21] although he found no conclusive proof. It is certainly not beyond reasonable possibility, as a number of unknown fur trappers and traders had made that trip before 1831.

That Catlin painted portraits of Oto, Omaha and Grand Pawnee tribesmen of the Platte River region is beyond doubt. Donaldson indicates that the artist visited these tribes in 1833 and that the portraits were painted that year, but Donaldson is known to be incorrect in a good many such instances. John C. Ewers, the meticulous anthropologist and Catlin authority of the Smithsonian Institute, is satisfied that most of them were done in 1831.[22]

Among the most important and interesting pictures which Catlin evidently painted on that obscure trip up the Platte, is one of *La-doo-ke-a*, The Buffalo Bull, of the Grand Pawnee tribe (color plate, page 38 and also in the group on page 36). This noted warrior is shown with his *medicine* or *toten* of the head of a buffalo painted on his face and breast. Another is that of *Om-pah-ton-ga*, The Big Elk, principal chief of the Omaha tribe (color plate, page 37). This famous red warrior was visited by Captain Long during his expedition of 1819, on which occasion the Indian leader delivered a speech asserting that not one of his tribe had ever stained his hands with the blood of a white man. His hospitality and friendship became well known to the white travelers who later passed through his country. Catlin also painted *No-way-ke-sug-gah*, He Who Strikes Two At Once, a distinguished Oto warrior (color plate, page 37). While this is a rather unfinished picture it shows him vividly in beautiful garb, trimmed with a profusion of scalp-locks and eagle quills, pipe in hand, and with a necklace of grizzly bears' claws around his neck. Whether these pictures were actually made in 1831 or 1833 is a matter of far less importance than is their historic value.

During the first two years that George Catlin spent along and beyond the Western Frontier, he added a great deal to the documentary record of the period, both in the portraits he painted and the information he recorded. But now he was ready to enlarge his field of painting and literary reporting to the field of primitive Indian ceremonies and other activities of their tribal lives. The great accomplishment, and the great adventure, was still to come. It began in the early spring of the following year.

New York Public Library

LA-DOO-KE-A, The Buffalo Bull and Other Pawnees

Smithsonian Institution

NO-WAY-KE-SUG-GAH, He Who Strikes Two at Once
An Oto Warrior

Smithsonian Institution

OM-PAH-TON-GA, The Big Elk
Chief of the Omahas

Smithsonian Institution

LA-DOO-KE-A, The Buffalo Bull
Grand Pawnee Warrior

4

Up the Wild Missouri

Newberry Library, Chicago

RETURN FROM WASHINGTON

CATLIN made many friends in St. Louis, both through General Clark and because of his own warm personality. Among these was Pierre Chouteau, the influential western manager of John Jacob Astor's powerful American Fur Company. Chouteau ruled all of the company's fortified fur trading posts along the entire Missouri, the Platte, and the company's spreading domination of the whole Northwest. During the summer of 1831 the company was readying a 130-foot river steamboat for a pioneering voyage. She was a beamy, double-deck, two-stacker to be known as the *Yellow Stone*, and it was hoped she would be able to carry her great load of supplies up the two thousand miles of the muddy Missouri to the mouth of the Yellow Stone River, where the company's farthest trading post, Fort Union, was located. From there the trappers and traders fanned out into the still little-known territories of the Blackfeet, the Crows and the other virgin areas of the westernmost prairies and Rockies.

As early as 1819 a river steamboat had ascended the Missouri as far as Council Bluffs, Iowa, but from there the supplies and trade goods had been carried across the country by pack-horses or dragged up the river in keelboats. This was a slow and expensive means of transportation. If the *Yellow Stone* could make it through to distant Fort Union, the voyage would mark the beginning of a new era in the fur trade as well as in the development and control of the Northwest by the American Fur Company. Everyone around St. Louis was talking about the undertaking and speculating on its chances of success, and everyone with the slightest excuse was anxious to ride up-river on the big boat. George Catlin was determined to go along. Chouteau had promised to try and find room for him, although this would not be certain until shortly before the start.

When winter set in the artist once more made the trip back East to spend some time with Clara, although this time he returned to St. Louis long before spring had come. He had been told that the *Yellow Stone* would be headed up-river as soon as the ice was out, in order to take advantage of the high water, and he was taking no chances on being late. During the intervening time he had developed an exciting plan. He would travel on the steamboat as far as she went, and there he would leave the boat and paint the Indian tribes of the vicinity and make trips out into the surrounding region. After this was done he would obtain a canoe and drift leisurely down the river alone, all the way back to St. Louis, paddling ashore to visit the various forts and stopping wherever there was an Indian village or other attraction worthy of being painted. On the way up he could survey the situation and decide where it would be best to stop on the way down.

The *Yellow Stone* left St. Louis on March 26th, 1832. Actual dates were apparently of relative unimportance to George Catlin, as were such matters as the festive departure on this occasion. In his *Letters and Notes*, he merely states: "In the spring of 1832 I ascended the Missouri, on the steamer *Yellow Stone*." However, such an historic event could hardly have passed without something of a celebration by the residents of St. Louis. As the pioneering steamboat went puffing and chugging out into the muddy water of the Mississippi and headed for the nearby mouth of the Missouri, there must have been much shouting and yelling from the crowd that had gathered along the river front, and from the boat's deck cannons surely boomed with big puffs of smoke.

It was a colorful assortment of individuals who crowded the two decks of the river steamer as she pulled away from St. Louis and headed for the mouth of the Missouri a few miles up-stream. They were mostly *engagees* of the American Fur Company — roughly picturesque French-Canadian river-men, grizzled Yankee trappers of English and Scottish ancestry, and half-breeds and mongrels of other sorts to do hard labor necessary to enlarge the company's existing forts and build new ones. The only persons aboard who were not directly engaged in some phase of the owner's enterprise were George Catlin and Major John F. A. Sanford, the U. S. Indian Agent for the tribes of the Upper Missouri and its tributaries. With the Major was a group of native tribesmen whom he had taken to Washington, D. C. the previous winter and was now returning to their villages. Among them was a picturesque

Smithsonian Institution

STEAMBOAT "YELLOW STONE" LEAVING ST. LOUIS

Smithsonian Institution

EE-AH-SA-PA, The Black Rock. A Sioux Chief

character, whose story rivals fiction and who is at the same time an all too realistic symbol of the Indian's tragic fate upon his amalgamation into the white man's ways of life. His name, as Catlin recorded it, was *Wi-jun-jon*, The Pigeon's Egg Head (it was really *Ah-jon-jon*, The Light) and he was the son of a chief of the Assiniboin tribe, whose village was a short distance below Fort Union.

Wi-jun-jon had been a warrior of distinction among his people — young, proud, valiant and handsome. He had fought many battles, and his fine buckskin garb had been adorned with numerous scalps from the heads of his enemies, all of which had been taken with his own hands. Major Sanford had selected him to represent his tribe in the delegation that was taken to meet the "Great White Father" in Washington.

The party had descended the Missouri in mackinaw-boats — large flat-bottomed row-boats used for travel on the rivers during the early days. As they came to the first habitations of white men, *Wi-jun-jon* and another Indian decided they would make a record of the cabins and houses they saw, in order to show the evidence when they got back home from the journey. First they cut notches in the wooden stem of the pipe each carried, but as they advanced down the river the number of cabins increased so rapidly that soon the pipe-stems were completely covered with little notches. Then they began putting the tally marks on the handles of their war clubs, which also became notched all over. Still determined to preserve a record of all they saw, the Indians each cut a long stick on the river bank, when the party stopped to camp. As the mackinaw-boats got closer to St. Louis, the two began spending most of their time cutting little notches on the long sticks. When the town of 15,000 inhabitants finally came into view, the Indians, finding themselves in a state of complete confusion, held a conference and all the sticks were thrown overboard into the river.

Upon their arrival in St. Louis, Major Sanford took them to see General Clark. George Catlin was in town at the time and painted some of their portraits. Here is the artist's own description: "*Wi-jun-jon* was the first who reluctantly yielded to the solicitations of the Indian agent and myself . . . though his pride had plumed and tinted him in all the freshness and brilliance of an Indian toilet . . . He was dressed in his native costume, which was classic and exceedingly beautiful; his leggings and shirt were of mountain goat skin, richly garnished with quills of the porcupine and fringed with the locks of scalps taken from his enemies heads . . . his head was decked with the war eagles' plumes, his robe was of the skin of a young buffalo bull, decorated with scenes of the battles of his life."

Shortly afterward they were taken on to Washington and elsewhere, to be feted and entertained as distinguished visitors, and duly impressed with the white man's importance, benevolence and power. *Wi-jun-jon* took to all this with a vainglorious enthusiasm. He loved every bit of it, and soon became the foremost on all occasions — the first to enter every pre-arranged reception and the last to leave; the first to bow to the pretty ladies; the first to drink his toast in fire-water, and repeat it; the first to shake President Andrew Jackson's hand and present the gift which he had brought for the occasion and then to make an oration which was so long it had to be abruptly stopped in the middle. With the group he visited New York and other cities, saw the white man's forts and big guns, steamboats that crossed the ocean, tall buildings, policemen, saloons, concerts, dancing ladies in theatrical shows; and learned that whiskey tasted as good from a glass as a bottle. None of Major Sanford's Indians enjoyed their indoctrination into the civilized ways of the white man nearly as much as *Wi-jun-jon*, The Pigeon's Egg Head, son of a chief of the Assiniboin tribe.

After a whole winter of luxurious living as guests of the Great White Father, the Indians were brought back to St. Louis just in time to ride back to their primitive villages on the first trip of the steamboat *Yellow Stone*. There could have been no more fitting climax. The trip had wrought a deep and lasting change on every one of them — but on none so much as *Wi-jun-jon*. When they marched aboard to take their place in the very front of the upper deck, The Pigeon's Egg Head as usual led the delegation — and what an appearance he made! He was dressed in a suit of full-dress American regimentals!

Here again is Catlin's own description: "He had in Washington exchanged his beautifully garnished and classic costume for a full dress *en militaire*. It was, perhaps, presented to him by the President. It was broadcloth of the finest blue, trimmed with lace of gold. On his shoulders were mounted two immense epaulettes; his neck was strangled with a shining black stock; and his feet were pinioned in a pair of water-proof boots with high heels, which made him step like a yoked hog. On his head was a high-crowned beaver hat, with a broad silver lace band, surmounted by a huge red feather, some two feet high; his coat collar, stiff with lace, came higher up than his ears, and over it flowed downwards to his haunches, his long Indian locks, stuck up in rolls and plaits, with red paint. A large silver medal was suspended from his neck by a blue ribbon, and across his right shoulder passed a wide belt, supporting by his side a broadsword. On his hands he had drawn a pair of kid gloves, and in them held a blue umbrella in one and a large fan in the other. In this fashion was poor *Wi-jun-jon* metamorphosed, on his return from Washington (see color plate page 56); and, in this plight was he strutting and whistling 'Yankee Doodle,' about the deck of the steamer that was wending its way up the mighty Missouri, and taking him to his native land again, where he was soon to light his pipe and cheer the wigwam fireside with tales of novelty and wonder." George Catlin was later to witness that comic-opera return of the prodigal Pigeon's Egg Head to his Assiniboin village and to report on its tragic consequences.

Smithsonian Institution

HA-WON-JE-TAH, The One Horn
First Chief of the Sioux

Smithsonian Institution

TCHAN-DEE, Tobacco
Second Chief of Oglala Sioux

For the first few hundred miles that the *Yellow Stone* puffed and grunted her way against the swirling current of the muddy Missouri, there was little that was difficult for the boat or exceptional for Catlin. Then they stopped at the village of the Poncas, near the mouth of the Niobrara River in present Nebraska. This marked the transition point beyond which the Indian tribes were as yet little affected by the spreading defilement of the white man's civilization. Here the local chief came aboard and Catlin found an interpreter through whom he could have a talk with him. "The chief . . . is a noble specimen of native dignity and philosophy," the artist wrote.[24] "He related to me with great coolness and frankness, the poverty and distress of his people; and philosophically predicted the certain extinction of his tribe, which he had not the power to avert . . . that the buffaloes which the Great Spirit had given them for food, and which formerly spread all over the green prairies, had all been killed or driven out by the white men . . . that his young men, penetrating their enemies' country for buffaloes, were cut to pieces and destroyed in great numbers. That his people had foolishly become fond of fire-water and had given away everything in the country for it — that it had destroyed many of his warriors and soon would destroy the rest. . . ."

The Poncas were at the time preparing to move their village farther west, where game was more plentiful. While the *Yellow Stone* was tied to the bank they took down their skin wigwams and departed. "My attention was directed to a very aged and emaciated man of the tribe, who I was told was being left behind," Catlin continues the story. "Once a chief and man of distinction, he was now too old and feeble to travel, and was being left to starve, or meet such death as might fall to his lot — and his bones to be picked by wolves. Almost naked, he sat by a small fire . . . with a few sticks within reach, and a buffalo skin stretched over his head — with only a few half-picked bones laid within his reach and a dish of water, but without weapons or means to replenish them . . . I advanced to the old man and sat by his side; and though he could not distinctly see me, he shook me heartily by the hand and smiled, evidently aware that I was a white man and that I sympathized with his misfortune. I shook hands again with him and left him, steering my way towards the steamer, which was ready to resume her voyage up the Missouri."

After the first thousand miles the journey became an expedition into a wild and untamed land. The heavily loaded steamer bumped against hidden sandbars and struggled in a constant fight to put league after league behind. Herds of buffalo, and elk and other game began appearing in increasing numbers on the rolling plains, fleeing in wild confusion at the sound and scent of the puffing *Yellow Stone*, which for the first time in history was saluting the shores of the Missouri with the din of her powerful steam engine. When the boat went puffing by the occasional Indian villages where the people had never before seen or heard of a steamboat, they seemed at a loss to know what to do. At the approach to every large village the twelve-pound cannon and three four-pound swivels on the deck, which were being taken to Fort Union, were all discharged in rapid succession, as a boastful salute. This threw the inhabitants into a state of utter amazement and confusion. Some lay their faces against the ground and cried out to the Great Spirit; some hurried to kill their favorite horse, as a sacrifice to appease their Almighty, while others knocked each other down in their wild and disorderly flight to the distant hills. Warriors, women, children, patriarchs and medicine-men fled like frightened animals from the sight and noise of the steamboat, the belching cannons and the discharge of steam from the safety valve which the captain ordered discharged for the hilarious amusement of those who watched from the decks.

George Catlin spent all the daylight hours on deck, making notes on the places where he would stop on his trip down the river, drawing sketches of scenes along the way, and forming his own opinion of the domineering attitude of the fur men, who were so ambitious to rule the whole country and make the Indians subservient to their greedy desires. He listened silently to the traders' speculation on how many beaver skins they should demand for a bottle of the cheapest whiskey, to what extent it might be diluted and still produce the desired effects of "fire-water," and how best to cultivate the habit for its use. He heard them argue as to what was the best method of employing the red men to kill the largest possible number of buffalo and to bring in the hides for the least possible amount of cheap trade goods. He also speculated on the ultimate effect of this rising tide of the white man's civilization, which would certainly flood the length and breadth of the wonderful homeland of a primitive and picturesque race, which it would doom to destruction. More than ever before, he was determined to be the pictorial historian of the western Indians and to champion their cause in the courts of human understanding and justice. But for now there was exciting adventure close ahead. He would soon be in the land of the notorious Sioux, where the *Yellow Stone* would make a prolonged stop, and there the realization of his years of dreaming and planning would actually begin.

"From day to day we advanced . . ." Catlin wrote in his journal,[25] "until at last our boat was aground; and a day's work of sounding told us at last there was no possibility of advancing further until there should be a rise in the river . . . Mr. Chouteau started off twenty men on foot, to cross the plains for a distance of two hundred miles to Laidlaw's Fort [Old Fort Pierre], at the mouth of the Teton River [about twelve hundred miles above St. Louis, at the location of the present capital city of South Dakota]. To this expedition I immediately attached myself; and having heard that a numerous party were there encamped . . . I packed on the backs and in the hands of several men, such articles for painting as I might want . . . with my sketchbook slung on my own back, and my rifle in hand, and I started off with them."

Smithsonian Institution

THE BEGGARS' DANCE OF TETON SIOUX

Smithsonian Institution

BUFFALO CHASE OF THE SIOUX

5

In the Land of the Sioux

Newberry Library, Chicago
SIOUX WARRIOR

THE long overland trip gave Catlin an opportunity to test his legs and his stamina against the half-breed and French-Canadian *engagees*, whose lives had been mostly spent in this way. It was a grueling introduction for a novice, but there was much to compensate the artist. They saw immense herds of buffalo, and although the party was without horses, they were able to approach the animals frequently enough to keep abundantly supplied with fresh meat. At the end of about a week, they found more than six hundred skin lodges of the Sioux nation encamped around Fort Pierre (page 48).

"I am now in the heart of the country belonging to the Sioux or Dahcotas, and have Indian faces and Indian customs in abundance around me," Catlin wrote.[26] "This tribe is one of the most numerous in North America and one of the most war-like to be found. They number some forty or fifty thousand, and are undoubtedly able to muster at least eight to ten thousand well mounted and well armed warriors. Many of them have been supplied with guns, although the greater part hunt with bows and arrows and lances, killing their game from their horses while at full speed . . . Their personal appearance is fine and prepossessing, tall and straight, and their movements graceful. At least one half of their warriors stand six feet or more in height. . . .

"The great family of Sioux occupy a vast tract of country extending from the bank of the upper Mississippi River to the Rocky Mountains and are a migrating tribe, divided into forty-two bands or families, each having its own chief . . . There are no parts of the Great Plains which are more abundantly stocked with buffaloes and wild horses, nor any people more bold in destroying the one for food and appropriating the other for their use . . . There has gone abroad . . . an opinion which is too current in the world, that the Indian is necessarily a poor, drunken, murderous wretch; which account is certainly unjust as regards the savage . . . That the Indians in their *native* state are drunken, is false; for they are the only temperance people, literally speaking, that I ever saw, or ever expect to see. These people manufacture no spiritous liquor themselves, and knew nothing of it until it was brought into their country and tendered to them by Christians."

Fort Pierre had been named for Pierre Chouteau, to whom Catlin was indebted for his passage on the steamboat *Yellow Stone* and who had been on that first voyage. The fort was one of the most important of the American Fur Company's posts, being in the center of the extensive Sioux country and drawing to it an immense quantity of fur and buffalo robes which were transported to Eastern cities to be sold at a great profit. The well-fortified compound enclosed nearly a dozen spacious buildings — stores and storage rooms and comfortable living quarters for Laidlaw, the Scotch factor, whose home was "neatly conducted by a fine looking, modest and dignified Sioux woman, the affectionate mother of Mr. Laidlaw's flock of attractive children."[27] George Catlin's observations and experiences among the Sioux are scattered through his various writings — sometimes brought into the record as reminiscenses or side-lights to other experiences. He also made a stop at Fort Pierre on his leisurely journey down the Missouri. For the sake of consistency and of giving a more comprehensive portrayal of this important tribe at that early period, the present writer has undertaken to combine, coordinate and condense the information. It would take a whole volume to present all of the notes and pictures that the artist documented regarding this tribe alone, but it is hoped that what is included here will give a fair impression of those people as they were before the days of the white man's civilization, whiskey and degeneration. It is all from the record that Catlin compiled — the earliest first-hand, comprehensive one that we have.

Due to the difficulties of navigating the *Yellow Stone* up the river, the stay at Fort Pierre was much longer than had been anticipated. This gave Catlin an excellent opportunity to observe and paint among the unusually large number of Sioux that were gathered there. At a time such as this, particularly when several of the independent bands or tribes were assembled, the occasion invariably became a gala festival of competitive games, dances and religious ceremonies. As none wanted to leave until the mysterious steamboat arrived, the scene became a sort of wild and primitive country fair. From daylight to dark and long into the night the almost constant thump of the drums and the wild chants and yells of the dancers could be heard. This was a wonderful opportunity for the boastful to display their skills and to show their bravery under the self-inflicted tortures of their religion.

The first painting that Catlin made was a large portrait of *Ha-won-je-tah*, The One Horn, first chief of the Sioux (page 43). This Indian took the name One Horn from a small shell — shown hanging on a plain thong around his neck — which had been handed down from his father and which he told the artist he valued more than anything else he possessed. His hair, which was very long and profuse, was divided into two parts, and lifted up and tied over the

Smithsonian Institution

FORT PIERRE, WITH SIOUX CAMPED AROUND

Smithsonian Institution

THE BEAR DANCE

top of his head, giving it the appearance of a turban. He had a wide reputation as the foremost hunter of the tribe and was said to be able to run down a buffalo on his own legs and then drive his arrow into its heart. It was proverbial among his people that One Horn's bow was never drawn in vain, and his wigwam was abundantly decorated with the scalps he had taken from his enemies' heads in the many battles he had fought.

None of the Indians had ever seen a life-like portrait of anyone put on canvas. When One Horn's was finished, several of the other chiefs were invited into the skin wigwam which Catlin was using as a studio. At first it frightened them and they clamped their hands over their mouths in sudden amazement. When they went away the things they said caused such a sensation throughout the encampment that the artist had to hang the picture outside where all could see it. So great was the Indians' amazement at the mysterious ability of the visitor from afar, that they immediately conferred upon him the distinguished title of *Ee-cha-zoo-kah-wa-kon*, The Medicine Painter. Thus he was elevated to the honorable position of medicine-man. But the Sioux medicine-men, of whom there were a number, took a quite different attitude. They loudly denounced the painting, predicting bad luck and premature death to anyone who would permit his body and soul to be put in such a form. "He can't even sleep at night!" they argued, from the fact the eyes in the picture were always open. The women and children who looked at the picture of their great chief went away moaning and crying, and the bravest of the warriors quickly slipped away when Catlin even looked at them. It seemed as though the artist's work had come to a very abrupt end and that the people might even do him bodily harm for bringing damnation to their chief. The white traders of the fort had been highly amused at the Indians' actions until the whole situation took such a serious turn. Then it required a lot of extremely persuasive talking to assure One Horn that no harm could come from having his portrait painted and that it was really a great honor to him. When finally convinced, he made a long speech to all the people. He explained that this great medicine-man of the white man's race had come a great distance just to paint the pictures of the most distinguished men of the Sioux, that he might take them home for the white chiefs to

New York Public Library

DANCE OF THE CHIEFTAINS

see. The Indians' attitudes changed quickly, like those of children, and while many of them were still deeply suspicious, some of the other leading chiefs and warriors went to their wigwams to put on their finest garments to sit for their portraits to be painted.

The next dignitary to be painted was *Ee-ah-sa-pa*, The Black Rock, a chief of the *Nee-caw-wee-gee* band (page 41). This tall, fine looking man came wearing his elegant head-dress of war-eagle feathers and ermine skins, surmounted with a pair of thinly shaved and polished buffalo horns, denoting his position as leader and warchief of his division of the tribe. And then there was *Tchan-dee*, The Tobacco, second chief of the powerful Oglala band (page 43). This man had a wide reputation as one of the bravest warriors of the entire Sioux nation.

Catlin's improvised studio became the continual rendezvous of the most notable individuals of all the various bands, who insisted on crowding in to watch the Medicine Painter put human beings upon canvas and to wait their turn. The artist was obliged to follow a strict form of protocol, painting his subjects according to their rank and importance. He ran into another difficulty, however, when he proposed to paint a woman. At first the chiefs and warriors were greatly amused at such a suggestion, and then they became highly indignant. Their women had never taken scalps, nor done anything better than build fires and dress skins. Even to think of honoring them, as the Mystery Painter had the chiefs, was an insult to all! This new difficulty was finally settled with a satisfactory explanation.

"The vanity of these men, after they had agreed to be painted, was beyond description," wrote Catlin.[28] "An Indian often lies down from morning till night in front of his portrait, admiring his beautiful face, and faithfully guarding it from day to day to protect it from accident or harm . . . owing to their superstitious notion that there may be life to a certain extent in the picture, and that if harm or violence be done to it, it may in some mysterious way affect their health or do them other injury."

One of the most frequent pastimes of all the Plains Tribes was dancing, and this was particularly true among the Sioux. Both vocal and instrumental music was an important part of the dances. The dance-steps were only about four basic kinds of stamping of the feet, although the sequence of the steps and the forms of the scenes had wide variety, and were accompanied by the most violent jumps and contortions. There was little or no harmony or melody in the music, and the songs were made up chiefly of wild chants, harsh gutterals, yells, barks and high-pitched screams, although these were given out in perfect time. There were also occasions when the Indian would lie down by his fireside with his drum cuddled affectionately in his hands, and tap it almost imperceptibly to the soft accompaniment of a stifled voice in a dulcet tone. These quiet songs had to do with thoughts of primitive romance, worshiping the Great Spirit or paying devotion to their personal "medicine."

So great was the regard for George Catlin and the *medicine* of his art, that they held a Dance of the Chieftains in his special honor. The interpreters explained that this was the highest favor which the Sioux could pay him. It was performed by a representative group of the chiefs and medicine-men, all dressed in their finest garments, with head-dresses of war-eagle feathers, and was staged in front of the head chief's wigwam with all the people gathered around to witness the affair. In the painting which was done of this, the artist shows himself standing at one side with the head chief, holding his sketch-pad in hand. The picture that is reproduced (page 50) is a drawing that Catlin later made of the original oil painting.

He witnessed and painted the *Bear Dance* (page 49). Like the other tribes, these people were very fond of bear meat, and required large quantities of bear grease to oil their long black hair as well as their bodies. They also enjoyed the challenge of killing these dangerous animals with their primitive weapons (page 15). Normally the dance was given by the prospective hunters several days in succession before setting out. They all joined in the song to the Bear Spirit, which they believed had an invisible existence and must be conciliated to insure success. The chief medicine-man led the dance, with the entire skin of a bear placed over his body, and some of the others wore bears' heads as masks. They all imitated the various movements and sounds of the animal they were preparing to meet in hand-to-claw combat, while dancing and chanting to the accompaniment of the drums.

There was also the *Beggars' Dance* (page 45) which was a pantomime appeal to the Great Spirit to open the hearts of the prosperous, that they should give of their wealth to the poor (*not* the dancers) assuring the givers that the Great Spirit would be kind to those who were generous to the destitute and helpless. And there was also the ceremony of *Smoking the Shield* (page 51) in which a young brave who was making his war-shield invited his friends and well-wishers to dance and feast around the shield while the rawhide was being

New York Public Library

SMOKING THE SHIELD

New York Public Library

THE SCALP DANCE

New York Public Library

LOOKING AT THE SUN

shrunk and hardened over a special fire built in the ground. Catlin gives a lengthy and detailed description of this,[29] as he also does of the other incidents.

The *Scalp Dance* (page 52) was the most significant of all. This wild demonstration was normally given to celebrate the victory of a war party and was performed at night by the light of torches and the weirdest vocal accompaniment that is imaginable. When the victors returned, bringing home scalps of their enemies, they generally "danced them" for several nights in succession. A number of young women were selected to hold up the scalps while the warriors danced around them, jumping and stamping and barking the most extravagant boasts of their prowess in war. It was an extremely primitive public manifestation of personal and tribal exultation. To the Sioux there was no greater accomplishment than success in warfare, and the scalps of an enemy were the highest badges of merit.

The taking of scalps was an honorable custom among the Plains Tribes, and a scalp was considered a fair prize whether taken in battle or otherwise. It was this practice, probably more than any other, which created terror and hatred toward the Indians by the early white immigrants in the West. The victim was not necessarily slain. Sometimes they were left alive to return and endure disgrace among their own people. A bona fide scalp, custom dictated, must contain the crown of the head, taken by slicing the knife around it through the skin and tearing off a piece about the size of the palm of a hand. Sometimes the victor's teeth were used to tear off the trophy. Scalps were carefully dried and often ornamented, to be long preserved and highly prized. Each scalp was usually stretched over a small hoop attached to a stick, or it was hung from a favorite garment, attached to the handle of a war-club, to the bridle-bit of a war horse or to the scalp-pole of their skin wigwams (see page 59). Besides the scalp, the victor frequently took the rest of the hair if he had the time, and brought it home for his wife to divide in small scalp-locks to fringe the seams of his shirt, leggings and other garments. Sometimes the scalps were buried after they were properly "danced." There were generally fresh scalps in the camps of the Sioux at the time of Catlin's visit.

Even more impressive were the religious torture ceremonies he witnessed. These voluntary self-tortures were performed by a young man of the tribe for the purpose of gaining respect and they are a strong indication of the tribal ethos and personal temperament of the Sioux. Among these was what they called *Looking at the Sun* (page 53) which is best described in the words of George Catlin himself: "I went to a little plain at the base of the bluffs, where were grouped some 15 to 20 lodges of the *Tiny-ta-to-ah* band. We found him naked, except for his breech-cloth, with splints or skewers run through the flesh of both breasts, leaning back and hanging with the weight of his body to the top of a pole which was fastened in the ground and to the upper end of which he was fastened by a thong which was tied to the splints. In this position he was leaning back, with nearly the whole weight of his body hanging to the pole, the top of which was bent forward, allowing his body to sink about half-way back to the ground . . . He held in his left hand his favorite bow, and in his right, with a desperate grip, his medicine bag. In this condition, with the blood trickling down over his body, which was covered with white and yellow clay, and amidst a large crowd who were looking on and encouraging him, he was '*looking at the sun*' without paying the least attention to any one about him. In the group around him were several medicine-men, beating their drums and shaking their rattles, and singing as loud as they could yell, to encourage him and strengthen his heart to stand and look at the sun from its rising in the morning till its setting at night; at which time, if his heart and strength have not failed him, he is cut down, receives liberal donations of presents . . . and the name of a medicine-man, which insures him respect through the rest of his life . . . If he faints and falls, of which there is imminent danger, he loses his reputation as a brave, and suffers disgrace in the estimation of the tribe."[30]

Smithsonian Institution

TAH-TECK-A-DA-HAIR, The Steep Wind
A Distinguished Sioux Warrior

Smithsonian Institution

TIS-SE-WOO-NA-TIS, She Who Bathes Her Knees
Wife of a Cheyenne Chief

Smithsonian Institution

WI-JUN-JON, The Pigeon's Egg Head
Going to and Returning from Washington

6

When Red and White Men Meet

Newberry Library, Chicago

SIOUX MEDICINE MAN

"THERE IS blood and butchery in the story," wrote George Catlin in relating his experience with *Shon-ka*, The Dog, chief of the *Ca-za-zhee-ta* or Bad Arrow Points band of the Sioux, "and it should be read by everyone who would form a correct notion of the force of Indian superstition. Three mighty warriors, proud and valiant, were killed and all in consequence of one of the portraits I painted . . . my brush was the prime mover of all these misfortunes, and my life was sought to heal the wound."[31] It began during the artist's first visit to Fort Pierre, but it was not until months afterward that he learned how it finally ended.

The attitude of the Sioux regarding their being painted remained a mixture of personal vanity and superstitious apprehension. Following a protocol that was considerably influenced by personal favoritism, the head chief dictated the order in which each of the subordinate chiefs should be painted, and they in turn did likewise with their own followers. This led to rivalries and complications and as Catlin could not possibly paint them all, he saw trouble ahead. Furthermore, the medicine men had become increasingly jealous of the artist. Once again some of the high-priests were carrying on their harangues against him, repeating their predictions of terrible consequences for those who permitted themselves to be painted, saying that after they were dead the pictures would still live as captives in the hands of the white men and cause them everlasting trouble. It was in the midst of this conflict of ideas, after Catlin had painted many portraits and tribal scenes, that the following incident occurred.

The artist was painting *Mah-to-tchee-ga*, The Little Bear, a distinguished chief of *Onc-pa-pa* band (page 61). For the sake of artistic variety, he was doing a profile portrait. As usual, there was an audience squatting and standing around inside the studio tepee watching the proceedings. The picture was nearly finished when *Shon-ka*, The Dog, of the Bad Arrow Points, came in and seated himself on the ground in front of the artist's subject, where he could have a full view of the picture in the process of completion. *Shon-ka* was an ill-natured, surly man, who was strongly disliked among the other bands, and this was no doubt responsible for his being slighted in the protocol established by the head chief. *Shon-ka* was obviously in a bad mood when he came in, and had sat sullenly for only a few moments when he uttered in a sneering tone: "*Ma-to-tchee-ga* is but half a man!" This brought a sudden silence. There was no movement, except the eyes of the chiefs who were seated and standing about. *Mah-to-tchee-ga*'s lips tightened a bit and then he spoke in a calm but demanding voice. "Who says that?" The reply came quickly. "*Shon-ka* says it; and *Shon-ka* can prove it." At this the eyes of *Mah-to-tchee-ga* turned slowly until they were fixed with unrestrained contempt upon the chief of the Bad Arrow Points. "Why does *Shon-ka* say it?," he demanded. "Ask *We-chash-a-wa-kon* (the artist). He can tell you. He knows you are but *half a man*, for he has painted but half of your face and knows that the other half is good for nothing!" This brought a flush to *Mah-to-tchee-ga*'s face and his eyes snapped. His reply to the challenge was sharp and uncompromising: "When The Dog says that let him prove it! *Mah-to-tchee-ga* can look at any one, and he is now looking at an *old woman* and a *coward!*"

Shon-ka abruptly got to his feet and wrapping his robe about himself with a flourish, strode out of the lodge in a manner which left no doubt that the matter was not ended. *Mah-to-tchee-ga*'s eyes followed him until he passed out of sight, then he pleasantly resumed his position and sat until the final touches were added to his portrait. When Catlin indicated that he was finished and that the chief should look at the picture, he stood for a few moments admiring his likeness; then he graciously presented the artist with a very elegant buckskin shirt, beautifully painted and decorated with porcupine quill-work and fringed with many enemy scalp-locks. Then he strode out of the lodge. As soon as he left, the others also went outside, for it was quite evident that something drastic was about to happen.

Mah-to-tchee-ga went directly to his own tepee, where he got out his muzzle-loading, flint-lock rifle and loaded it with powder and wad, and dropped a round lead ball down the barrel. Then in the custom of his people, he threw himself face-down upon the ground in humble supplication to the Great Spirit for aid and protection. His wife, seeing him so agitated, and fearing evil consequences, without knowing the circumstances and desiring to preserve the peace in the encampment, picked up the rifle and quietly shook it until the ball rolled out upon the ground.

Mah-to-tchee-ga was still moaning his prayers when the voice of *Shon-ka* was heard outside the tepee. "If *Mah-to-tchee-ga* be a *whole* man, let him come out and prove it! It is *Shon-ka* who calls him!" The prayer was abruptly ended and grabbing his gun, *Mah-to-tchee-ga* darted out between the closed flaps of his lodge. They both fired their guns almost simultaneously. The Dog fled uninjured, but *Mah-to-tchee-ga* fell to the ground, with the side of his face shot away — the side which had been left out of the portrait.

The whole encampment was immediately thrown into a state of agitation. A thousand red warriors went running to their tepees, stripping off their superfluous garments as they went, setting up a wild chorus of yells and war-cries that rose in intensity and volume. They quickly appeared with their bows and arrows and guns. The Bad Arrow Points promptly assembled around *Shon-ka*, to protect their leader, and they all raced for their horses as the arrows and rifle balls of vengeance began to fly in their direction. It wasn't long before the fight had moved out onto the prairie, though still within full view of everyone around the fort. The warriors and braves of *Shon-ka*'s Bad Arrow Points made their escape, although it was later learned that The Dog had his arm broken by one of the rifle balls. Meanwhile, the squaws of his band had been taking down their tepees to make a hurried departure.

Mah-to-tchee-ga died of his wound. His wife was inconsolable, believing that she had been the innocent cause of her husband's death. All the warriors and friends of the victim's band swore vengeance until The Dog should pay the penalty with his own life. The eyes of the superstitious multitude encamped around Fort Pierre were turned upon George Catlin as the direct cause of what had happened. The traders and other white men put themselves in the best possible state of defense; they urged the artist to pack up his belongings as quickly as possible; and plans were rushed for the prompt departure of the *Yellow Stone*, which got under way the following day.

Catlin did not learn the rest of the story until quite a while later. When he risked a return to Fort Pierre about four months afterward, he was informed that the followers of *Mah-to-tchee-ga* had taken to the war-path and followed the Bad Arrow Points for a good many days. There were several encounters. In one of the battles, the dead chief's brother, *Tah-teck-a-da-hair*, The Steep Wind (color plate page 55, also in group on page 61), was killed. The death of this valiant and highly esteemed warrior, as well as of all the others who died in the feud, was made the direct responsibility of the white Medicine Painter who had painted the picture of *Mah-to-tchee-ga* with only half a face. A solemn council was held and with all the solemnity of Indian justice, George Catlin was also doomed to death, along with The Dog. It was not until after the artist returned to St. Louis that he learned *Shon-ka* The Dog was finally tracked down and killed near the Black Hills. This ended the little war and the bands were good friends again. If Catlin had been anything of a sensationalist, he could easily have painted several very dramatic pictures of this episode.

While Catlin was at Fort Pierre, the trading post had been visited by a small party of Cheyennes, with which the Sioux carried on a semi-friendly relationship. The Cheyennes lived farther to the West, going to the edge of the Rocky Mountains. Being in a region particularly abundant in wild horses, they had a remunerative trade in these animals with both the Sioux and Mandans, although they were the constant enemies of the Blackfeet, their neighbors to the north, and the Pawnees to the south. In the visiting party was an attractive Indian woman, the head chief's wife, whom the artist had the opportunity of painting without the complications he had formerly encountered. Her name was *Tis-se-woo-na-tis*, otherwise known as She Who Bathes Her Knees (color plate page 55).

New York Public Library

SIOUX WOMEN DRESSING HIDES

The artist also had enjoyed the excellent opportunity of accompanying and observing the marvelous abilities of the Sioux in hunting buffaloes on the surrounding plains. He saw the great herds as they originally were and watched the Indian hunters pursue them as they did long before the white man came into the country. Catlin gave us the first really comprehensive eye-witness account that we have of these dramatic hunting scenes, which have since become one of the most noteworthy bits of lore in the story of our Old West. Coming as he did on the steamboat *Yellow Stone*, which provided a means of transporting heavy loads of buffalo hides, he saw the beginning of that extensive trade, which rapidly led to the complete destruction of the great herds — and he clearly foresaw the tragic results.

"The word buffalo is undoubtedly the most incorrectly applied to these animals," he wrote,[32] "for they bear about as much resemblance to the Eastern (European) buffalo, as they do to a zebra or a common ox . . . The American bison, or (as I shall hereafter call it) the buffalo . . . graze in almost incredible numbers over vast tracts of this country . . . The Sioux are a bold and desperate set of horsemen; and great hunters . . . The Indian generally strips himself and his horse of his shield and quiver and every part of his dress which might be an encumbrance . . . grasping his bow in his left hand, with five or six arrows ready for instant use. In his right hand or attached to his wrist is a heavy whip, which he uses without mercy. The Indian has little use for the rein, which hangs on the neck, while the horse is trained to approach the animal from the right side, permitting the rider to shoot his arrow to the left; which he does at the instant when the horse is passing — bringing him opposite the heart, which receives the deadly weapon 'to the feather.'

"When pursuing a large herd, the Indian generally rides in the rear, until he selects the animal he wishes to kill, which he separates from the throng by dashing his horse between the rest and forcing it off by itself; where he can approach it without the danger of being run down and trampled to death . . . At the moment the horse has approached the nearest distance required and has passed the animal, he sheers away to prevent coming onto the horns of the infuriated beast, which often are instantly turned and presented for a fatal reception. These frightful collisions often take place, notwithstanding the sagacity of the horse and the caution of the rider [see color plate page 146]. The Indian also generally has a *laso*, dragging behind his horse's heels — a long thong of rawhide, ten or fifteen yards in length and made of several braids. This is used chiefly to catch the wild horses, by throwing over their neck a noose which is made at the end and with which they are 'choked down.' In running buffalo, or in time of war, the *laso* drags on the ground, so that if the man is dismounted, which is often the case, he has the power of grasping to the *laso* and securing his horse again." These trailing *lasos* can be seen in the picture on page 64.

That the buffalo was not always hunted for its meat and hide alone is indicated by an incident which the artist witnessed while at Fort Pierre. A party of several hundred Indians on horseback crossed the river about mid-day to attack an immense herd nearby. They returned at sundown, with about *fourteen hundred fresh buffalo tongues*, which had been taken at the suggestion of the white traders and for which they received in payment a few gallons of whiskey that was quickly consumed by the hunters. "Not a skin or a pound of the meat, except the tongues, was brought in," wrote Catlin, "which fully supports me in the seemingly extravagant prediction that I have made as to the extinction of the buffalo . . . The Indians look to the white man as wiser than themselves and able to set them examples — and see none of these in their country but sellers of whiskey and setting the example of using it themselves. They easily acquire a taste, where whiskey is sold for sixteen dollars a gallon and soon impoverishes them, and must soon strip the skin from the last buffalo's back to be vended to the Traders for a pint of diluted alcohol . . . The Indian and the buffalo are joint and original tenants of the soil, and fugitives from the approach of civilized man . . . It is not enough in this polished and extravagant age, that we get from the Indians his lands, and the very clothes from his back, but the food for his mouth must be stopped, to add a new article to the fashionable world's luxuries . . . that white men may figure a few years longer, enveloped in buffalo robes — spread them over the backs of their sleighs and trail them ostensibly amid the busy throng, as a thing of elegance that had been made for them! . . . It may be that *power* is *right*, and *voracity* a virtue; and that these people, and these noble animals, are righteously doomed to an issue that *will* not be averted."

Due to the long delay at Fort Pierre, the *Yellow Stone* was pushed as rapidly as possible toward its destination at Fort Union, about eight hundred miles farther up the Missouri. Very few stops were made and these were brief, for the high water of spring and early summer would soon be at an end and the big steamboat might become stranded until the following year. There was one stop on that trip, however, to which George Catlin looked forward with apprehension and curiosity. That was when *Wi-jun-jon*, The Pigeon's Egg Head, returned to the Assiniboin village of his chieftain father, after visiting the white man's cities. When the *Yellow Stone* was still a good many miles from the village, *Wi-jun-jon* was on the forward most part of the boat's upper deck gazing with loving eyes upon the familiar scenery and waiting impatiently for the first distant view of his home. He was, of course, still dressed in the military uniform which had been given to him by the President of the United States and to which he had added such embellishments as had caught his child-like fancy. The whole garb was by now very badly wrinkled and soiled, from being slept in so many nights and being used so long to wipe his hands on. The tall plume which once stood above his big

New York Public Library

THE LITTLE BEAR, THE STEEP WIND, AND THE DOG

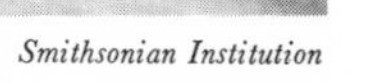

Smithsonian Institution

CHIN-CAH-PEE, The Fire Bug
Wife of *Wi-jun-jon*

Smithsonian Institution

TCHA-AES-KA-DING
Blackfoot Boy

beaver hat, drooped over his face in jaded fashion; the kid gloves were almost black; and his fan was badly broken. But he still wore the broadsword and high-heeled boots, and had two bottles of whiskey in his pockets and under his arm a small keg of it; and he was, beyond all doubt, the most astonishingly garbed Indian who ever traveled the Missouri.

Wi-jun-jon's village was only a short distance below Fort Union. It was the principal settlement of the Assiniboin tribe of between seven and eight thousand proud and dignified people, who controlled the large territory from just below the mouth of the Yellowstone River northward and eastward into Canada. Finally the steamboat arrived there and tied up to the bank, where well over a thousand of the tribesmen were gathered to welcome home the son of their chief. They were also anxious to hear what he had to tell about his long journey to visit the Great White Father and see the sights of the white man's cities and their civilized society. Awaiting the return was his wife, *Chin-cah-pee*, The Fire Bug (page 62) and his children and many relatives and friends. But what they saw, and later heard, was far far beyond their wildest anticipations or ability to understand.

"I saw him walk ashore," wrote Catlin[33], ". . . with a keg of whiskey under his arm and blue umbrella in his hand. In this plight and metamorphose he took his position on the bank, amongst his friends, his wife and other relatives, not one of whom exhibited for half an hour or more the slightest symptoms of recognition, although they knew well who was before them. He also gazed upon them . . . as if they were foreign to him and he had not a feeling or thought to interchange with them. Thus the mutual gazing upon and from this would-be stranger continued . . . when a gradual but cold and exceedingly formal recognition began to take place and an acquaintance took place, which ultimately resolved itself." Bit by bit *Wi-jun-jon* condescended to tell his story and with insatiable Indian curiosity the tribesmen grasped for every word. This amazing sensation among the Assiniboines was only beginning when the *Yellow Stone* pulled away to hurry on to its destination but as Fort Union was only a short distance away, George Catlin later learned the outcome.

Daily and nightly the Assiniboines crowded around their Pigeon's Egg Head to listen to what he said — which was to them so unintelligible and beyond comprehension that they set him down as an unbelievable liar and deranged impostor. He had been, they said among themselves, among the whites who are great liars, and all he had learned was to come home and tell lies. He rapidly sank into disgrace, although he blithely continued to strut about and act the fox and bear as best he could, and to lecture on the manners and customs of the pale-faces. Soon, however, his keg of whiskey was dry of its charms to his best friends; his once beautiful military costume, which his wife thought useless below the waist, had been cut off to make herself a pair of leggings; and she had appropriated the lace band of the hat for a pair of splendid garters. Finally about all that he had left was the umbrella, which he affectionately held onto and kept spread over his head on nearly all occasions, both day and night. Even when he went out on the buffalo hunts he did little more than strut about or sit and talk about what he had seen. This went on for months — and eventually *Wi-jun-jon*, The Pigeon's Egg Head, was killed as the most preposterous liar and no-good individual that the tribe had ever known.

Smithsonian Institution

SIOUX INDIANS HUNTING BUFFALO

7

Life in a Primitive State

Newberry Library, Chicago

THE RED THUNDER

IN A LETTER dated "Yellow Stone, 17th June, 1832," George Catlin wrote: "I arrived at this place yesterday, in the steam-boat 'Yellow Stone,' after a voyage of nearly three months from St. Louis, a distance of two thousand miles . . . The Fur Company have erected here, for their protection against the savages, a very beautiful Fort, and our approach to it, under the continual roar of cannon for half an hour, and the shrill yells of the half affrighted savages who lined the shore, presented a scene of the most thrilling and picturesque appearance." The lengthy letter was sent to William L. Stone, Editor of the *New York Commercial Advertiser*, who saw fit to "take the liberty of publishing his letter entire" in the issue of Tuesday, July 24, 1832 — although Catlin's name was nowhere mentioned in connection with it. Between this date and February 20th, 1833, there were five letters from the artist published, the others carrying his signature. These described his entire trip up and down the Missouri River, and they were later greatly elaborated into a substantial part of George Catlin's two-volume work, *Letters and Notes On the Manners, Customs and Condition of the North American Indians*, published by the Author, London, 1841.

Fort Union was situated at the mouth of the Yellowstone River, very close to the present North Dakota-Montana state border. It was established in 1829, just three years before Catlin's arrival, by Kenneth McKenzie, a Scotsman of adventurous spirit and great courage, who had pioneered the American Fur Company's conquest of the Upper Missouri country. By 1832 the fort had become the principal trading rendezvous of a large number of primitive Indians of several tribes, who came long distances to visit the place. Sometimes a whole tribe came together. Sometimes several tribes were there at the same time, and bitter enemies though they might be, the vicinity of the fort was recognized as a peaceful meeting place. At the time of Catlin's arrival, there were large numbers of Blackfeet, Crows, Assiniboines, and Knisteneaux (Crees) encamped there. (Page 67.) The fort itself was two hundred feet square, built of stone and was inside a stockade. Kenneth McKenzie ruled his broad domain like a medieval baron. "He lives in a good and comfortable style," wrote Catlin. "Inside the fort are eight or ten log houses and stores, and he generally has 40 to 50 men and 150 horses about him . . . His table groans under the luxuries of the country — with buffalo meat and tongues, beavers' tails, and marrow fat; but *sans coffee*, *sans bread and butter* . . . and with good wine, also; for a bottle of *madeira* and one of excellent port are set in a pail of ice every day and exhausted at dinner." Kenneth McKenzie was a shrewd and despotic trader who set the pattern for the white man's conquest in the Northwest. He offered the pioneer documentarian every opportunity to pursue the purpose of his visit.

"I am travelling in this country," Catlin wrote,[34] "not to advance or prove theories, but to see all I am able to see and tell it in the simplest and most intelligent manner." He was strictly a realist. How easy it would have been for him to play to the gallery of popular taste and paint pictures of the many sensational scenes he witnessed and in which he personally played a part, or to glamorize his Indian warriors and make his Indian maidens beautiful, as the fiction writers did. But he followed the same basic, honest precept in making his Indian pictures as he had in painting the portraits of DeWitt Clinton and the Virginia Constitutional Convention. "It is but to paint the splendid panorama of a world entirely different from anything seen or painted before; a vast country of green fields, where men are all red; where meat is the staff of life; where no laws but those of honor are known; where buffaloes range, and the elk, mountain sheep, and fleet-bounding antelope . . . where the wolves are white and bears grizzly . . . where the rivers are yellow and white men are turned savages . . . the dogs are all wolves, women are slaves, men are lords . . . For all those . . . yet uncorrupted by the vices of civilized acquaintance . . . for the character and preservation of these noble fellows I am an enthusiast, and it is for these uncontaminated people that I would be willing to devote the energies of my life."

Catlin was very careful in the matter of documentation of his pictures. He may have made an occasional error in an Indian name or a particular date, or enlarged a design to give it emphasis and detail. In as many instances as possible, he acquired and carried home the costumes which his subjects wore. It should be kept in mind that Catlin was working among a people of whose ethnology and history he knew practically nothing and whose languages he was only beginning to understand; that he was extremely short of funds; and that he painted an almost unbelievable number of pictures in a very short period of time. To aid in the documentation of his work, he carried with him printed certificates of authentication, which he filled out and had signed on the spot by reputable Indian agents, fur company agents, and Army officers, who had witnessed the actual painting. An example of this is:

"*No. 131 — Blackfoot, PE-TOH-PE-KIS (The Eagle Ribs) I hereby certify That this portrait was painted from life, at Fort Union, mouth of Yellowstone, in the year 1832, by George Catlin, and that the Indian sat in the costume in which it is painted.* [Signed] *John F. A. Sanford, United States Indian Agent.*"

This particular Indian is shown in Catlin's drawing of him on page 70 of this book.

The Blackfeet and Crows were the principal tribes with which the American Fur Company at Fort Union were concerned, for these two extensive groups controlled a vast area extending in a broad sweep westward into the Rocky Mountains. This was a great beaver country — and beaver skins had been the richest harvest since the fur trade began in America. The Blackfeet, including the Piegans, and the "Bloods" of the north extended into British territory and into the still unexplored Rocky Mountains. Catlin estimated their number at about 16,500. They were a very war-like and predatory people, fine of physique, highly intelligent in their primitive pursuits, and richly clad in the prosperous manner of their culture. Although the white man's conquest of the region was only beginning, the Blackfeet resented the intrusion and were openly defiant of it. They were willing to come to Fort Union and trade, but they repeatedly warned the traders that they would not tolerate the company's trappers trespassing in their domain. They had said they would kill men whom they found taking their beavers and other game. This warning had been disregarded at the cost of fifteen to twenty men each year. There was nowhere on the American frontier a stronger, more determined conflict of interests between red men and white. "Trinkets and whiskey, however," the artist wrote,[35] "will soon spread their charms amongst these people, as it has amongst other tribes; and white man's voracity will sweep the prairies and the streams of their wealth; leaving the Indians to . . . starve upon, a dreary and solitary waste."

Catlin was provided a studio in one of the bastions of the Fort. "My easel stands before me," he wrote,[36] "and the cool breech of a twelve-pounder makes me a comfortable seat, whilst her muzzle is looking out one of the port-holes. The operations of my brush are mysteries of the highest order to these red sons of the prairie, and my room the earliest and latest place of concentration of these wild and jealous spirits; who all meet here to be amused, and pay me signal honors; but gaze upon each other, sending their side-long looks of deep-rooted hatred and revenge around the group. However, whilst in the Fort, their weapons are placed within the arsenal, and naught but looks and thoughts can be breathed here; but death and grim destruction will visit back those looks upon each other, when these wild spirits again are loose and free to act upon the plains . . .

"The chiefs have had to place 'soldiers' (as they are called) at the door, with spears in hand to protect me from the throng . . . and none but the worthies are allowed to come into my apartment, and none to be painted except such as are decided by the chiefs to be worthy of so high an honor . . .

"I have this day been painting a portrait of the head chief of the Blackfoot nation . . . The name of this dignitary is *Stee-mick-o-sucks*, The Buffalo's Back Fat. [Color plate page 73] . . . Whilst sitting for his picture he has been surrounded by his own warriors, and also gazed at by his enemies . . . a number of distinguished personages of each of which tribes have laid all

Smithsonian Institution

FORT UNION, MOUTH OF THE YELLOWSTONE

day around the sides of my room; reciting to each other the battles they have fought, and pointing to the scalplocks worn as proofs of their victories, attached to the seams of their shirts and leggings. This is a curious scene to witness, when one sits in the midst of such inflammable and combustible materials, brought together unarmed, for the first time in their lives; peaceably and calmly recounting the deeds of their lives, and smoking their pipes upon it, when a few days or weeks will bring them on the plains again, where the war-cry will be raised, and their deadly bows will again be drawn on each other . . .

"I have also painted *Pe-toh-pe-kis*, The Eagle Ribs [previously referred to] . . . Of all the Blackfeet whose portraits are now standing in my room, he is one of the most extraordinary. Though not a chief, he stands here in the Fort and deliberately boasts of eight scalps which he says he has taken from the heads of trappers and traders with his own hands. His dress is really superb, almost literally covered with scalp-locks, of savage and civil. His head-dress is made of ermine skins and horns of the buffalo . . . worn only by the bravest and the most extraordinary of the nation . . . I have also painted, of the Blackfeet, *Mix-ke-note-skin-a*, The Iron Horn [page 69] . . . and half a dozen others . . . Also the grandson of the head chief, *Tcha-aes-ka-ding*, [shown on page 62] a boy of six years of age, and too young as yet to have acquired a (tribal) name, has stood forth like a tried warrior; and I have painted him at full length, with his bow and quiver, and his robe made of raccoon skin. His father is dead, and in the case of the death of the chief, he becomes the hereditary chief of the tribe. This boy has been thrice stolen away by the Crows, and thrice re-captured by the Blackfeet, at considerable sacrifice of life, and at present he is lodged with Mr. McKenzie, for . . . protection, until he shall arrive at the proper age to take the office to which he is to succeed. . . ."

Besides portraits of the chiefs and warriors, Catlin also transferred to canvas the likeness of the principal medicine-man of the Blackfoot tribe — the high-priest, prophet, doctor, magician and supernatural controller of the whims of human destiny. No one in an orthodox Indian community exerted a broader and stronger influence over its citizens, than the medicine-man, and none of these was more characteristic of his profession than this distinguished functionary of the Blackfeet. His name was *Wun-nes-tow*, The White Buffalo. The artist painted him full-length, in his inauspicious and civil appearance (page 17); also in all the strange regalia of his mystic profession (color plate page 74) and made a graphic drawing of an actual performance of his rites over the body of one of his tribesman (page 71) who was killed in a dramatic incident which the artist witnessed.

"Medicine" played an extremely important part in the primitive culture and therefore in the daily lives of every tribe and its individuals. Medicine meant mystery, or supernatural influence, rather than drugs, although it was often used by the medicine-man as doctors and physicians. The tribes and the clans had their sacred "medicines," which were strange material objects, like the hide of a white buffalo or maybe an unusual fossil, which might be wrapped in finely tanned and beautifully decorated doeskin and kept in a very elaborate case or bundle in the same manner as civilized church congregations keep their own religious treasures. Every Indian individual in his primitive state had his own personal medicine-bag, to which he prayed, paid the greatest respect and looked to for personal protection throughout his life. Each man's personal medicine was generally acquired as a part of his transition from adolescence into manhood. To "make his medicine," he might wander out into the wilderness alone, absenting himself from all others for several days, and lie on the ground or wander about, abstaining from food and drink, crying to the Great Spirit, and waiting for some dream or extraordinary experience which could be construed as a sort of supernatural vision which would determine what his medicine should be. He might dream about a bird, or reptile, or animal, or maybe see or find something unusual. In his fear or hunger he might

Smithsonian Institution

MIX-KE-MÓTE-SKIN-NA, The Iron Horn
Blackfoot Warrior

Smithsonian Institution

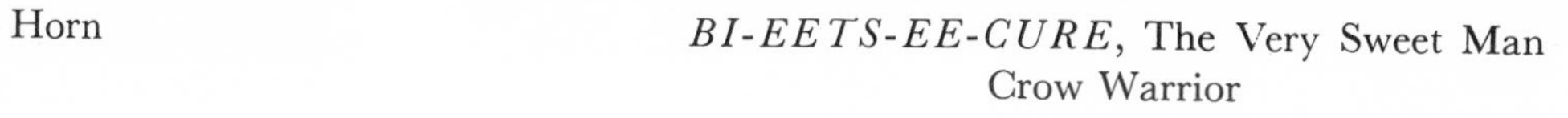

BI-EETS-EE-CURE, The Very Sweet Man
Crow Warrior

have some hallucination — or even *pretend* to do so. But he had to "make his medicine" before he returned home, and that would form the basis of his medicine-bag, to be his for life and valued beyond all price, even to the extent of his very existence. In death, this guardian spirit was buried with him — to conduct him safely into the beautiful heaven to which all good Indians aspired.

The medicine-man was the high priest, the symbol and the embodiment of everything that the Indian recognized and worshiped in his "medicine." The performance of *Wun-nes-tow* in administering the "last rites" to a murdered chief of the Blackfeet, which Catlin witnessed, came about in the following manner as told in the artist's own words:[37] "A party of Knisteneaux came here (Fort Union) from the north, for the purpose of making their summer trade with the Fur Company; and a party of Blackfeet, their natural enemies, came from the west, also to trade. These two belligerent tribes encamped on different sides of the Fort, and they spent some weeks here at the Fort and about it, in apparently good feeling and fellowship; unable in fact to act otherwise, according to the regulation of the Fort. . . .

"The Knisteneaux had completed their trade . . . When they were ready to start, with their goods packed to travel, their arms were given them, and they started; having bid friends and foes a hearty farewell . . . and though one of them loitered about the Fort, until he got an opportunity to poke the muzzle of his gun between the piquets; when he fired it at one of the Chief of the Blackfeet, who stood within a few paces, talking with Mr. McKenzie, and shot him through the center of the body. The Blackfoot fell and rolled about upon the ground in the agonies of death. The Blackfeet seized their weapons and ran in a mass out of the Fort, in pursuit of the Knisteneaux, who were rapidly retreating to the bluffs. I ran to my

New York Public Library

PEH-TO-PEE-KISS, The Eagle Ribs; War Chief of the Blackfoot
With his Wife and Child (right), and *Peh-No-Mah-Kan*

New York Public Library

BLACKFOOT MEDICINE-MAN PERFORMING HIS RITES

painting room, overlooking the plain, where I had a fair view of the affair; and a skirmish ensued which lasted half an hour . . . The Blackfeet returned to the Fort, and I saw the medicine-man performing his mysteries over the dying man [page 71].

"The man who was shot was still living — still lying on the ground in the agonies of death, and no one could indulge the slightest hope for his recovery; yet the *medicine-man* must needs be called . . . Several hundred spectators, including Indians and traders, were assembled around the dying man, when it was announced that the *medicine-man* was coming; we were required to form a ring, leaving a space of some 30 or 40 feet in diameter around the dying man, in which the doctor could perform his wonderful operations; and a space was opened to allow him free room to pass through the crowd without touching anyone. His arrival was announced by the death-like 'hush! — sh! —' through the crowd; and nothing was to be heard, save the light tinkling of the rattles upon his dress, as he slowly moved through the avenue left for him . . . [Color plate page 74.]

"He approached the ring with his body in a crouching position, with a slow and tilting step. His body and head were entirely covered with the skin of a yellow bear, the head of which (his own head being inside of it) served as a mask; the huge claws of which were dangling on his wrists and ankles; and in one hand he shook a frightful rattle and in the other brandished his medicine spear; to the rattling din and discord of all of which he added the wild and startling jumps and yelps of the Indian, and the appalling grunts, snarls and growls of the grizzly bear, in ejaculatory and guttural incantations to the Good and Bad Spirits, in behalf of his patient, who was rolling and groaning whilst he was dancing around him, jumping over him, and pawing him about and rolling him in every direction. . . . This strange

New York Historical Society

CATLIN SKETCHING BUFFALO UNDER WOLF SKIN

operation proceeded for half an hour, before the numerous and death-like silent audience, until the man died; and the medicine-man danced off to his quarters and packed up, and tied and secured from the sight of the world, his mystery dress and equipments. His dress, in all its parts, is one of the greatest curiosities in the whole collection of Indian manufactures which I have yet obtained in the Indian country. It is a strange medley and mixture, perhaps, of the mysteries of the animal and vegetable kingdoms that ever was seen. Besides the skin of the yellow bear (an anomaly in that country and great medicine) there are attached to it the skins of many animals, which are also anomalies or deformities, which render them medicine — the skins of snakes, frogs and bats — beaks and toes and tails of birds — hoofs of deer and antelopes — in fact the odds and ends and fag ends, and tails and tips of almost everything that swims, flies or runs, in this part of the world."

All this was the "medicine," the mystery and superstition which dominated the primitive Indians, among whom George Catlin was living and to whom he came as a documentary pioneer to portray them factually for future generations.

Smithsonian Institution

STU-MICK-O-SUCKS, The Buffalo's Back Fat
Head Chief of the Blackfeet

Smithsonian Institution

BLACKFOOT MEDICINE MAN
WUN-NES-TOW, The White Buffalo

8

The Magnificent Male

Newberry Library, Chicago
THE TWO CROWS

THERE WAS hardly an able-bodied tribesman throughout the whole Northwest who was not an enthusiastic hunter, as well as a bold and daring warrior, and a magnificent male on constant parade. Next to his prowess in battle, the Indian was most proud of his skill in wielding his primitive weapons in pursuit of dangerous game. Almost always astride a spirited horse's back, these red knights of the northern prairies took real delight in dashing at full speed into a stampeding bunch of buffalo to sink arrows or spears into the side of a shaggy quarry, or to parry the claws of a powerful grizzly bear while swinging a heavy war club at his head. Big game hunting was not only a sport, but one of life's necessities. Here was a potent lure for a visiting enthusiast like Catlin, who from early boyhood had grown up in the wooded hills of Pennsylvania with a gun in his hands. Here also was equally attractive material for a pioneer documentary artist's sketch book and canvas. Catlin frequently joined the hunting parties that went out from Fort Union, both as participant and observer. Whether Blackfeet, Crows or Assiniboines, they welcomed him into their company and took child-like delight in putting on their best display for the edification of this congenial and kindred spirit. He also rode alone to their encampments, to be welcomed as a friendly guest.

For those who have not personally traveled alone among primitive people, it is difficult to understand how a man can get along without understanding the language, particularly when the visitor is endeavoring to gather information regarding activities and customs that are strange to him. Among such people, however, the language and communication of ideas is reduced to the simplest form, and instinctive understanding is far more highly developed than it is among civilized groups. George Catlin had an inquisitive nature and an extremely analytical mind. Because of the very sympathetic relationship he enjoyed with the Indians, he saw more and learned more, even without benefit of an interpreter at his side, than most other white men would have. He also had a remarkably good memory to supplement the hasty sketches and detailed notes in his sketch books, and they could be filled in with further information by the white traders who were more familiar with the Indians' mode of life. Always extremely careful about details, he never left a questionable fact without searching for proof. Almost everywhere that he went he not only carried sketch-books, but also his pieces of unmounted canvas, which when painted and dry were rolled up and packed in a round tin case that was slung on his back.

In hunting the buffalo, the methods of the Blackfeet and Crows were very similar to the Sioux. His notes made while in the Fort Union area give a description of the weapons used: "The bow with which they are armed is small and apparently an insignificant weapon, though one of almost incredible power in the hands of its owner, whose sinews have been from childhood habituated to its use," he wrote.[38] "The length of these bows is generally about three feet and sometimes not more than two and a half. They have no doubt studied to get the requisite power in the smallest compass possible, as it is more easily used on horseback than one of greater length. The greater part of these bows are made of ash and lined on the back with layers of buffalo or deers' sinews to give greater elasticity. There are many also (amongst the Blackfeet and Crows) which are made of bone, and others of the horn of the mountain sheep. Those made from bone are decidedly the most valuable and cannot be procured short of the price of one or two horses . . . and their arrows are headed with flint or bone, of their own construction, or with steel, as they are now chiefly furnished by the Fur Traders. The quiver, which is uniformly carried on the back and made of the panther or otter skin, is a magazine of these deadly weapons, and generally carries two varieties. The one to be drawn upon a human enemy, generally poisoned and with long barbs designed to hang in the wound after the shaft is withdrawn, in which they are but slightly glued; and the other is used for their game, with the blade firmly fastened to the shaft and with the barbs inverted, that it may easily be drawn from the wound and used again."

There appeared to be an inexhaustible abundance of buffalo and other game throughout this whole vast region — all far removed from the destruction of the white man's civilization. But even here George Catlin clearly foresaw the inevitable, and he advanced the following prophetic proposal: "What a splendid contemplation it would be, by some great protecting policy of our government, to preserve them in their pristine beauty and wildness, in a *mag-*

Smithsonian Institution

A CROW TEPEE

New York Historical Society

VILLAGE LIFE ON THE PLAINS

nificent park, where the world could see them for ages to come. What a beautiful specimen for America to preserve and hold up to the view of her refined citizens and the world, in future ages! A *National Park*, containing man and beast, in all the wild freshness of their native beauty! I would ask no other monument to my memory, than the founder of such an institution."[39] This proposal encompassed a strip of territory along the eastern edge of the Rocky Mountains, and it was the first suggestion of its kind. He later advocated this proposal in the lectures that were given with the exhibition of his Indian Gallery when he returned to the East, and in the published accounts of his experiences. Like other of Catlin's farsighted proposals, this was not realized until a good many years afterward, when it became at least partially fulfilled in what is today Yellowstone National Park — just as his plan for creating a "museum of mankind" later materialized as our great U.S. National Museum and Smithsonian Institution. Catlin not only advanced these proposals, but he devoted untiring efforts to their fulfillment throughout the rest of his long life.

There was a great deal around old Fort Union to stimulate the Medicine Painter's interest. Each tribe had its own attractions. The Crows were not as large nor as powerful as the Blackfeet, although they were equally proud and as skilled and desperate warriors, and there was no tribe which equalled them in the elegance with which their men garbed themselves for war or peace. An example of the classic masculine display with which the primitive Crows adorned themselves is shown in the artist's portrayal of *Ba-da-ah-chon-du*, He Who Jumps Over All (colorplate page 92, also a later drawing of the same subject on page 18). This dignitary is mounted on his fine horse, both elaborately costumed in beautiful headdresses of war-eagle feathers and handsomely bedecked in paraphernalia from head to feet, with their remarkably long hair trailing in the breeze. Here was the pre-white-man Plains Indian at the height of his primitive culture.

The Crows, according to Catlin's estimate at the time, were a nation of probably not more than 7,000 in all, with about 800 braves and warriors. Among the more extensive tribes, such as the Sioux and Blackfeet, it was a fair calculation to count one in five as fighting men. Among the Crows and other smaller but equally warlike groups, the proportion was smaller, due to the larger number who were continually being killed in battle. Among the latter there were sometimes two or three women to every man.

Like the other Plains Indians who moved about from place to place, following the herds of buffalo and waging almost constant warfare against their neighbors, the Crows lived mostly in tepees or lodges made of tanned buffalo hides. "The Crows, of all the tribes, make the most beautiful lodges," wrote Catlin. "They often dress the skins almost as white as linen, and beautifully garnish them with porcupine quills, and paint and ornament them in a variety of ways, as to render them exceedingly picturesque . . . I have procured a very beautiful one of this description [see page 76] highly ornamented and fringed with scalp-locks, and sufficiently large for 40 men to dine inside. The poles are 30 in number . . . The tent when erected is about 25 feet high, with the great or Good Spirit painted on one side and the Evil Spirit on the other." This particular tepee was transported back to St. Louis and was later exhibited in his Indian Gallery in New York and other Eastern cities, as well as in Europe. "These lodges are taken down in a few minutes by the squaws . . . and easily transported to any part of the country where they wish to encamp [see page 78] . . . as they range over the plains . . . to procure and dress their skins . . . and also for the purpose of killing and drying meat; making pemican and preserving the marrow-fat for their winter quarters; which are generally taken up in some heavy-timbered bottom, deeply imbedded within the

Smithsonian Institution

MOVING CAMP

surrounding bluffs, which break the winds and make their long winter months tolerable. They sometimes erect their skin lodges amongst the timber and dwell within them during the winter months; but more frequently cut logs and make rude cabins, in which they can live much warmer and better protected from the assaults of their enemies."

Smithsonian Institution

CROW WOMAN
Hair Cut for Mourning

The moving of the camp was directed by the chief. He would send his runners or criers, who were continually close at hand to carry out his biddings, through the village to announce the order. At the appointed moment every skin tepee would begin dropping to the ground. In the meantime all the necessary horses and dogs, of which there was invariably a great number, had been assembled to be speedily loaded with the burdens allotted to them. This was entirely the squaws' work. The lodge poles were divided into two bunches, with the small ends of each bunch fastened upon the shoulders of a horse, leaving the butt ends to drag on the ground on either side. Just behind the horse a short pole was tied across at right-angles to keep the poles spread apart; and upon this conveyance was placed the rolled or folded lodge, and upon it all the household possessions of the family. On the top of it all would be perched as many of the wives and children as could find a place to sit. Each horse was generally led or driven by a squaw, with a large pack on her own back, although sometimes she would sit astride the horse, perhaps with an infant at her breast and another youngster behind her, clinging to the horse. Furthermore, every dog that was large enough, and not wild enough to evade being captured and put in harness, would be pressed into service pulling his own load on a small *travois.* Two poles of about fifteen feet in length would be lashed to his shoulders, similarly to the horses, on which were tied the bundles allotted to him. In this manner the cavalcade would string out to move across the country. The men, all mounted on the best horses, would ride along in front, and at the flank or rear, looking on with the indifferent dignity of their elevated station as masters and warriors.

The Crow men were known for their tall and fine physique, and for their beautiful white, elaborately decorated garments. They were the virile, masculine, *beau monde* of the Plains tribes. Subjected as they were to the rains and sleet and wet snows, their skin clothing and tepee materials had to be specially prepared, and none excelled the Crows in this fine art. Their beautifully decorated dress of deer and elk and buffalo skins, which were repeatedly wet upon their backs, dried almost as soft as when made; and the tepee skins, which stood through all the inclement weather of summer and winter, were taken down as pliable as when first put up. Modern tanning methods seldom accomplish the fine results that were attained by the Crow squaws. The usual method of preparing a hide was quite simple in formula, but exceedingly efficient in its application. A hide was immersed, for the proper length of time, in a brine of ashes and water, after which the hair was scraped off. The hide was then stretched upon a frame or on the ground with stakes driven through the edges, and the brains of buffalo or elk were rubbed all over it. After remaining thus for a few days, the flesh side was scraped and "worked" until dry and soft. Then it was put through a process of "smoking" over a fire-hole fed with rotten wood and covered with a tight canopy of hard hide to retain the smoke and heat. By this process, expertly carried out, a chemical reaction was achieved which produced the desired results.

Catlin described the Crow men as "fine looking, with an ease and grace added to their dignity of manners . . . most of them six feet tall or more . . . and many have cultivated their hair to such an almost incredible length that it sweeps the ground as they walk."[40] (See color plates on pages 91–92). They usually bathed every morning in the river, after which they returned to their tepees, where their hair was oiled with a profusion of bear grease and combed with a porcupine's tail. In the performance of their toilette their squaws served as aids and attendants. The extraordinarily long hair was worn only by the men. "The present chief of the Crows, who is called 'Long Hair,' has received his name as well as his office from the circumstance of having the longest hair of any man in the nation," the artist continues. "I have not as yet seen this extraordinary gentleman, although he is known to several reputable persons with whom I am acquainted, who have assured me they had measured his hair by correct measure and found it to be ten feet seven inches in length; closely inspecting every part of it at the same time and satisfying themselves that it was the natural growth. On ordinary occasions it is wound with a broad leather strap, from the head to its extreme length, and then folded up into a block of some twelve inches in length; which when he walks is carried under his arm, or placed in his bosom within the folds of his robe; but on any great parade or similar occasion, his pride is to unfold it, oil it with bear's grease and let it drag behind him, black and shining as a raven's wing."

The Crow women had a glossy profusion of hair, although they were obliged to keep it cut rather short so as not to compete with their lords and masters. They were, like all other Indian women, the slaves of their husbands, in all the domestic duties and drudgeries of tribal life. The women, with few exceptions, were not allowed to join in religious ceremonies, nor in dances or other amusements. Being themselves the processors of all the skins used for garments, some of the squaws wore dresses made of fine tanned doe-skin, attractively decorated, although even in this respect they were not allowed to compete with the men.

Like the Blackfeet, the Crows strongly resented the white trappers and hide-hunters who trespassed in their country, catching beavers and other valuable fur-bearers and destroying the buffalo and other game on which the people depended for food and clothing. Such intrusions had been the basis of Indian tribal wars for centuries past. The white intruders could only be considered the same as other violators of the Indian's traditional rights of domain. The Fur Company had been warned time and again, although the Crows had shown great tolerance and friendship. "They have in some instances plundered and robbed the trappers and traders in their country," explained Catlin, "yet thieving in their tribal estimation is considered one of the most disgraceful acts a man can do. They call it 'capturing,' when they sometimes run off a trader's horses, considering it honorable as a retaliation for the unlicensed trespass committed in their country by mercenary white men . . . I look upon the Indian, in his native state, the most honest and honorable people that I have ever lived amongst . . . For the never-ending and boundless system of plunder, and debauching that is practiced upon these rightful owners of the soil by acquisitive white men, the retaliation by driving off and appropriating a few horses is but a lenient punishment."

During approximately a month that Catlin spent in the vicinity of Fort Union he was incessantly busy painting portraits and scenes of native life among the various tribes of the region, as well as filling page after page of his sketch-books and note-books with detailed reminders of every conceivable form of tribal life. He was constantly under a severe handicap. The only artist's materials available were those he had brought with him from St. Louis; and the conditions under which he worked and by which he preserved and transported all these materials were extremely difficult and hazardous. Even the most experienced of the *engagees* of the Fur Company generally reduced their personal property to little more than a gun and a skinning knife. What this pioneer artist accomplished and eventually brought safely back to St. Louis is truly amazing. Not the least remarkable feat was the two-thousand-mile trip that he made with his paraphernalia in a small skiff down the entire extent of the Missouri River, painting at nearly every important wild Indian settlement along the way. No white man of arts and letters had ever done anything like it before.

For the down-river journey George Catlin acquired two companions. They were Jean Ba'tiste, a Frenchman, and Abraham Bogard, a Mississippian. Both of these men were seasoned frontiersmen who had long served in the employ of the American Fur Company, trapping beaver and other furs far back in the little known wilderness. Now due a holiday from their hazardous adventures, they welcomed the jaunt down the river so they could spend their precariously earned pay in the drinking places and flesh-pots of St. Louis.

"When I had completed my rambles and sketches in those regions . . ." he wrote, "we launched off one fine morning, taking our leave of the fort and the friends within it. . . . Our canoe, which was made of green timber, was heavy and awkward, but our course being with the current promised us a fair and successful voyage. Ammunition was laid in in abundance, a good stock of dried buffalo tongues, a dozen or two of beavers' tails and a goodly supply of pemican. Bogard and Ba'tiste occupied the middle and bow, with their paddles in their hands, and I took my seat in the stern at the steering oar. . . . Besides which our little craft carried several packs of Indian dresses and other articles which I had purchased of the Indians, and also my canvas and easel, and our culinary articles, which were few and simple, consisting of three tin cups, a coffee pot, one tin plate, a frying pan, and a tin kettle. Thus fitted out and embarked, we swept off at a rapid rate under the shouts of the savages and the cheers of our friends who lined the bank as we gradually lost sight of them and turned our eyes toward St. Louis . . .

"We had another *compagnon du voyage*. Mr. McKenzie had made me a present of a full-grown, domesticated war-eagle, the noble bird which the Indians so much esteem for its valour and the quills to adorn the heads of chiefs and warriors. I had a perch erected for it some six feet high, over the bow of the skiff, on which it rested in perfect quietude, without being fastened, silently surveying all that we passed above and below; thus forming for our little craft a most appropriate figure-head. . . . He held to his perch and could not have been made to leave us — well fed with fresh buffalo meat and sometimes with fish . . . and he seemed to be owner and commander of the expedition. We always found him on his stand in the morning; and during the day as we were gliding along, when he tired of his position, he would raise himself upon his long and broad wings, and spreading them over us, would soar for miles together, a few feet over our heads, looking down at us."[41] Their one tin kettle was shortly lost overboard and the coffee pot burned up when left in a camp-fire while they all went in hasty pursuit of some game that appeared nearby. Catlin made a "sort of coffee a few times in the frying pan, but this proved a decided failure; and Bogard, who had a rabid taste for coffee, had the privilege of filling his pocket with ground coffee and sugar, which he daily ate from the hollow of his hand, while it lasted." Thus these picturesque and unusual argonauts moved steadily along the trail of high adventure — two on a lark and one making documentary history.

Smithsonian Institution

MANDAN VILLAGE

9

The Mysterious Mandans

Newberry Library, Chicago

MANDAN WARRIOR

CATLIN and his companions stopped at the main village of the Assiniboines and at the larger encampments of wandering tribesmen which struck Catlin's fancy, although he was restless to reach the villages of the mysterious Mandans, about two hundred miles down the river. It was there that the Lewis & Clark Expedition had spent the winter of 1804–'05 and the artist had heard a great deal about these unusual people from General Clark.

At first it seemed that St. Louis was very far away. But soon the three voyagers became absorbed in their idyllic journey through a wilderness world where a white man had rarely been seen before. Great herds of buffalo grazed along the water's edge and often blackened the green hills for miles away. There were nearly always antelope, elk and deer to be seen; frequently packs of big gray wolves roamed within view, searching for stragglers to be pulled down and torn apart; occasionally an arrogant grizzly; now and then mountain sheep perched on the cliffs that broke the monotony of gracefully rolling hills and spreads of prairie; and a great many ducks, geese, swans, cranes, prairie chickens and birds of many other varieties. Nearly every evening when the travelers went ashore to camp, they left their skiff for a little while to select some tender game for their supper and the following day, and the artist filled page after page of his sketch book with drawings and notes.

Time passed rapidly and on the seventh day they arrived at Fort Clark, the most important stopping place on the entire journey. "On this day, just before night, we landed our boat in front of the Mandan village," Catlin wrote,[42] "and amongst the hundreds who flocked towards the river to meet and greet us was Mr. Kipp, the agent of the American Fur Company, who has charge of their establishment at this place. He kindly ordered my canoe to be taken care of and my things be carried to his quarters, which was done at once."

George Catlin's experiences among the Mandans were unique in many respects. He observed and made pictures of practically every phase of their extraordinary culture, including the religious torture rituals and the associated ceremonial procedures which were not witnessed in their uninhibited entirety by any known white man, either before or afterward. In the latter instance, what he reported and recorded in his pictures was so radically unusual that its truthfulness was for a long time disputed, even by would-be authorities on the American Indians. Even after Catlin's unqualified veracity was established beyond doubt, there were those who had difficulty believing that such rituals were possible. Adding importance to his documentation is the fact that the Mandans were almost entirely exterminated by an epidemic of small-pox in 1837, or only five years after the artist's visit. "If Mr. Catlin had visited no other Indian tribe than the Mandans," wrote Thomas Donaldson, of the Smithsonian Institution, more than half a century afterward,[43] "his notes of and paintings of these Indians would alone preserve his memory." His opinion is well supported by the facts.

The Mandans were a small tribe of only about 2,000 individuals. They called themselves the *See-pohs-ka-nu-mah-ka-kee* or "People of the Pheasants." They lived in two permanent villages, about two miles apart, on the bank of the Missouri River near the present city of Bismarck, North Dakota. According to Catlin's description,[44] the principal village was located on a bank about forty feet above the bed of the river, where the bank formed an abrupt promontory. Thus the Mandans had only the back side to protect, which was effectually accomplished by a strong stockade of timbers about eighteen feet high and set firmly in the ground at sufficient distance apart to permit weapons to be fired between them. Running along inside the stockade was a three foot ditch, which further screened their bodies from the view and weapons of attacking enemies. The Mandans were very secure and had little to fear except from a meeting with unfriendly neighbors on the open prairie. Differing in many respects from the other roaming Plains tribes, the Mandans were not warlike, and judiciously located in a permanent and almost invulnerable village, they had advanced considerably further in the arts and had supplied their dwellings more abundantly with the comforts and luxuries of primitive life. They were known to the white men who had been among them as particularly friendly and cultured for Indians. "So forcibly have I been struck with the peculiar ease and elegance of these people," wrote the artist,[45] "together with the diversity of complications and various colors of their hair and eyes, and their unaccountable customs, that I am fully convinced that they have sprung from some other origin than that of other North American Indians, or that they are an amalgam of natives with some civilized race . . . There are a great many of these people whose complexions appear as light as half breeds; and among the women there are many whose skins are almost white, with the most pleasant symmetry of features; with hazel, gray and blue eyes . . . there may be seen every color of hair that can be seen in our country, with the exception of red and auburn . . . and in some instances almost white. About one in ten of the whole tribe are what the French call *cheveux gris* or gray-hairs."

The lodges of the village were grouped closely together, leaving just enough room for walking or riding between them. They were circular in form, from forty to sixty feet in diameter, depending on the number of inmates and importance of the families who occupied them. The foundations were prepared by excavating some two feet into the ground to form the floor of the dwelling. The superstructure consisted of a solid wall of timbers, about six feet in height, placed upright and imbedded in the ground, with earth packed solidly all around the outside. Resting upon the tops of these wall timbers were much longer ones, with their smaller ends tilted upward at a forty-five degree angle to the center and top of the dwelling. A sky-light of three or four feet was left at the apex. The roof was supported by beams passing around the inside and upheld by large posts extending from the floor. On the top was placed a covering of willow boughs, over which was placed earth, to a depth of two to three feet. The roof was finished off with a layer of clay, which when hard became impervious to water. These dome-shaped roof-tops were the lounging places for whole families in pleasant weather — a gossiping place for old and young, sages and warriors, wooing lovers, children and dogs.

The earth floors inside these dwellings were so hardened from use by bare and moccasined feet, and swept so clean, they had almost a polished appearance and would scarcely soil the whitest doe-skin. In the center and under the open skylight was the fire-place for cooking and heating (page 86). The family or families of plural wives, children, relatives and friends all slept in more or less curtained compartments around the side of the big room, which was always elaborately decorated with a wild profusion of finely tanned and beautifully garnished skin garments, head-dresses of war-eagle or raven feathers, weapons of war and hunting, paraphernalia for the various symbolic dances and various religious ceremonies, and the all-important "*medicine-bags*" which were the sacred and inviolate private possession of every male who had arrived at the age when he could proudly consider himself a man. On a post fixed in the ground in the small spaces between each sleeping compartment there was generally the woolly black head and horns of a buffalo that had been carefully made into an elaborate head-dress for use by the full-fledged warriors in the ceremonies of the *buffalo dance*.

"I have this morning perched myself upon the top of one of the earth-covered lodges," wrote Catlin;[46] "and having the whole village beneath and about me, [see page 82] with its sachems, warriors, dogs and horses in motion; its medicines and scalp-poles waving over my head; its green prairies in full view; with the din and bustle of the thrilling panorama that is about me . . . There are several hundred dwellings and they are purely unique . . . The living, in everything, carry an air of intractable wildness about them, and the dead are not buried but dried upon scaffolds. On the tops of the lodges are to be seen groups standing and reclining, whose picturesque appearances it would be difficult to describe . . . and beyond these, groups are engaged in games. Some are also to be seen manufacturing robes and dresses; and others, fatigued with amusements, have stretched their limbs to enjoy the luxury of sleep while basking in the sun . . . On the roofs of the lodges are also buffaloes' skulls, skin

Smithsonian Institution

SEEHK-HEE-DA, The White Eyebrows
Mandan Man with Yellow Hair

Smithsonian Institution

SAH-KO-KA, The Mint
Mandan Girl with Gray Hair

canoes, sleds and other things. And suspended on poles . . . above the doors of the lodges, are displayed the scalps of warriors . . . exposed as evidence of warlike deeds. On other poles are the warriors' whitened shields and quivers, with medicine-bags attached; and here and there a sacrifice of red cloth, or other costly stuff, offered up to the Great Spirit . . .

"In the center of the village is an open space of 150 feet in diameter and circular in form, which is used for all public games, festivals and exhibitions; and also for their annual *religious ceremonies*, which are soon to take place. The lodges around this open space front it, with their doors toward the center. In the middle of this circle stands an object of great religious veneration, on account of the importance it has in the conduction of those remarkable, annual religious rites [see color plate page 127]. This object is in the form of a large hogshead, some ten feet high, made of hand-hewn planks and hoops, and containing within it some of the villages' most precious community *medicines* — religiously preserved and highly venerated . . . Also, one of the lodges fronting on this public area and facing the strange object of their superstition, is the 'Medicine Lodge.' It is in this sacred building that those amazing ceremonies take place — in commemoration of the 'Great Flood.' I am told by the Traders that the cruelties of these scenes are frightful and abhorrent in the extreme; and that this huge lodge, which is now closed, has been built exclusively for this grand celebration."

All was not warfare, manly pursuits and serious attention to religious rites and colorful ceremonies, however, as the artist elsewhere relates in his *Letters and Notes*:[47] "There is another character familiarly known in this and every other tribe as an Indian *beau* or *dandy*. Such personages may be seen on every pleasant day, strutting around the village in the most beautiful and unsoiled dresses, but without the honorable trophies of scalp locks and claws of

New York Public Library

INTERIOR OF MANDAN DWELLING

Smithsonian Institution

HA-NA-TA-NU-MAUK, The Wolf Chief
Head Chief of the Mandans

the grizzly bear attached to their costume . . . They generally remain about the village, to take care of the women. They plume themselves with swan's down and quills of ducks, with plaits of sweet-scented grass and other unmeaning ornaments, which have no other merit than that of looking pretty and ornamental. These elegant gentlemen, who are few in each tribe, are held in very little esteem by the chiefs and braves . . . are denominated 'faint hearts' by the whole tribe. They seem, however, to be well contented with the celebrity they have acquired among the women and children, for the beauty and elegance of their personal appearance . . . These gay and tinselled bucks may be seen astride of their pied or dappled ponies, with a fan in the right hand, made of a turkey's tail, with whip and fly-brush attached to the wrist, and underneath them a white and beautiful and soft pleasure-saddle, ornamented with porcupine quills and ermine, parading about the village . . . When fatigued with this severe effort, the dandies will wend their way home; lift off their fine white saddle of doe's-skin, turn out their pony, take a little refreshment, smoke a pipe, and fan themselves to sleep and doze away the rest of the day."

Accustomed as the Mandans were to living in a permanent village and in dwellings which provided them an excellent retreat from inclement weather, it was natural that they should dress more elegantly than the nomadic tepee dwellers. There was a basic similarity of costume among most of the Northwestern tribes, although there were certain designs of decoration and modes of stitching or embroidering in nearly every tribe which distinguished it from the others. Because one tribe was constantly at war with another, there was a certain amount of interchange of property by capture and trade. The result was the wearing and copying of the fine examples of costume developed by neighboring artisans.

Polygamy was a custom common to the Plains tribes, particularly the Mandans. It was not exceptional to find a chief with from half a dozen to as many as fourteen wives, whose ages might run from young girls to old women — all more like slaves and chattels than companions in matrimony. Most of the manual labor was done by women and there was no such thing as hired help. It thus became a matter of necessity for a chieftain or other person of importance to have in his household a sufficient number of hand-maids or menials to perform the duties and drudgeries of his establishment, for his own personal comfort and the entertainment of his guests. Wives were an important part of every man's wealth, and the Indians had both the passion for the accumulation of wealth and the desire for the luxuries of life which is common to all races. The number of an Indian's wives rated him in affluence and

New York Public Library

MANDAN WOMEN BATHING

New York Public Library

THE STEAM-BATH

importance in the tribe. There was also the natural inclination of the male, which was highly developed among these people — and a man who produced a large number of male children provided his people with warriors essential to survival. A plurality of wives did not increase the expense of a household, but actually added to its prestige and prosperity.

Most of the white traders had Indian wives. Aside from the fact that there were no white women in the country at this time, it was good business if not a sheer necessity for promoting friendly relationships. If a trader or agent changed his location to another tribe, he generally also changed his wife. "The young women of the best families only can aspire to such an elevation," wrote Catlin,[48] "and most of them are exceedingly ambitious for such a connection . . . certain of a delightful exemption from the slavish duties when married under the circumstances, and generally allowed to lead a life of ease, covered with mantles of blue and scarlet cloth, with beads and trinkets and ribbons . . . the envied and tinseled belles of the tribe . . . Their women [the Mandans] are beautiful and modest — and amongst the respectable families, virtue is as highly cherished and as inapproachable as in any other society . . . and if either Indian or white man wishes to marry the most beautiful girl in the tribe, she is valued only equal perhaps to two horses, a gun with powder and ball for a year, five or six pounds of beads, or a couple of gallons of whiskey. The girls of this tribe, like most of the northwestern tribes, marry at the age of 12 or 14, and some at the age of 11."

At another place in the artist's notes on the Mandan women, he has the following to say:[49] "The strictest regard to decency, cleanliness and elegance of dress is observed. About half a mile above the village is the customary place where the women and girls resort every morning in the summer months to bathe in the river. To this spot they go by the hundreds at sunrise and on the beautiful beach they can be seen running and glistening in the sun, playing and leaping into the stream. The poorest swimmer amongst them will dash into the current of the Missouri and cross with perfect ease. A quarter of a mile back from the river, on an elevated terrace forming a semi-circle around this bathing place, are stationed several sentinels to guard and protect this ground from the approach of boys and men." A drawing of the Mandan women bathing in the river is reproduced on page 88. The artist is shown lying in the grass at a respectable distance away, but with a telescope in his hands. The bathing place of the men and boys was a similar distance on the opposite side of the village; and after the morning ablution the bathers returned to their homes to rub their bodies and hair with a profusion of bear grease.

The Mandans were also habitual users of steam-baths, of which each village had several that were accessible to all. They consisted of a sort of wicker bath-tub, which was carried to and from the public "sudatory" for use. (See page 89) The steam-baths were constructed of buffalo hides, with a furnace of large stones which the squaw heated in a nearby fire and doused with cold water after they were placed in position. The bottom of the bathing basket was usually strewn with a thin mat of wild sage and other aromatic and medicinal herbs, to flavor the exhilarating vapors which were inhaled deep into the bather's lungs. Finally he would dash out and plunge into the cold water of the river, after which he would wrap his buffalo robe about himself and hurry home, to be vigorously rubbed with bear grease. Then a pleasant nap, and he would dress in his finest garments to go forth to a social visit, a feast, to join in a dance, or maybe just to gossip and parade himself about the village. The Mandans were strongly addicted to the pleasures of feasting, personal display and talking about their own masculine conquests as well as those of their ancestors. Nothing, however, absorbed the interest of the Mandans as deeply as the legendry of the past which was interwoven with their sadistic religious rites.

Letters and Notes

USE OF SCALPS

American Museum of Natural History

CROW WARRIORS BATHING IN YELLOWSTONE

American Museum of Natural History

CROW CHIEF AT HIS TOILET

American Museum of Natural History,
American Heritage Magazine

BA-DA-AH-CHON-DU, He Who Outjumps All
A Crow Chief

10

A Guest Among Friends

Newberry Library, Chicago
MANDAN

AS WITH the previous tribes, Catlin's art created a sensation which fluctuated between superstitious adulation and open rebellion against the visiting white man. Following the protocol which experience had taught him was necessary, he had first painted portraits of the two foremost dignitaries of the tribe. The titular head of the Mandans was *Ha-na-ta-nu-mauk*, The Wolf Chief (page 87). Familiarly known to the early French traders as "*Chef de Loup*," he was a haughty and overbearing man, more feared than loved by his people. Having inherited his high office from his father, he had managed to hold onto his authority in spite of his shortcomings as a governor and warrior. The second person to be put on canvas was *Mah-to-toh-pa*, The Four Bears (page 95). Although second chief, he was the most popular man of the tribe. He was of admirable deportment and elegant appearance, a valiant leader and warrior. Catlin described him as "the most extraordinary man, perhaps, who lives at this day in the atmosphere of nature's noblemen . . . wearing a robe with the history of his battles upon it, which would fill a book of themselves, if properly translated."

The first two portraits were painted in the privacy of Catlin's improvised studio in the Fur Company fort and were not viewed by the sitters until both were finished. The two chiefs were shown the paintings together, and recognizing each other's likeness, they were amazed. They both clamped their hands over their mouths in the Indian expression of intense surprise, as each gazed from the painting to subject; and then with even greater curiosity at the artist's palette and its jumble of moist paints out of which these realistic portraits had been transferred to canvas. No Mandan medicine-man had ever performed such an amazing feat! "*Te-ho-pe-nee Wash-ee!*" (Great Medicine White Man!) they both exclaimed. Then they left the studio — to go to their own lodges and smoke a pipe in deep meditation upon this strange thing which had happened to them.

It was not long until a crowd began gathering around Catlin's studio as word spread about the new magic. By the time the two chiefs returned, several hundred people were pushing and mumbling and staring at the door. The Wolf Chief and The Four Bears brought several other tribal dignitaries and medicine-men to see the pictures, and a strong guard of braves had to be called into service to keep the curious crowd from pushing inside. The public clamor became so great that Catlin was asked to take the portraits outside and hold them up for all to see. Instantly recognizing their chiefs, some commenced yelping, others crying out or covering their mouths, while still others darted away and disappeared inside their own lodges to decide for themselves what to think about the paintings. They all agreed that the visiting white man had *made living beings! They had seen their two chiefs alive, in two places at the same time!* All agreed that such an operation could not be performed without some kind of serious harm to the chiefs as well as to the whole community. Catlin was therefore proclaimed a very dangerous white medicine-man who could make living persons by looking at them, and destroy life in the same way if he chose. Some demanded that he should immediately be driven from the village before he did more harm.

A tribal council was hurriedly called, at which the situation was argued with all the seriousness with which they would declare war against the Sioux. Mr. Kipp, whose judgment was highly regarded, made a strong appeal before them on Catlin's behalf. He assured the members of the council that it was a great honor to have their portraits painted, so that the artist might take the pictures to the great villages of the white men and show what fine people the Mandans were. Catlin himself was called to explain the meaning and purpose of his work. Finally, after prolonged explanation and serious arguing, the council decided that what the artist was doing was "good" and not "bad" — and this dictate of their supreme council was ordered promulgated throughout the village. The council members shook the artist's hand and prepared a fresh pipe to be smoked to his good health and to a friendly visit among them. He was presented with a *she-she-quoi*, or medicine-man's rattle and staff, hung with grizzly bears' claws, bats' wings, sage and ermine skins and highly perfumed with the scent of the skunk. A dog was also sacrificed and its bloody body hung with due ceremony over Catlin's studio door. Then other dignitaries went to have steam-baths and garb themselves in their finest garments to sit for their portraits.

There were some, however, who did not agree with the council's decision. When the painting in the studio was resumed, one important dissenter appeared outside the door and began haranguing the crowd. This was *Mah-to-he-ha*, The Old Bear, principal medicine man of the tribe. He commenced howling that all who were being painted were fools and when they died they would never be able to close their eyes in peaceful rest. Catlin met this new challenge in a diplomatic manner. Early the following morning, when alone in the studio, he sent for The Old Bear. Through an interpreter he told the medicine-man that ever since he had arrived in the village he had been admiring his wonderful appearance. He had learned what a distinguished person The Old Bear was; and he had practiced painting the others until he felt that his skill was equal to doing full justice to such a marvelous man. Now, he said, he was ready to paint *Mah-to-he-ha*. The Old Bear was so flattered by this eulogy that he shook Catlin's hand with the greatest enthusiasm and squatted down to smoke a pipe with him. Then he went away to have the most thorough steam-bath he had ever had, and to dress in the finest manner for the auspicious occasion.

"He made his appearance, having spent the whole fore-part of the day at his toilette . . ." wrote Catlin.[50] "Bedaubed and streaked with paints of various colors, with bear's grease and charcoal, with medicine-pipes in his hands and fox tails attached to his heels, entered *Mah-to-he-ha*, The Old Bear. With him came an entourage of his profession . . . in the *materia medica* and *hoca poca*. He took his position in the middle of the room, waving his eagle calumets in each hand and singing his medicine-song . . . looking me full in the face until I completed his picture, which I painted full length [color plate page 110]. His vanity was completely gratified by the operation. He lay for hours together, day after day in front of the picture, gazing upon it; lit my pipe for me as I was painting; shook my hands a dozen times each day; and enlarged upon my medicine virtues and talents . . . and became my strongest supporter in the community."

MAH-TO-TOH-PA, The Four Bears; Second Chief of the Mandans

Equally important to Catlin's prestige was the friendship which developed with *Mah-to-toh-pa*, The Four Bears. This distinguished and popular person took a real liking to the artist, and as an indication of this esteem, the second-chief tendered him a private feast. After his morning steam-bath and after being rubbed, greased, polished, painted and dressed in his most elegant finery, The Four Bears came into the studio. "Passing his arm through mine", wrote Catlin,[51] "he led me in the most gentlemanly manner through the village and into his own lodge . . . I was seated on a handsome robe, painted with hieroglyphics; and my host seated himself on another a little distance from me; with the feast prepared in dishes resting on a beautiful rush mat placed between us." (Page 97). The food consisted of three dishes. A large wooden bowl held a roast of choice buffalo ribs, another was filled with a sort of pudding made of wild turnip flour and flavored with dried wild currants and an earthen tray was heaped with pemican and marrow fat. Laid beside this primitive feast was a handsome pipe and a tobacco pouch filled with *knick-kneck* (Indian tobacco made of the bark of the red willow). When they were seated, the host lit his own pipe and after a few puffs presented the stem to Catlin to puff on. Then drawing his knife, Four Bears cut a small piece of meat and cast it into the fire (his way of saying grace). After this, the host indicated that the artist should draw his own knife and begin eating. "I ate my dinner alone," relates Catlin "for such is the custom of this land . . . a chief never eats with his guests; but while they eat he sits by at their service and ready to wait upon them." The Four Bears sat cross-legged, cleaning his pipe and preparing it for a smoke when his honored guest had finished. After he had taken enough *knick-kneck* from the pouch, he also took out a dried beaver castor, which was used to add flavor to the tobacco. Shaving off a small quantity, he mixed it with the tobacco in his hand. When the pipe was filled, a small amount of powdered buffalo dung was sprinkled on top, and then *Mah-to-toh-pa* sat with the pipe in his lap, waiting the time to light it. Finally, as Catlin put it, "we enjoyed together for a quarter of an hour the most delightful exchange of good feelings, amid clouds of smoke and pantomimic gesticulations." (There is no mention of use of the sign language.)

Throughout the little feast the chief's six or seven wives were seated in silence around the sides of the dwelling, waiting to obey their master's orders instantly and to execute them quietly. When Catlin rose to leave, the beautiful pipe was presented to him, as was the elegantly decorated buffalo robe on which he had sat. The hieroglyphics painted upon it were representations of the battles of the famous warrior's life and the fourteen enemies he had killed. (The artist's line drawings of these are used as spot illustrations in this book.)

The Mandans spent far less time in warfare, and much more in pleasant amusements than most tribes. There was hardly a day on which some masculine competition was not staged in the "public square" or on the prairie just outside the stockade. These contests were invariably accompanied by gambling among both participants and audience. All the Plains Indians were inveterate gamblers. Like the other tribesmen, the Mandans were extremely proud of their fine horses and loved to display their skill in horsemanship. Horse-racing was one of the most popular pastimes. Each contestant would wager his "entrance fee" of a shield, robe, pipe or other article according to the established value of the race. The prizes as well as the contest were supervised by appointed judges.

Another favorite competition was the "Game of Arrows" (page 98). In this each contestant would add his wager to a winner-take-all prize. One by one each man would shoot his arrows into the air, endeavoring to see who could put the largest number in the air before the first struck the ground. Frequently as many as eight arrows were put up before the first one fell. There were also other competitions in marksmanship with bow and arrow.

The Mandans had their own versions of most of the dances found among the other tribes, and some that were peculiar to themselves. Most of these were put on with a more elaborate display than other tribes, and their costumes, kept in the protection of permanent earth lodges, were generally of finer quality, while the dancing was of a higher degree of rhythm and perfection. One of the most characteristic of these was the *Buffalo Dance* (page 103). This was held for the purpose of "making the buffalo come," and a variation of it was a part of the Mandan's annual religious torture ceremonies. Because they did not travel long distances from their fortified village, they frequently had to resort to "medicine" to bring the migrating buffalo herds close to them. Every man was therefore obliged to keep the mask or head-dress of a buffalo hanging in his lodge, and always be ready to participate in the dance. These were held in the public area in the center of the village. Only ten to fifteen men would begin the dance, each wearing his own head decoration, and carrying his favorite hunting bow or spear. The dancers were accompanied by beating drums, rattles and the incessant wild song and shouting prescribed for the occasion, and the dance would go on without interruption day and night for as many days as it took to bring the buffaloes. The other men would stand around, wearing their own buffalo head-dresses, with weapons in hand, ready to take the places of those who became too exhausted to continue. When a dancer reached the end of his endurance, he began bending his body lower and lower, until one of the others would draw his bow and hit him with a blunt arrow. Falling to the ground like a wounded buffalo, he would be dragged out of the way by the bystanders, who went through a pantomime of skinning and cutting him up just as a dead buffalo was handled. His place would immediately be taken by a new dancer. In the meantime, the hunting scouts would have been riding across the prairie as far as they dared to go. When they finally

CATLIN DINING WITH *MAH-TO-TOH-PA*

New York Public Library

THE GAME OF ARROWS

discovered buffalo, they would signal back to watchers perched on top of the highest lodge in the village, and the news would be excitedly shouted down to the dancers. Amid lusty shouts of thanks to the Great Spirit, the dancers would run home to hang up their head-dresses and go dashing away on their best ponies to join the hunt.

Even more typical of the unusual Mandans were their mortuary customs. At death the deceased was dressed in his best attire, with the body oiled, painted, feasted and supplied with weapons, pipe and tobacco, provisions and his personal "medicine." Securely sewed into a case made of the freshly skinned hide of a buffalo, the body was placed on a scaffold, with its feet toward the rising sun in an area outside the stockade that was known as "The Village of the Dead." (below) Long after the burial, however, the most unusual part of the custom took place. It is given here in Catlin's own description: "When the scaffold on which the body rests, decays and falls to the ground, the nearest relatives, having buried the rest of the bones, takes the skull, which is perfectly bleached and purified, and places it with others in circles of a hundred or more on the prairie . . . eight or ten inches from each other, with the faces all looking to the center — where they are religiously protected and preserved in their precise positions from year to year . . . Each skull is placed upon a bunch of wild sage . . . The wife knows, by some mark or resemblance, the skull of her husband or her child, and there seldom passes a day that she does not visit it, with a dish of the best cooked food that her lodge affords, which she sets before the skull at night and returns for the dish in the morning . . . and she lingers to hold converse and company with the dead . . . sitting or lying by the skull of child or husband, talking to it in the most pleasant and endearing language that she can use . . . and seemingly getting an answer back . . . frequently bringing her needlework with her . . . chatting incessantly with it, while she is garnishing a pair of moccasins."[52]

Thomas Gilcrease Institute

THE VILLAGE OF THE DEAD

New York Public Library

MAH-TO-HE-HA, The Old Bear. Mandan Medicine Man

11

O-KEE-PA—The Torture Ceremony

THE EVIL SPIRIT
"O-kee-pa"

ALL the mysticism, religious devotion, and endeavor to be in the good graces of the Great Spirit, found its ultimate expression in what the Mandans called *O-kee-pa*. Among the rituals of the peoples of the earth it would be difficult to find any practice of self-imposed penance more excruciating. Sacrifice was an important part of the Plains Indians' religion. It was widely practiced and took many forms, from the simple offering of a bit of meat cast into the fire before eating, or the burning of the first ear of corn before the harvest, to inflicting of pain approaching the brink of death. But nothing equaled the ordeal of the *O-kee-pa*.

"The Mandans sacrificed their fingers to the Great Spirit," wrote Catlin,[53] "and of their worldly goods the best and most costly; if a horse or dog, it must be the favorite one; if an arrow from the quiver, they will select the most perfect one . . ." Most frequently the sacrifice was offered on behalf of an individual, although others were on behalf of the tribe. "Of *these* there are three erected over the great medicine lodge . . . They consist of ten or fifteen yards of blue and black cloth each, purchased from the Fur Company at fifteen to twenty dollars per yard, which are folded to resemble human figures, with eagle feathers on their heads and masks on their faces. These singular figures . . . are erected about thirty feet high over the door of the mystery-lodge, and there left to decay. There hangs now by the side of them . . . the skin of a white buffalo." (See pages 82 and 127.) The white buffalo was an extremely scarce animal. In all the vast herds there were possibly as few as one in 5,000,000; and the hide was so highly valued that it was generally possessed only as a tribal "medicine."

George Catlin was fully aware of the extraordinary character of the pagan rites of the *O-kee-pa*, which he was privileged to witness and record in pictures. He was one of the few white men to be an eye-witness, and he and his companions were probably the only ones who ever saw the ceremonies in their entirety. He was accompanied by James Kipp, whose eleven years of residence among the Mandans made him an interpreter of great proficiency. After the ritual was over the artist had his companions sign the following deposition: "We hereby certify, that we witnessed, in company with Mr. Catlin, in the Mandan Village, the ceremonies represented in the four paintings, and described in his Notes, to which this Certificate refers; and that he has therein faithfully represented those scenes as we saw them transacted, without any exaggeration. [Signed, witnessed and dated:] J. Kipp, Agent Amer. Fur Company; L. Crawford, Clerk; Abraham Bogard — Mandan Village, July 20, 1832."

New York Public Library

PREPARING FOR THE TORTURE CEREMONY

"From what I can learn," wrote Catlin,[54] "no one but the medicine-man knows the exact date when it is to commence." It was the day when the willow leaves became full-grown, for according to tradition, "the twig that the bird brought in [in the Mandan story of the Great Flood] was a willow bough and had full-grown leaves upon it." The bird was the mourning dove, which they called the *medicine-bird* and was never disturbed or harmed in any way.

"On the morning when these mysteries commenced . . ." the artist begins the description[55] "I entered the medicine-house as I would have entered a church . . . but little did I expect to see its floor strewed with the blood of its fanatical devotees . . . in worshipping the Great Spirit . . . whom they worship with great sincerity . . . I was sitting at breakfast in the house of Mr. Kipp, when we were startled by the shrieking and screaming of the women, and barking and howling of dogs . . . 'Now we have it!' exclaimed my host. 'The grand ceremony has commenced!' . . . I seized my sketch book and all of us were in an instant in front of the medicine-lodge . . . All eyes were directed to the prairies to the west, where was beheld in the distance a solitary figure making his way towards the village. The whole village joined in the expression of great alarm . . . bows were strung and trimmed to test their elasticity — horses were caught and run into the village — warriors were blackening their faces — and every preparation was made, as if for combat."

During the din and confusion the lone figure approached and entered the village with a slow, dignified step. He proceeded into the public area, where all the chiefs and warriors received him with pomp and ceremony, shaking hands with him and pronouncing his name: *Nu-mohk-muck-a-nah* (the *first* or *only* man). He was in reality *Mah-to-he-ha*, The Old Bear, who was to preside as high priest and master of ceremonies. His body was virtually naked and painted with white clay, over which he wore loosely a robe of four white wolf skins; on his head was a decoration of raven's wings; in his left hand he carried a large pipe which was guarded as something of great importance. After greeting the chiefs and others, he went to the medicine lodge and officially opened the door. He then designated four men to go inside to clean it out, strew willow-boughs and wild sage upon the floor and arrange the buffalo and human skulls and the other articles that were to be used in the torture rites.

While these preparations were being made in the medicine lodge, *Nu-mohk-muck-a-nah* went through the village, stopping in front of each lodge, screeching until the principal occupant came out. Then he related the catastrophe which had happened on earth when the waters overflowed, saying that he was the only person saved from this calamity; and that he had landed his big canoe on a high mountain in the west, and had come to open the medicine-lodge, which must receive from every lodge a present of some sharp cutting instrument that might be sacrificed to the water so the Great Flood would not come again. (How familiar this sounds!)

Throughout the first day the entire village assembled in gala attire in the public area and in front of the medicine-lodge, to watch the procedures solemnly. The principal event was the *Bel-lohck nah-pick*, or the Bull Dance (color plate page 127). Somewhat similar to the Buffalo Dance, though much more elaborate, it was on this occasion repeated four times on the first day, eight times on the second day, twelve times on the third and sixteen times on the fourth or final day. It was danced by twelve men around the sacred altar, a large wooden barrel-like structure located in the center of the public area and called the "big canoe." Eight of the dancers wore the skins of buffalo, with horns and hoofs and tail, and they imitated the movements of the animal. Their bodies were nearly naked and painted with black, red or white paint. Each carried a rattle and a long white staff, and on his back was a large bunch of

New York Public Library

THE BUFFALO DANCE

green willow boughs. These eight men were divided into four pairs, occupying the four cardinal points around the altar. Between each pair was another dancer, with a rattle and staff, and naked except for a beautiful head-dress and an apron of eagles' feathers. The bodies of two of these were painted black, with pounded charcoal and grease, and were called "the night" — and the numerous white spots with which they were dotted were called the "stars." The other two men were painted vermilion, to represent "the day," and were streaked with white "ghosts which the rays of the sun were chasing away." (Color plate page 128.) These twelve men were the only dancers. During the intervals between the dances they retired to a nearby lodge to rest and to re-paint their bodies for the next performance.

Throughout the day, and particularly between the dances, the entire populace abandoned themselves to a grotesque and noisy display of fanatical exuberance, which at times took on the appearance of a primitive masked ball and sometimes spread out onto the surrounding prairie. The first day came to an end with the *Nu-mohk-muck-a-nah* carrying all the hatchets and knives he had collected, to the properly cleaned and prepared medicine-lodge. Then this strange character slipped away to hide through the night. There had to be absolute silence throughout the village until he appeared again at sunrise.

Very early on the second day the *Nu-mohk-muck-a-nah* danced through the village and was joined by all the young men who were candidates for the ordeal and the honors awarded to those who could endure it. One by one these aspirants joined in single file behind the medicine-man, and the line finally entered the sacred medicine-lodge. Each young man's body was practically naked, and covered with paint and clay of various colors. Each carried in his right hand his personal medicine-bag. On his left arm was his war shield and in his left hand, bow and arrow, with the quiver slung on his back. Upon entering the medicine-lodge they seated themselves around the sides, with their weapons hung on the wall above them. It was then that *Mah-to-he-ha*, The Old Bear, took George Catlin by the arm and led him to a special seat inside, to witness the rites along with Kipp and the two other white men.

"*Nu-mohk-muck-a-nah* lit and smoked his medicine-pipe," relates the artist, "and then delivered a short speech to the candidates, stimulating and encouraging them to trust the Great Spirit for protection during the severe ordeal they were about to pass through. After this he called into the lodge an old medicine-man, whose body was painted yellow and whom he appointed master of ceremonies for the rituals which were to follow. This individual was called '*O-kee-pe Ka-se-kah*' [Conductor of the Ceremonies]. His authority was invested by the presentation of the special medicine-pipe, carrying with it all the power of conducting the rites." *Nu-mohk-muck-a-nah* then shook hands with him and departed for the mountains in the west, presumably to remain there until next year. After he had left the medicine-lodge, the newly appointed high-priest lay down by the fire in the center, with his pipe beside him, and began crying out to the Great Spirit incessantly (page 102). Thereafter none of the candidates was permitted to leave the medicine-lodge, or communicate with anyone outside, and all had to abstain from food, drink or sleep until the end of their four day ordeal.

Above the buffalo and human skulls arranged on the floor, there was a flimsy scaffold about five feet high. On this rested some small medicine objects which were, as Catlin put it, "the *sanctissimus sanctorum*, from which seemed to emanate all the sanctity of the proceedings and to which all seemed to be paying the highest devotional respect . . . Immediately under the little frame and on the floor of the lodge was placed a knife, and by the side of it a bundle of splints or skewers, which were in readiness for the infliction of the forthcoming cruelties . . . also a number of stout cords of rawhide hanging down from the top of the lodge . . . There were also other accoutrements of *medicine* and torture placed about the high-priest and this earthy temple of baptistry. Here the candidates must now remain, each in his appointed spot,

New York Public Library

"*O-KEE-PA*": Mandan Torture Ceremony

his thoughts and his idealistic hopes continually fired by the oratory of the high-priest and a thousand challenges to their manly courage, until the bloody climax of the fourth day."

On the final day the performance of the Bull Dance and the public display came to a climax about noon. Everyone gathered in the public area or crowded the dome-tops of the lodges nearest the medicine-lodge. Suddenly a terrible scream burst above the shouting and singing, as a strange character appeared across the prairie. He was running rapidly, darting about like a boy chasing a butterfly. As he approached the entrance to the stockade, it could be seen that his almost naked body was painted black, with white rings here and there, and he had large white markings like canine teeth drawn on his face. Besides being hideous, he uttered most frightful shrieks and screams as he dashed through the village, frightening the women, who themselves screamed for protection as they raced to elude him. This character was known to everyone as *O-kee-hee-de*, the Satanic Majesty of the Evil Spirit (page 101).

In the published descriptions of religious rites enacted by primitive people, certain incidents are occasionally left untold, for reasons of prudence and modesty. This is especially true of the Victorian era. Such was the case with *O-kee-hee-de*, the Evil Spirit. Although omitted by Catlin in his books, the ritual is plainly described in a "*Folium Reservatum*," of which a small number of copies were privately printed to supplement his book *O-Kee-Pa*. The following is the artist's own account of these remarkable ceremonies:

"The bizarre and frightful character described as *O-kee-hee-de* . . . who entered the area of the buffalo dancers to the terror of the women and children, had a small thong encircling his waist, a buffalo's tail behind; and from under a bunch of buffalo hair covering the pelvis, an artificial penis, ingeniously (and naturally) carved in wood of colossal dimensions, pendulous as he ran, and extending somewhat below his knees. This was, as his body, painted jet black, with the exception of the glans, which was a glaring vermilion. On entering the crowd . . . he directed his steps toward the group of women, who retreated in the greatest alarm . . . for at his near approach to them he elevated his wand, and as he raised it over their heads, there was a corresponding rising of the penis, probably caused by some invisible thong connecting the two together.

"The medicine-pipe of the master of ceremonies (of the Buffalo Dance) being thrust before his eyes, its charm held him motionless, until the women and children had retreated a safe distance . . . After several repeated attempts of this kind, and being defeated in the same way in each, he returned to the buffalo dance . . . and placing himself in the attitude of a buffalo bull in the rutting season . . . he mounted on to one of the dancing buffalos . . . He approached and leaped upon four of the eight, in succession . . . producing the highest excitement and amusement in the crowd.

"The scene finished, *O-kee-hee-de* appeared much fatigued and exhausted, which brought the women and children around him, they being no longer afraid of him . . . His wand was broken and he was driven into the prairie, where he was again beset by a throng of women and children, and the frightful appendage was wrested from his body and brought by its captor triumphantly into the village . . . Lifted onto the front of the Medicine Lodge, directly over the door . . . she harangued the multitude for some time . . . then ordered the Buffalo Dance to be stopped, and the '*Pohk-hong*' (or torturing rites) to commence."

The dancers and musicians went into the Medicine Lodge where the candidates were now to face their ordeal. The guards at the door also admitted several sturdy men who were to serve as attendants and assist in inflicting the cruelties. The last to enter were the tribal chief and the other dignitaries who were to be official witnesses and were to decide how bravely each of the various young men conducted themselves. Two of the attendants took positions in the center of the lodge, one with the scalping-knife and the other with the bundle of skewers. Then, one at a time the candidates came forward — already weak from fasting and thirst and being without sleep for four days and nights. Here is Catlin's own description of the procedure: "An inch or more of the flesh on each shoulder, or each breast, was taken up between the thumb and finger by the man who held the knife; and the knife, which had been hacked and notched to make it produce as much pain as possible, was forced through the flesh below the fingers, and was followed by a skewer which the other attendant forced through the wounds (underneath the muscles, to keep them from being torn out), as they were hacked. There were then two cords lowered from the top of the lodge, which were fastened to these skewers, and they immediately began to haul him up. He was thus raised until his body was just suspended from the ground, when the knife and additional splints were passed through the flesh in a similar manner on each arm below the shoulder, also below the elbow, on the highs, and below the knees.

"This extremely painful operation was performed, in all instances, on the same parts of the candidates bodies and limbs . . . Each one was then instantly raised with the cords until the weight of his body was suspended by them, and then, while the blood was streaming down their limbs, the attendants hung upon the other skewers the young man's shield, bow and quiver, etc., and in many instances the heavy skull of a buffalo was attached to each arm and leg . . . Each one was then raised until all the weights swung clear, leaving the feet some six or eight feet above the ground . . . and their heads sunk forward on their breasts, or thrown backwards, in a frightful condition (see pages 105, 109 and 128).

"The fortitude with which every one of them bore this part of the torture surpassed

New York Public Library

"*O-KEE-PA*": The Last Race

credulity . . . When completely suspended . . . the attendants commenced turning them around with a pole . . . in a gentle manner at first, but gradually increasing, faster and faster, until the brave fellow could control the agony no longer and burst out in the most heart-rending cries . . . to the Great Spirit to support him . . . until by fainting, his voice falters and his struggling ceases, and he hangs, apparently, a still and lifeless corpse!"

The attendants and the witnesses watched each candidate intently until he hung as if dead and his medicine bag, which he had clung to, dropped to the ground. Then the signal was given and the young man was lowered to lie lifeless on the floor of the medicine-lodge. The cords by which he was suspended were pulled out, leaving the other weights hanging to him. No one was allowed to assist him in any way, for he was now "trusting his life to the keeping of the Great Spirit."

When the young man had regained consciousness and had enough strength to do so, he got to his feet or crawled around the lodge past the witnesses. If he still had enough super-courage and fortitude left, he went to where another of his elders sat by a dried buffalo skull, with a sharp hatchet in his hand. Here the candidate extended the little finger of his left hand upward and uttered a prayer to the Great Spirit; and then laid the finger on the buffalo skull, to be chopped off as a further sacrifice.

During all this the crowd waited in the public area and on the tops of the lodges. As soon as six or eight of the candidates had passed through the entire ordeal inside the medicine-lodge, they were led outside, with all the weights still dragging from their mutilated bodies. There, within public view, each one was taken in charge by two athletic men, fresh and strong, who wrapped rawhide straps around the candidate's wrists and, grasping the straps firmly in their own hands, began to race him furiously around the altar in the center of the public area. With the skulls and other weights dragging behind, the candidate struggled to follow as bravely as possible, until human endurance could carry him not another step and he fell once again like a dead man on the ground. This was called *Eh-ke-nah-ka-nah-pick*, the Last Race (page 107).

This ended the ordeal. Each individual was left to lie where he fell in the public area, until he was again able to rise to his feet without aid. Then, staggering like a drunken man, he made his way through the crowd to his own home, where family, relatives and friends waited to welcome him with admiration rather than sympathy — for now their young man had become a full-fledged Mandan.

Letters and Notes

SCALPING

American Museum of Natural History

CATLIN PAINTING THE FOUR BEARS

American Museum of Natural History

MANDAN TORTURE CEREMONY

Smithsonian Institution

MANDAN MEDICINE MAN
MAH-TO-HE-HA, The Old Bear

12

A Many-Sided Enchantment

Newberry Library, Chicago

THE BLOODY HAND

THE Little Mandan Village, although only about two miles up-river from the larger one, served as something of a summer resort for the more affluent families of the larger. Otherwise it ran its own affairs, even to the holding of a separate *O-kee-pa*. George Catlin visited the smaller settlement and was there received with the usual hospitality. "In this village I have been unusually afflicted by the friendly importunities of one of the reverensing parasites," he wrote,[56] "who among various other offices of kindness has insisted on offering his body for my pillow, which for several nights I have not had the heart to reject . . . I have been suffering from an influenza, which has induced me to sleep on the floor wrapped in a buffalo robe with my feet to the fire in the center of the room, to which the genuine politeness of my constant and watchful friend has regularly drawn him where his irresistible importunities have brought me, night after night, the only alternative of using his bedaubed and bear-greased body for a pillow."

About eight miles farther up the Missouri, on the Knife River near its mouth, lived the Minnetarees. Known as the "People of the Willows," this small tribe of not more than 1500 souls, more correctly identified as the Hidastas, were of Sioux stock, although their language was closely akin to that of the Crows. At the time of Catlin's visit they were friendly with the Mandans. Their three villages were located quite close together and the dwellings were earth-covered like their neighbors', the "People of the Pheasants."

With his two picturesque companions Ba'tiste and Bogard, the artist paddled their skiff back up river and landed in front of the forty or fifty large earth-domed lodges of the principal village of the Minnetarees (page 113). Located on a flat bench at the top of a high bank, it overlooked the Knife River. The two smaller villages were on lower ground on the opposite side of the Knife. They were almost hidden in the luxuriant cornfields which surrounded them. "The scenery along the bank of this little river, from village to village," wrote Catlin,[57] "is rendered curious by the wild and garrulous groups of men, women and children who are continually wandering along the winding shore, or dashing and plunging through the river's blue water, enjoying the pleasure of swimming, of which both sexes seem to be passionately fond. Others are paddling about in their tublike canoes made of the skins of buffaloes (known as bull-boats); and every now and then are to be seen their steam-baths."

Following the usual protocol, the white visitors first made an official call on the head of these people. "The chief sachem of this tribe," Catlin's account continues, "is a very ancient and patriarchal looking man by the name of *Eah-tohk-pah-shee-pee-shah*, The Black Moccasin (page 115). I have been for some days an inmate of his hospitable lodge, where he sits tottering with old age and silently reigns sole monarch of this little community, who are constantly dropping in to cheer his sinking energies and render him their homage. His voice and sight are nearly gone; but the gestures of his hands are yet energetic and youthful, and he freely speaks the language of his kind heart. I have been treated in the kindest manner by this old chief." This same man was first chief of the Minnetarees during the winter of 1804–'05 when the Lewis & Clark expedition was at the Mandan Village. Their journal refers to him as "*Ompsehara* or Black Moccasin;" and as George Catlin sat with the now aged patriarch, he took great pleasure in telling about the friendly visit of the artist's distinguished predecessors.

When Catlin decided that he and his two companions should visit the other villages of the Minnetarees, the old chief insisted that one of the younger women of his numerous household should take them across the river in a bull-boat. This brief trip developed into an interesting experience. When the tublike skin boat was put into the water the woman made signs for the three white men to get into it. The artist wrote: "When we were in and seated flat on its bottom, with scarce room to adjust our legs or feet, she waded out, pulling it along towards the deeper water, carefully with the other hand attending to her dress, which seemed to be but a light slip and floating upon the surface until the water was about her waist, when it was cast off over her head and thrown ashore, and she plunged forward, swimming and drawing the boat with one hand, which she did with apparent ease. In this manner we were conveyed to the middle of the stream, where we were soon surrounded by a dozen or more beautiful girls, from twelve to eighteen years of age, who had been bathing on the opposite shore. They all swam in a bold and graceful manner, as confidently as so many otters or beavers; and with their long black hair floating on the water, whilst their faces were glowing with jokes and fun, which they were cracking about us and which we could not understand. In the midst of this delightful aquatic group we three sat in our little skin-bound tub (like the 'three wise men of Gotham, who went to sea in a bowl,' etc.), floating along on the current . . . amusing ourselves with the playfulness of these creatures floating about under the clear blue water, catching their hands on the side of our boat, occasionally raising half of their bodies out of the water, and sinking again, like so many mermaids.

"In the midst of this tantalizing entertainment, in which Ba'tiste and Bogard, as well as myself, were all taking infinite pleasure . . . we found ourselves in the delightful dilemma of being turned round and round for the expressive amusement of the villagers, who were laughing at us from the shore . . . The group of playful girl swimmers had peremptorily discharged from her occupation our fair conductress who had undertaken to ferry us safely across the river, and they had also ingeniously laid their plans . . . to exhort from us some little evidence of our liberality, which it was impossible to refuse them after so liberal and bewitching an exhibition . . . I had some awls in my pockets, which I presented to them, and also a few strings of beautiful beads, which I placed over their delicate necks as they raised them out of the water by the side of our boat; after which they all joined in conducting our craft to the shore . . . until the water became so shallow that they waded along with great coyness, as long as their bodies could be half concealed under the water, when they gave our boat a last push to the shore, and raising a loud and exultant laugh, plunged back into the river."

After the white visitors had been properly feasted and entertained in the lodge of the chief of the smaller village, and had made the rounds of visiting some of the other lodges, they were invited to attend a series of games and horse-races that were arranged in their

Smithsonian Institution

MINNETAREE VILLAGE

honor at a beautiful spot on the prairies a short distance away. All the men and women went out to watch the younger men in these displays of skill and strength. As Catlin was always far more than a curious tourist when among the Indians, he borrowed a horse and rode in some of the races, to the great entertainment of all. "When I had enough of these amusements," the artist relates, "I succeeded with some difficulty in pulling Ba'tiste and Bogard from amongst the group of women and girls, where they seemed to be successfully ingratiating themselves, and we trudged back to the little village of earth-covered lodges, which were hemmed in and almost obscured by fields of corn and luxuriant growth of wild sun-flowers . . . whose spontaneous growth had reared their heads like a dense forest."

It was the time of year when the ears of corn were of proper size for eating and when they held the annual festivities to render thanks to the Great Spirit for the return of this joyful occasion. The artist witnessed the Corn Dance (page 117), in which the first ears picked were sacrificed, accompanied by elaborate ceremonies and the singing of songs of thanksgiving. The dance also marked the beginning of a great feast, which continued until the fields of corn were entirely exhausted. The Minnetarees were expert hunters and Catlin also rode out on the prairie for an exciting buffalo chase.

By now fall was in the air and St. Louis was still a long way off. So the artist and his two companions paddled their little skiff rapidly back to the big Mandan Village, where they gathered their various belongings, including Catlin's precious cargo of paintings and the Indian paraphernalia he had collected, and they prepared to continue the journey. "In taking this final leave of them," Catlin wrote in a final summary of his opinion of the Mandans, "which will be done with decided feelings of regret, I shall look back upon them and their curious modes with no small degree of pleasure; inasmuch as their hospitality and friendly treatments have fully corroborated my fixed belief that the North American Indian in his primitive state is a high-minded, hospitable and honorable being".[58]

Some thirty years afterward, Catlin described two significant incidents which occurred at the time of his departure. Although omitted from his *Letters and Notes*, they were included in his *Life Amongst the Indians*, which was not published until 1861:[59] "The last I saw of my friends the Mandans was at the shore of the river in front of their village . . . the whole tribe upon the beach. My friend *Mah-to-toh-pa*, and The Wolf Chief, and the *Great Medicine*, all successively embraced me in their arms; the warriors and braves shook hands with me, and the women and children saluted me with shouts of farewell; Ba'tiste and Bogard and myself were again on our way to St. Louis.

"At this exciting moment a young warrior whom I recognized followed opposite us at the water's edge, and leaning over tossed into the canoe a parcel which he took from under his robe; and seeing me attempting to unfold it, he waved his hand and shook his head, making a sign for me to lay it down, which I did . . . After we had gotten away I opened the parcel and found the most beautiful pair of leggings I had ever seen, fringed with a profusion of scalp-locks and handsomely garnished with porcupine quills. These I instantly recognized as the identical pair I had been for some time trying to purchase and for which I had offered the young warrior a horse . . . What a beautiful moral from this — having parted with me without the least prospect of ever seeing me again, enveloped in an intricacy of thongs which he intended I should not be able to untie until the current had carried me beyond the possibility of making him any compensation for them, he had compelled me to accept as a *present* what he could not *sell* to me for the price of a horse!

"We travelled fast, and just as the village of the Mandans was dwindling into nothing, we heard the startling yells and saw in the distance behind us the troop that was gaining upon us . . . their hands extended and robes waving for us to stop. In a few minutes they were op-

EEH-TOHK-PAH-SHEE-PEE-SHAH, The Black Moccasin
Head Chief of the Minnetarees

posite to us on the bank and I steered my boat to the shore . . . '*Mi-neek-e-sunk-te-ka* (The Mink),' they exclaimed, 'is dying! The picture which you made of her is too much like her — you put so much of her into it, that when your boat took it away from our village, it drew part of her life with it — she is bleeding from the mouth — she is pucking up all her blood — you are drawing the strings out of her heart and they will soon break. We must take her picture back and then she will get well again. Your *medicine* is great, it is too great; but we wish you well.' Mr. Kipp came with the party and interpreted the above. I unrolled my bundle of portraits and though I was reluctant to part with it, (for she was a beautiful girl) yet I placed it in their hands, telling them I wished her well; and I was exceedingly glad to get . . . under way again . . . They rode back at full speed with the portrait; but I have since learned that the girl died and that I am forever to be considered the cause of her misfortunes."

As a further footnote to George Catlin's story of the Mandans, it is appropriate to include here a brief account of the artist's version of the destruction of that tribe.[60] The information on which this was based came directly to the artist from Kipp, the trader, who related the incidents when he visited Catlin in New York City in the fall of 1838: "In the summer [of 1837] the small-pox was accidentally introduced among the Mandans by the fur-traders; and in the course of two months they all perished, except some thirty or forty, who were taken as slaves by the Riccarees . . . who moved up the river and took possession of their village soon after the calamity . . . The Riccarees . . . after living some months (in the village) were in turn attacked by a large party of their enemies the Sioux, and whilst fighting desperately in resistance, in which the Mandan prisoners had taken an active part, the latter had contrived a plan for their own destruction, which was effected by their simultaneously running through the stockade onto the prairie, calling out to the Sioux to kill them (both men and women) . . . 'that their friends were all dead and they did not wish to live' — that they here wielded their weapons as desperately as they could, to excite the fury of their enemy, and that they were all thus cut to pieces and destroyed . . ."

From Kipp, the artist also learned of the fate of his good friend the proud and valorous *Mah-to-toh-pa*, The Four Bears. "This fine fellow sat in his lodge and watched every one of his family die about him (of the smallpox), his wives and his children . . . when he walked out, around the village, and wept over the final destruction of his tribe; his braves and warriors . . . all laid low; when he came back to his lodge, where he covered his whole family with a number of robes, and wrapping another around himself, went out upon a hill at a little distance, where he laid for several days, despite all the solicitations of the traders, resolved to starve himself to death. He remained there until the sixth day, when he had just strength enough to creep back to the village, when he entered the horrid gloom of his own wigwam, and laying his body alongside of the group of his family, drew his robe over him, and died on the ninth day . . . So have perished the friendly and hospitable Mandans."

The Riccarees of Catlin's journal are known today as the Arikaras. In 1832 they occupied about 150 earth-covered lodges, similar to those of the Mandans, on the Missouri River just north of the mouth of the Grand River. Lewis & Clark had found these people extremely hospitable, but their experiences with white traders had already changed that attitude. Before Catlin left Fort Union, news arrived there that a party of trappers and traders had burned two Arikaras to death in retaliation for something they had done, and McKenzie had warned the artist and his two companions to slip past their village very cautiously at night. While Catlin was at the Minnetaree villages he met a small party of Arikaras who were there on a friendly visit. Among these he painted a beautiful girl, *Pshan-shaw*, The Sweet-scented Grass (page 118) and also a chief of the tribe, *Stan-au-pot*, The Bloody Hand (page 111). But the three travelers approached the Arikara village cautiously, for it was well known that these people had sworn terrible death to every pale face who fell into their hands.

The three travelers in their skiff enjoyed their journey down the Missouri "until at length the curling smoke of the Riccarees announced their village ahead of us . . ." relates Catlin,[61] "and we instantly dropped under some willows along the shore, where we listened to the yelping, barking rabble, until night had drawn her curtain (although the moon arose, in full brightness) when we put out in the middle of the stream . . . We lay close in our boat with a pile of green bushes over us, making us nothing but a 'floating tree-top.' On the bank in front of the village was being enacted a scene of thrilling nature. A hundred torches were swung about, giving us a full view of the group that were assembled and some fresh scalps hung on poles . . . in the nightly ceremony composed of the frightful shrieks and yells and gesticulations of the *scalp-dance* . . . After I had got some hundreds of miles below them I learned that they were dancing two white men's scalps taken in revenge against the traders.

"In addition to this multitude of demons, there were some hundred of cackling women and girls bathing in the river at the lower end of the village; at which place the current drifted our small craft in close to the shore, till the moon lit their shoulders and they stood half-submerged like mermaids and gazed upon us! '*A canoe, a canoe!*,' they screamed. In a moment the songs of the scalp-dancers were stopped! The lights went out and village was in darkness . . ." Immediately the warriors grabbed their weapons and started in hot pursuit of the boat which was endeavoring to slip past their village. The camouflage was hurriedly discarded and the three white men paddled frantically to escape. All the rest of the night they struggled to keep ahead of the Arikaras. Nor did they stop or relax in the desperate dash until the end of the following day. This was George Catlin's first experience with the Plains Indians in their character of the future — a character which the white man was responsible for creating.

New York Public Library

THE CORN DANCE

Smithsonian Institution

PSHAN-SHAW, The Sweet-scented Grass
Arikara Girl

13

White Man's Civilization

Newberry Library, Chicago

"BLACK HAWK"

EVERY DAY of the long journey down the Missouri River provided its own memorable sights and exciting incidents. Catlin, however, refrained from glamorizing his story with lengthy accounts of the thrilling experiences that happened along the way, and he skipped over what others would have made the most of. "We all had our rifles and used them often," was the way he put it. "We frequently went ashore amongst the herds of buffalo and were obligated to do so for our daily food . . . Our canoe was generally landed at night . . . when we straightened our limbs on our buffalo robes . . . out of the walks of Indians and grizzly bears . . . The sportsman's fever was aroused and satisfied; the swan, ducks, geese, and pelicans; the deer, antelope, elk, and buffalo, were stretched by our rifles; and sometimes — 'pull, boys, pull! a war party! for your lives pull, or we are gone!' "

At one time the skiff got into the midst of an immense herd of buffalo swimming across the river on their southward migration. Even the danger of this situation failed to excite him: "It was in the 'running season,' and we had heard the 'roaring' (as it is called) of the herd when we were several miles from it. When we came in sight . . . the river was filled and in parts blackened with their heads and horns, as they were swimming about, following up their objects, and making desperate battle. I deemed it imprudent for our canoe to be dodging amongst them and ran it ashore for a few hours, when we laid waiting for the river to clear, but we waited in vain. Their number, however, got somewhat diminished at last, and we pushed off, and successfully made our way amongst them."[62]

Moving down the Missouri across the territory which is today the state of South Dakota and along the borders of Nebraska, Iowa, Kansas and into Missouri, the artist made brief stops at the principal river villages of Poncas, Ioways and Omahas. He had become acquainted with some of these tribesmen on the previous trip of 1831; and he made additional paintings and sketches to augment his growing collection, which was already the most important pictorial record of its kind that had ever been made. By the time the weary travelers reached Cantonment Leavenworth, they were ready to enjoy the relaxation and the luxuries that well-established military post offered them.

Fort Leavenworth, the present site of a federal penitentiary in the northeastern part of Kansas, was in 1832 the westernmost outpost of the United States military forces in the Northwest. It was under the command of Colonel Davenport, whom Catlin described as "a gentleman of great urbanity of manners, with a Roman head and a Grecian heart, restrained and tempered by the charms of an American lady, who has elegantly pioneered the graces of civilized refinement into these uncivilized regions." The artist's journal also gives this further picture of life in that military outpost on the American frontier: "In this delightful cantonment there are generally stationed six or seven companies of infantry and ten or fifteen officers, several of whom have their wives and daughters with them, forming a very pleasant little community, who are almost continually together in social enjoyment of the peculiar amusements and pleasures of this wild country . . . such as riding on horseback or in carriages over the beautiful green fields of the prairie, picking strawberries and wild plums, deer-chasing, grouse-shooting, horse-racing, and other amusements . . ." He describes a prairie-hen hunt which he made with one of the officers of the garrison, on which they shot seventy-five of these fine birds in one afternoon, with the aid of a fine pointer dog, and they "had legitimately followed the sportsman's style."

Although Leavenworth was on the outer fringe of the white man's civilization, it was a gathering place for a number of the still wild tribes, some of whom traveled long distances to trade there or just to see the soldiers of the Great White Father. Among these primitives were the Pawnees, Omahas, Iowas, Otos, Missouris, and Kansas. There were also the semi-civilized remnants of other tribes that had been moved into the region from their former lands farther east, such as the Delawares, Peorias, Potawatomies, and the Kaskaskias. Of all these tribes the Pawnees were by far the wildest, most warlike and powerful — and Catlin had by now developed a penchant for the primitives. The Pawnees were divided into four principal groups — the Grand Pawnees, Wolf Pawnees, Tappage Pawnees and Republican Pawnees;

Smithsonian Institution

ENCOUNTER WITH BUFFALO ON MISSOURI

and they dominated a wide area extending up the Platte River and its tributaries into the prairies bordering the distant Rocky Mountains.

It has been said earlier that Catlin made an extensive trip up the Platte into Pawnee country in 1831. John C. Ewers, the Smithsonian expert on Western Americana art as it specifically involves ethnology, inclines to 1831 as the time when Catlin painted the portraits of *La-doo-ke-a*, The Buffalo Bull (page 38) and other notable Pawnees. Unfortunately there is no known journal for that trip and no certainty as to just which pictures he painted at that time, although the artist provides some brief but interesting notes on the Pawnees in his account of the visit to Fort Leavenworth on the down-river journey of 1832. He explains why these tribesmen, like the Osages, Iowas, Kansas, and Sauks and Foxes, followed the custom of shaving their heads and ornamenting them with a crest of deer's hair, rather than wearing the long hair and elaborate head-dresses of eagle feathers and other appurtenances of most tribes of the Great Plains. "The hair is cut off as close to the head as possible," Catlin relates,[63] "except a tuft the size of the palm of the hand, on the crown of the head; and in the center of which is fastened a beautiful crest of the hair of the deer's tail (dyed red) and often surmounted with the war-eagle's quills . . . The little crest is called the scalp-lock and is scrupulously preserved as a challenge to their enemies if they can get it as a trophy, in case they are conquered or killed in battle. It is considered cowardly and disgraceful for a warrior to shave it off. This crest is colored blood-red; as is also the upper part of the head and generally considered part of the face — as red as they can possibly make it with vermilion."

It was at this time that an epidemic of small-pox swept through these tribes, resulting in wholesale destruction of the Pawnees as well as their neighbors. Catlin had something to say about that: "When that most appalling disease was accidentally introduced amongst them by the Fur Traders and whiskey sellers, ten thousand or more of them perished in the course of a few months . . . Terror and dismay are carried with this awful disease, in the midst of which they plunge into the river when in the highest state of fever; or throw themselves from precipices; or plunge their knives to their hearts, to rid themselves of the pangs of slow death. Amongst the formidable Pawnees, the Fur Traders are still doing some business; but from what I can learn, the Indians are dealing with considerable distrust with a people who introduced so fatal a calamity amongst them."

While the officers and their ladies at Fort Leavenworth were enjoying their social life, interspersed with hunting deer and prairie hens in "the sportsman's style," there was serious trouble brewing on the upper Mississippi. The white man's treaties, land deals and his whole civilization were becoming self-evident realities to many of the Indians along this western frontier. Black Hawk, the patriarchal leader of the Sauks and Foxes, had already taken an irrevocably defiant stand and, with his tribal supporters, had issued a vehement call for all-out war against the white man. This had been preached before in the tepees and council lodges, but there was always a majority of the child-like primitives who were too fond of the token payments for land purchases, and the whiskey and other things the white man had to offer.

After their rest at Fort Leavenworth George Catlin and his companions hurried on to St. Louis for the season was getting late. His tiny boat was heavily loaded with the treasures of his paint brush, sketch pads and notebooks. Getting them safely back to St. Louis would be the fulfillment of a long and devoutly cherished dream — or at least the first phase of that dream. It was a happy day when the three weatherworn, ragged, bearded and grimy river travelers paddled their little skiff among the huge transport boats to the flourishing city of 15,000 inhabitants.

John C. Ewers has compiled some interesting statistics on George Catlin's trip into the

New York Historical Society

A BUFFALO BULL

terra incognita of the Upper Missouri.[64] From the first day the artist was among the Sioux at Fort Pierre, he spent exactly eighty-six days traveling, painting and making notes. This averages eighteen miles per day. In addition he participated in buffalo hunts, watched prolonged and complicated primitive ceremonials, talked with officials of the American Fur Company and gathered an immense amount of information as well as a large collection of Indian paraphernalia. He also painted more than one hundred thirty-five pictures — some sixty-six Indian portraits from life, thirty-six scenes of Indian life, twenty-five landscapes and at least eight hunting scenes. "Only a man of boundless energy, roused to a feverish pitch of creativity, could have performed all of these tasks in so short a period," states the conservative Smithsonian ethnologist. "Surely there must have been days when Catlin created more than a half-dozen pictures." And it should also be kept in mind that this artist was working under a most terrific handicap — he had only the artistic materials he could take with him on the long journey into an absolute wilderness; he had only the crudest means of caring for and transporting everything; and he had extremely meager funds with which to carry out his work. That he got as much of it as he did safely back to St. Louis, is little short of a miracle.

No blowing of whistles heralded the arrival of the tiny boat that had come all the way from Fort Union. To those who may have noticed the travelers, they were three river-rats coming from somewhere that was of no importance to anyone but themselves. They landed the skiff at one of the wharfs, and Bogard and Ba'tiste helped Catlin carry his paintings and Indian paraphernalia to an inexpensive hotel. When the artist returned a few hours later to care for his little boat he found that it had already been stolen! Here is his comment about that: "Although my little boat, to which I had contracted a peculiar attachment, had often laid unmolested for weeks and months at the villages of the red men, with no laws to guard it; and where it had also often been taken out of the water and carried up the bank and turned against my wigwam; and by the red men again safely carried to the water's edge and put afloat upon the water when I was ready to take a seat in it . . . to this place [St. Louis] I had also transmitted by steamer and other conveyances, about twenty boxes and packages at different times, as my note-books showed; and I have, on . . . enumerating them, been lucky enough to recover about fifteen of the twenty, which is a pretty fair proportion for this desperate country and the very *conscientious hands* they often are doomed to pass through!"

Thus did George Catlin return to the white man's civilization. And his companions on the long trip through the wilderness fared in a similar manner. "Ba'tiste and Bogard (poor fellows) I found, after remaining in St. Louis a few days, had been about as unceremoniously snatched off as my canoe had been; and Bogard, in particular, as he had made show of a few hundred dollars he had saved by his hard earnings in the Rocky Mountains. He came down with a liberal heart, which he had learned in an Indian life of ten years, with a strong taste which he had acquired for whiskey at twenty dollars per gallon; and with an independent feeling, which illy harmonized with rules and regulations of a country of laws; and the consequences soon were that by the 'Hawk and Buzzard' system, and Rocky Mountain liberality, the poor fellow was soon 'jugged up'; where he could deliberately dream of beavers and the free breezes of the mountain air."[65]

For Catlin to have decided at this point that his mission was complete, would not have been beyond reason. He had painted and learned more about the primitive Indians of the West than any other person. The strong sentimental urge to return to the wife he loved with the deepest devotion would in itself have been excuse enough. He knew very well how easy it would be to return to the East and pick up again the comfortable and profitable career of painting portraits of the famous and wealthy. But he considered his accomplishments on the Upper Missouri only the encouraging beginning of his career, and he was more determined than ever to devote his entire life to the fulfillment of his plan, which, experience had now convinced him, was of even greater importance than he had previously dreamed.

Upon his return to St. Louis, the artist had learned that the Black Hawk War had been brought to an end. At eleven o'clock on the 27th of August, 1832, that redoubtable war chief of the Sauks and Foxes, Black Hawk, along with his sons and The Prophet and others of their supporters had been delivered as prisoners to General Joseph M. Street at Prairie du Chien. Ironically, they had been brought in by a party of Winnebagoes under the one-eyed *Du-cor-*

Knoedler Galleries, New York

A BUFFALO STAMPEDE

ree (Decorie) — a Judas in the service of General Street. As they were officially delivered, *Du-cor-ree* addressed a little speech to the General, which is highly significant: "My Father — we have done what you told us to do. We always do what you tell us, because we know it is for our good. My Father — you told us to get these men, and it would be the cause of much good for the Winnebagoes. We have brought them . . . If you had told us to bring their heads alone, we would have done so . . . We know you, and believe you are our friend. We want you to keep them safe. If they are hurt, we do not wish to see it. Wait until we are gone, before it is done. My Father — many little birds have been flying about our ears of late, and we thought they whispered to us that there was evil intended for us; but now we hope these evil birds will let our ears alone . . . My Father — you say you love your red children. We think we love you as much, if not more than you love us. We have confidence in you . . . We now put these men in your hands; we have done all that you told us to do."[66]

Black Hawk also had something to say on that occasion: "My warriors fell around me . . . I saw my evil days at hand. The sun rose on us in the morning; at night it sank in a dark cloud . . . This was the last sun that shone on Black Hawk. He is now a prisoner to the white man, but he can stand torture. He is not afraid of death. He is no coward. He is an Indian. He has done nothing of which an Indian need be ashamed. He has fought the battles of his country against the white man, who came year after year to cheat his people and take away their lands . . . The white man despises the Indians and drives them from their homes. But the Indians are not deceitful . . . Black Hawk is satisfied. He will go to the world of spirits contented. He has done his duty . . . The white men do not scalp the heads, but they do worse, they poison the heart. It is not pure with them."[67]

The captives, under military guard, were put aboard the steamboat *Winnebago*, commanded by Captain Hunt, and were transferred to the prison at Jefferson Barracks, about ten miles below St. Louis. Catlin promptly obtained permission to visit them and paint their portraits. The hostages included Black Hawk and The Prophet and eleven other head men of the Sauks and Foxes, with about fifty less famous warriors.[68] When the artist arrived at their place of internment, he found that each of the Indians had a heavy iron band securely fastened to his ankle, to which was attached a heavy iron ball and chain, which he had to carry whenever he moved about! (See drawing on page 125).

Catlin does not have a great deal to say about this particular occasion or its implications, although the scenes he witnessed on that visit to Jefferson Barracks undoubtedly had a deep effect upon him. "When I painted this chief" [color plate page 164], he relates,[69] "he was dressed in a plain suit of buckskin, with a string of wampum in his ears and on his neck, and held in his hand a medicine bag, which was the skin of a black hawk, from which he had taken his name, and the tail of which made him a fan, which he was constantly using." The artist had little more to say about The Prophet, *Wah-pe-kee-suck*, also known as The White Cloud (color plate page 164): He was "a very distinguished man, and one of the leading men of the Black Hawk party, and studying favor with the whites, as indicated by the manner in which he was allowing his hair to grow. The Prophet . . . is about forty years old and nearly six feet high, stout and athletic . . . the priest of assassination or secret murder." While Catlin was painting *Nah-pope*, The Soup, (see drawing on page 125) that warrior seized the ball and chain that were fastened to his leg, and raising them in the air exclaimed with haughty scorn: "*Make me so, and show me to the Great Father!*" When the artist refused to paint the portrait *Nah-pope* wished, the Indian kept varying his position and distorting his face with grimaces, to prevent Catlin's catching a true likeness.

BLACK HAWK AND FOLLOWERS IN BALLS AND CHAINS
Jefferson Barracks, 1832

Knoedler Galleries, New York

CATLIN HUNTING BUFFALO FOR FOOD

Smithsonian Institution,
American Heritage Magazine

MANDAN "O-KEE-PA",
The Bull Dance

Lithograph

BULL DANCE PARTICIPANTS
(*O-KEE-PA*)

Lithograph

MANDAN TORTURE CEREMONY
(*O-KEE-PA*)

14

Return to the Primitive

Newberry Library, Chicago

OSAGE WOMAN

HIS long journey into the wild country of the Upper Missouri left George Catlin obsessed with the idea of devoting all his energies for the rest of his life to documenting the Indians of the West and to championing their cause throughout the world. He fully realized that this was not a popular cause, and that it was also a very poor way of trying to make a living. But everything else now became relatively unimportant.

Although Catlin was extremely attentive to documentary accuracy in his paintings and notes, he was peculiarly indifferent to specific dates and to including in his journal his exact itinerary. This makes it extremely difficult to make a chronological arrangement of certain phases of his story. Examination of his published *Letters and Notes* frequently leads to even greater confusion, for they are extremely disorganized. His only attempt at a published itinerary of his travels is a brief summary he prepared as an appendix to the 1871 exhibition catalogue of his Indian cartoons. One statement which the artist made in that obviously hasty sketch of his career has been seized upon by his critics. It reads: "In the summer of 1833 I ascended the Platte to Fort Laramie, visiting the two principal villages of the Pawnees, and also the Omahas and Ottoes, and at the fort saw a great many Arapahoes and Cheyennes, and rode to the shores of the Great Salt Lake, when the Mormons were yet building their temple at Nauvoo, on the Mississippi (38 years ago)."[70]

There is no reason why Catlin could not have made a trip to the popular rendezvous at the mouth of Laramie Creek on the Upper Platte. Indians, trappers and traders had for a number of years been gathering there, and a good many nondescript white men had gone to and returned from the Great Salt Lake. Distance and difficulty of travel never meant very much to Catlin. And there are Indian portraits to support the supposition that at some time the artist was among the tribesmen who inhabited the Upper Platte, although the fact that such an important part of his travel is nowhere included in his various journals is not easily understandable.

Thomas Donaldson, who himself makes numerous errors in the dates he recorded, quotes, in his voluminous Smithsonian catalogue and notes on *The George Catlin Indian Gallery*, the artist's statement of 1871, which he evidently accepted, and adds: "Of Mr. Catlin's movements in 1833 no journal was ever printed. The Pawnee portraits are Nos. 55–61 and 99–111. Some of the portraits above enumerated, the landscapes, games and customs were undoubtedly painted during this year, but cannot be designated, as several years' work are in the numbers given or referred to."[71] Elsewhere Donaldson states: "Mr. Catlin first visited the Pawnees on the Platte River in 1833."[72] He also adds the footnote under the listings of some of the pictures: "Painted by Catlin in 1833." This particular year and its implications have been the subject of considerable controversy, without adequate proof or disproof.

The comment that Catlin makes in his *Letters and Notes* after recording his return from the Upper Missouri in the fall of 1832, is as follows: "I start in a day or two, with a tough little pony and a pack horse, to trudge through the snow drifts from this place [St. Louis] to New Madrid and perhaps further; a distance of three hundred miles to the South — where I must venture to meet a warmer climate — the river open and steamers running, to waft me to the Gulf of Mexico. Of the fate or success that waits me, or the incidents of that travel, as they have not transpired, I can as yet say nothing; and I close my book for further time and future entries."[73] What followed this in his journal, however, apparently refers to a visit to the Florida coast during the winter of 1833–'34, just prior to the fully recorded journey into the far Southwest. There is nothing whatever about the summer of 1833. The *Pittsburgh Gazette* of April 23, 1833 carried a story indicating that George Catlin had "during the last week frequently exhibited a portion of his extensive collection of Indian portraits . . . and will leave in a few days for the Arkansas river."

The next indication of the artist's whereabouts and activities appears in the *New York Commercial Advertiser* for the date of June 20, 1833, which published another letter received from him: "St. Louis, — 4th, 1833. Since arriving at this place I have been shut up like a hermit in his cave, retouching and finishing my numerous sketches of the country, physiognomy, manners and customs which I collected on my tour through the vast and wild regions of the 'Upper Missippi.'"

A careful check of the files of the St. Louis *Missouri Republican*, for the issues from April 9th to November 30th, 1833, was made by Brenda R. Gieseker, Chief Librarian of the Missouri Historical Society. This search revealed only two references to George Catlin, under the dates July 9th and 12th, and both of these relate to the artist's visit to the Upper Missippi River during the previous year. As Catlin had by this time gained a considerable local reputation, it is reasonable to assume that a journey to Great Salt Lake during the summer of 1833 would have produced some newspaper mention. A further search in the library's manuscript volumes of the American Fur Company ledgers of the R. Chouteau Moffitt Collection, relating to activities on the Platte, also failed to reveal that George Catlin was in that region in 1833. However, documentary evidence that George Catlin did *not* make a trip up the Platte River or to Great Salt Lake in the year 1833, has been found. In the artist's personal papers, memorandums, letters, etc., which have remained unclassified in the Smithsonian Institution, there is a ragged account book filled with a disorganized collection of receipts. These represent a wide range of purchases and expenditures of cash, from shirts to Christmas presents and room rent in various hotels. Most of these receipts are on odd slips of paper, torn from the ends of letters or any other source available at the time needed. Literally hundreds of these are individually folded and pasted into the account book, and a great many more are tied into bundles. A careful examination of all of these receipts has pretty conclusively established George Catlin's whereabouts during practically every week of the year 1833. The following receipts, all in the artist's own handwriting and bearing the signatures of the persons to whom the moneys were paid, are all place-named Cincinnati, Ohio, and dated 1833: "June 26 — for 6-2/7 weeks Board for Self and Lady @ $10.- $67.17" . . . July 20 — Painting 100 frames"

Smithsonian Institution

HAW-CHE-KE-SUG-GA, He Who Kills the Osages
Chief of the Missouris

Smithsonian Institution

KEE-MO-RA-NIA, The No English
A Beau of the Peorias

. . . "July 26 — 4-2/7 weeks Board, Self and Lady @ $10." . . . "Aug. — 3-3/7 weeks board" . . . "Sept. 23 — 76 frames" . . . "Sept. 26 — 4-3/7 weeks board at Pearl Street House" . . . "Sept. 28 — Shipping 2 boxes (of paintings) to Major O'Fallon in St. Louis" . . . "Oct. 7 — Printing 150 Super Royal (sic) bills and mounting same on boards — Reynolds, Allen & Disney" . . . "Oct. 26 — 1 frock Coat, $37. . . . 1 pr. pants $14." . . . "Nove. 12 — 3-1/7 weeks Board, Self and Lady, @ $10." Furthermore, there is a receipt place-named Louisville, Kentucky and dated December 5, 1833, for: "Louisville Hotel — 1 Bottle Champaign and Board, Self & Lady for 18 November — 3-3/7 weeks".

Further proof is found in the *Western Monthly Magazine*, which was published in Cincinnati. Its editor and publisher was Judge James Hall, who later became distinguished for the monumental three volume work of 1837 which is today known as *McKinney and Hall's History of the Indian Tribes of North America.*[74] Among the judge's other books in the same general field were *Legends of the West* (1832), *Sketches of History and Life and Manners in the West* (1835). James Hall was extremely well qualified to evaluate paintings or other documentary work of the character of George Catlin's. It is quite natural that these two, because of their deep mutual interests, should have become well acquainted during the half year that they were both residents of Cincinnati. In the October issue of Judge Hall's *Western Monthly Magazine*, he had a three page editorial on *Mr. Catlin's Exhibition of Indian Portraits*, from which the following excerpts are taken:

Knoedler Galleries, New York

BUFFALO CROSSING YELLOWSTONE IN WINTER

Smithsonian Institution

WINTER HUNTING ON UPPER MISSOURI

"There is now in this city a collection of paintings, which we consider the most extraordinary and interesting that we have ever witnessed, and one which constitutes a most valuable addition to the history of our continent, as well as to the arts of our country. Mr. Catlin, engaged some time since in the very arduous and novel enterprise, of visiting the distant tribes of our western frontier, for the purpose of painting from nature a series of portraits and landscapes illustrative of the country and its inhabitants, and has succeeded thus far beyond his most sanguine hopes . . . His gallery now contains about *one hundred and forty* pictures; and we are informed that he has in his possession an equal number in an unfinished state, which have not yet been submitted to public inspection. Those that we have seen include portraits of individuals of *twenty-seven* different tribes . . . We are happy to learn that Mr. Catlin's interesting labors are not to end with this collection. His enthusiasm is equal to his genius; and he is determined to persevere . . . until he shall have completed a gallery illustrative of the actual condition and physical character of our tribes. He will proceed to the western frontiers next spring."

This seems to establish beyond reasonable doubt that George Catlin was in Cincinnati from May to December of 1833, and that his wife was with him. It is quite obvious that he was working on his pictures — finishing some and probably repainting others from hasty sketches, while his memory was fresh.

There is no explanation why he made the erroneous statement of 1871, but it is impossible to believe that the statement was an intentional falsification. He did not need to add breadth to his vast travels. He was in 1871 a very weary, disheartened, disillusioned and ill old man of seventy-five who had lost virtually everything in life that he held precious. He had never considered specific dates of particular importance. That itinerary also contains other errors. But if he did go to Great Salt Lake it must have been in 1831.

There are no such doubts about the year 1834. The journey that Catlin made far into the Southwest is in some respects equal in importance to his accomplishments on the Upper Missouri. Furthermore he narrowly escaped paying the price of his own life for it.

It is apparent that the cold winter weather of the north affected Catlin's "lung ailment" and he and Clara had spent what is evidently a second winter on the sunny Gulf of Mexico. His brother James was connected with a bank in Pensacola, and from that Florida town Catlin wrote in January 1834: "Far more agreeable to my ear is the Indian yell and war-whoops, than the civilized groans about 'deposits,' 'banks,' 'boundary questions,' etc. . . . and I vanish from this fair country with the sincere hope that these tedious words may become obsolete before I return."[75]

The artist had obtained official permission to accompany an expedition of the First Regiment of Mounted Dragoons across the Southern Plains to the Rocky Mountains — a government undertaking that was the first of its kind in that vast region, as well as one of the most disastrous marches in the early days of the U. S. Army in the West. Catlin left his wife in New Orleans, from where she would later go by steamboat to St. Louis and then stay with some friends in Alton, Illinois, until his expected return there in the fall.

The military expedition of the First Dragoons in 1834 was the U. S. Government's first move toward the acquisition of the Mexican controlled region of the Southwest. George Catlin's authorization to accompany the Regiment was signed by his friend the Honorable Lewis Cass, then Secretary of War under President Jackson. Major Henry Dodge had received a presidential promotion to the rank of colonel and had been made commandant of the recently organized First Regiment of Dragoons to carry out the assignment. The regiment assembled at Jefferson Barracks and was largely composed of seasoned veterans, including the Battalion of Mountain Rangers who had participated in the Black Hawk War of 1832. Among them was the West Point graduate, Lieutenant Jefferson Davis. The Dragoons moved to Fort Gibson, the military outpost on the Arkansas River about seven hundred miles west of the Mississippi and not far from the present city of Tulsa, Oklahoma. Catlin had been instructed to join the expedition at Fort Gibson.

The dates, route, hardships and disasters of this expedition, and George Catlin's participation in it, are well documented in the official report to the U.S. Adjutant General's Office.[76] A further account is found in the book *Dragoon Campaign to the Rocky Mountains*, by a Dragoon (James Hildreth), published in New York in 1836. Its author quotes at length from some of the letters which Catlin sent back East for publication in the New York *Commercial Advertiser*, finding them "a better description of the incidents on the expedition" than his own words could express. The pictures and notes that Catlin made on that trip into the little known region of the Southwest combine to give us the earliest comprehensive portrayal of the Southern Plains Indians.

Smithsonian Institution

STEE-TCHA-KO-ME-CO, The Great King
A Chief of the Creeks

Smithsonian Institution

COL-LEE, Chief of the Cherokees

Smithsonian Institution

CLERMONT, First Chief of the Osages

15

On the Southern Plains

Newberry Library, Chicago

THE STONE WITH HORNS

CATLIN traveled by boat up the Mississippi to the Arkansas River and then on to Fort Gibson. The little river steamer *Arkansas* churned and bumped her way slowly up the shallow waterway for which she was named, frequently getting stuck in spite of the high water of spring. With the artist was a companion named Joe Chadwick, whom Catlin took along as a "man Friday." After numerous delays, they reached Fort Gibson, situated on the left bank of Grand River, about two and a half miles above its confluence with the Arkansas. The region was then known as Arkansas and later as Indian Territory, until the state of Oklahoma was admitted to the Union in 1907.

Fort Gibson was the southwestern outpost of the Territory dominated by the United States. Although the Fort had been established as a frontier military post almost ten years before, the white man had encroached on the region that lay beyond far less than on other parts of the West. Valuable furs were not nearly so plentiful in the more fertile country of the Northwest, and this important fact, as well as the hostile attitude of the Mexicans who considered the Southwest their own, had discouraged trappers and traders. But now the United States was ambitious to expand the boundary in that direction.

"In the vicinity of this post," wrote the artist in his journal,[77] "there are an immense number of Indians, most of whom have been removed to the present location by the Government, from their eastern original positions, within a few years past . . . I had two months at my leisure in this section of the country, which I used in traveling about with my canvas and note-book; visiting all of them in their villages . . . Cherokees, Choctaws, Creeks, Seminoles, Chickasaws, Senecas, Delawares, and several others."

Living in the vicinity of Fort Gibson was about a third of the once numerous and powerful tribe of Cherokees. Of Iroquois stock, these people formerly dominated the mountain regions now part of the present states of Virginia, North and South Carolina, Georgia, Tennessee and Alabama. Bit by bit, however, they had sold their agricultural lands to the Government, and had been pushed beyond the Mississippi. This movement was still in progress at the time of Catlin's visit. These Indians had previously done some farming, and when re-settled in the region about Fort Gibson they turned to cultivating corn and other crops. Some seven thousand of this tribe were living under the rule of their aged and dignified chief *Col-lee*. Although Catlin was not particularly interested in semi-civilized

Indians, he painted a fine portrait of this dignitary of the Cherokees (page 135). The picture plainly indicates the mixture of white and red blood in his veins.

There were also, according to the artist's estimate, about twenty thousand Creeks, who had recently taken up their new dominion adjoining the Cherokees, on the south side of the Arkansas River. They had previously occupied the greater portions of Alabama and Georgia. Like so many other tribes, they had become parties to one treaty after another, which had pushed them westward into the wilderness. Like the Cherokees, they had turned to agricultural pursuits, and some of the more prosperous had developed plantations of considerable size, on which they used large numbers of Negro slaves. Their most notable chief, at the time of the artist's visit in 1834, was *Stee-tcha-ko-me-co*, the Great King, more familiarly known as "Ben Perryman" (page 135).

The Osages in the vicinity were more to Catlin's liking. This tribe had steadfastly rejected everything in the way of civilized customs. They dressed in skins obtained from their own hunting and own processing. This tribe almost entirely abstained from the use of whiskey, which was everywhere the principal inducement for trading with the white men. "This is an unusual and unaccountable thing," commented Catlin.[78] "From what I can learn, the Osages were once fond of whiskey; but several of their very good and exemplary men have been for years past exerting their greatest efforts amongst these people . . . and I am fully of the opinion that this decided anomaly in the Indian country has resulted from the exertions of these pious and good men."

The Osages lived and hunted in the region around the headwaters of the Arkansas and Grand Rivers, to the west and south of Fort Gibson. They had three permanent villages of lodges built of bark and reeds at distances of about forty, sixty and eighty miles from the Fort, which was their main place of trade. There were usually quite a number of them encamped in the vicinity of the garrison. Their men were tall and statuesque, well over six feet in height; and in both warfare and the chase they were extremely skilled. They shaved their heads and decorated them in the manner of some of the other tribes to the north. They also frequently slit their ear lobes, which became greatly extended from the weight of strings of wampum and other ornaments. Catlin visited the villages of the Osages and he painted the portraits of several of their most important people. Among these was their young first chief, *Clermont* (page 136), the son of a very distinguished former chief of the same name. His attractive wife and child, as well as two of his warriors, are shown in a line drawing (page 139) that was done several years afterward. Catlin also painted a full length picture of the tribe's most noted and respected warrior, *Tal-lee* (color plate page 163) whom the artist described as a "handsome and high minded gentleman of the wild woods and prairies."

During the prolonged delay while George Catlin was waiting around Fort Gibson, the Choctaws appealed to him most. There were about fifteen thousand of these semi-civilized tribesmen who had recently been transplanted from their former homeland in Alabama and Mississippi to the country north of the Arkansas and Canadian Rivers. Although they had settled down to agricultural pursuits, with well managed farms and permanent towns, they had tenaciously preserved their tribal games, horse-racing, dancing, wrestling, foot-racing and ball-playing. The last mentioned was an extremely popular sport among many of the Plains Tribes and the artist became a hot fan. "I have made it a uniform rule," he states,[79] "whilst in the Indian country, to attend every ball-play I could hear of, if I could do it by riding a distance of twenty or thirty miles . . . to straddle the back of my horse and look on . . . with irresistible laughter at the succession of tricks, and kicks and scuffles which ensue, in the almost super-human struggle for the ball."

New York Public Library

CLERMONT, Head Chief of the Osages
With Wife and Child and Warriors

A "great ball-play" of the Choctaws was to be held. It was something of a tribal championship affair, and George Catlin made sure to be on hand from the opening ceremonies to the last hurrah. The description which he recorded in his journal provides an interesting comparison with present day baseball and our own derivative game of lacrosse.

"This game had been arranged three or four months before the parties met to play it," the artist-reporter's account of the preliminaries begins. "The two champions who led the contesting parties, had the alternate choosing of players from throughout the whole tribe and had sent runners with ball-sticks fantastically ornamented with ribbons and red paint, to be touched by each one of the chosen players, who thereby agreed to be on the spot at the appointed time and ready to play."

The playing field selected was an attractive area of flat prairie about six miles from the Choctaw Agency headquarters. On the appointed day several thousand of the Indians were gathered. There were two points of timber about half a mile apart, in which the two teams and their families and supporters encamped, with the playing field lying between. "At sundown the ceremony of measuring out the ground and erecting the goals was performed. Each party had their goal made with two upright posts about twenty-five feet high and six feet apart, set firmly in the ground, with poles across the top. These goals were about fifty rods apart; and at a point just half way between was a small stake driven in the ground, where the ball was to be thrown up at the firing of a gun . . . All this preparation was made by some old men, who had been selected to be the judges of the play. They drew a line from one goal to the other; to which came from the woods on both sides a great concourse of women and old men, boys and girls, dogs and horses; and bets were made on the forthcoming play. This betting was all done across the line, chiefly by the women, who seemed to have martialled out a little of everything that their houses and fields possessed. Goods and chattels — knives — dresses — blankets — pots and kettles — dogs and horses — guns; and all were placed in the possession of the *stake-holders*, who sat by them and watched them continuously preparatory to the play."

Throughout this first day of preparations and betting, none of the players appeared on the field. "But soon after dark a procession of lighted torches was seen coming from each encampment, as the players assembled around their respective goals; and at the beat of the drums and chants of the women, each party of players commenced the 'ball-playing dance.' Each group danced for a quarter of an hour around their goal, in their ball-play dress; rattling their ball-sticks together in the most violent manner and all singing as loud as they could. The women of each party, who had their goods at stake, formed in two rows along the line between the two parties and danced also, in a uniform step, and all their voices joined in chants to the Great Spirit, in which they were soliciting his favor, and also encouraging the players to exert every power they possessed in the struggle that was to ensue." The dance was continued at intervals throughout the night, without rest or sleep for any of the players or the audience.

Among the Choctaws each ball-player carried two ball-sticks. Among the Sioux and some of the other tribes, only one stick was used (see color plate page 181). The ball was caught in the small net at the end, and thrown from the net without being touched with the hands. The appearance of the sticks and the player's dress can be seen in the artist's portrait of *Tullock-chish-ko*, He Who Drinks the Juice of the Stone (page 141), who was the most distinguished ball-player of the Choctaw nation. No player was permitted to wear moccasins, or any dress other than his breech-clout, supported by a beautiful beaded belt, a "tail" made of white horse-hair or eagle feathers, and a "mane" around his neck that was also made of horse-hair dyed various colors.

Smithsonian Institution

KIOWA GIRL AND BOY

Smithsonian Institution

CHAMPION CHOCTAW BALL-PLAYER

"In the morning at the appointed time the two parties and all their friends were removed from the playing field. Then the game was commenced, by the judges throwing up the ball at the firing of a gun. At that instant the struggle ensued between the players, who were six or seven hundred in numbers, and were mutually endeavoring to catch the ball in their sticks and throw it home between their respective goals [page 143]. Whenever this was successfully accomplished it counted one point for the game. In these desperate struggles for the ball, hundreds of strong young Indian athletes were running together and leaping, actually over each other's heads, and darting between their adversary's legs, tripping and throwing, and foiling each other in every possible manner, and every voice raised to its highest key in shrill yelps and barks! Every mode is used that can be devised to oppose the progress of the foremost who is likely to get possession of the ball; and these obstructions often meet desperate resistance, which terminate in violent scuffles and sometimes in fisticuffs; when their sticks are dropped and the parties are unmolested whilst settling matters between themselves . . . There are times when the ball gets to the ground, and such a confused mass rushing together around it . . . when the condensed mass of ball-sticks, and shins, and bloody noses, is carried around the different parts of the playing field . . . Each time the ball is passed between the goal posts of either party, one was counted toward their game and there was a halt of about a minute. Then the game was again started by the judges, and another similar struggle ensued . . . and so on until the successful party arrived at one hundred points, when the victors took the stakes." After the excitement of the public brawl was over, everyone assembled in the vicinity of the Agency house, and enjoyed a friendly get-together of dancing and other amusements.

The ball-play of the semi-civilized Choctaws was of little interest to Catlin. "I have become so much of an Indian of late that my pencil has lost all appetite for subjects that savor of tameness," he wrote.[80] ". . . I am going farther to get sitters than any of my fellow artists ever did, but I take an incredible pleasure in roaming through nature's trackless wild and selecting my models where I am free and unshackled by the killing restraints of society . . . I am encouraged by the continual conviction that I am practicing in the true school of the arts; and that, though I should get as poor as Lazarus, I should deem myself rich in models and studies for the future occupation of my life. Of this much I am certain, that amongst these sons of the forest, where are continually repeated the feasts and gambols equal to Grecian games, I have learned more of the essential parts of my art in these last three years than I could have learned in New York in a lifetime."

While waiting at Fort Gibson, Catlin and his man Joe Chadwick had got together their own supplies and horses for the journey. The artist was always extremely independent when it came to matters of supplies. Always a great admirer of fine horses, he procured an exceptional one this time. "For this expedition," he related twenty-seven years afterward,[81] "I purchased the finest horse then known in that section of the country, belonging to Colonel Birbank, an aged officer of the garrison at Fort Gibson, who had become a little afraid to ride him on parade, where he attracted the attention and admiration of all the officers, but, by his flourishing gaiety and prancing, he had too much excited the nerves of his rider, who was willing to sell him for the price of $250.; which I gave him. 'Charley' (the name he answered to) was an entire horse — a Mustang, of cream color; his black tail sweeping to the ground, and his black mane nearly so. He had been taken and broken by the Comanche Indians, who take great care never to break the spirit of those noble animals. I rode and galloped Charley about, gradually beguiling him into the new relationship, for some weeks before the regiment was ready to commence the march; and my friend Joe, on his nimble, slender-legged little buffalo chaser, which he had bought from an Indian hunter, was everywhere my companion."

Finally the regiment of dragoons was drawn up in battle array and reviewed by General Leavenworth, preparatory to starting the expedition into the *terra incognito* of the wild Comanches and Pawnee Picts, and the dominion of the hostile Mexicans. "Each company of horses has been selected of one color entirely," the artist related.[82] "There is a company of bays, a company of blacks, one of whites, one of sorrels, one of greys, one of cream color . . . This regiment goes out under the command of Colonel Dodge, and from his well tested qualifications and from the beautiful equipment at his command there can be little doubt that they will do credit to themselves and an honor to their country, so far as honors can be gained and laurels can be plucked from their wild stems in a savage country."

It had long been traditional for large expeditions of cavalry to ride forth from their stronghold amid a display of fanfare and flying banners. These cavalcades did not always return with the same pomp and ceremony; and the First Regiment of Dragoons that rode away from old Fort Gibson toward the Southwest was destined for a sad end.

"I start this morning with the dragoons for the Pawnee country; but God only knows where that is," wrote George Catlin in a letter to his in-law the Honorable Dudley S. Gregory, of Jersey City, dated at Fort Gibson on June 19, 1834.[83] "I have no time to write, for we are on the march and the bugle is echoing through the hills." The artist and his companion Joe had been assigned to the headquarters unit and they took their places with the commanding officers at the head of the long column. General Leavenworth, who had come to Fort Gibson to supervise the planning and organization of the expedition, had decided to ride out with the dragoons as far as the False Washita, a distance of about two hundred miles. To make up the time lost in delays getting started, the regiment pressed forward as rapidly as possible to that first resting place, from where the general had intended to return to the

Smithsonian Institution

BALL-PLAY OF THE CHOCTAWS

fort. During that time Catlin had very little opportunity to do much more than make hasty sketches and notes for his journal.

Writing in a *Letter* from the mouth of the Washita, Red River (July 1834), he had this to say:[84] "I arrived at this place three days ago . . . I am already again in the land of the buffaloes and fleet-bounding antelopes . . . We shall start from here in a few days. We are at this place, on the bank of the Red River, having Texas under our eyes on the opposite bank . . . The plains around us are literally speckled with buffalo. We are distant from Fort Gibson about 200 miles, which distance we accomplished in ten days . . . The 'bold dragoons,' marching in beautiful order, forming a train a mile in length. Baggage wagons and Indians (engagés) helped to lengthen the procession . . . bending its way over the hills like a huge black snake, gracefully gliding over a rich carpet of green . . . When we started from Fort Gibson, the regiment of dragoons, instead of 800 which it was supposed it would contain, had only organized to the amount of 400 men . . . to penetrate the wild and untried regions of the hostile Comanches."

Writing elsewhere about the first days of the journey, Catlin related:[85] "When we (Joe and I) started out we were fresh and ardent for the incidents that were before us; our little pack-horse carried our bedding and culinary articles, amongst which we had a coffee-pot and frying pan . . . and wherever we spread our bear skin and kindled our fire we were sure to take by ourselves a delightful repast and refreshing sleep. During the march, as we were subject to no military subordination, we galloped about wherever we were disposed . . . and running our noses into every wild nook and crevice we saw fit . . . we travelled happily, until our coffee was gone and our bread; and even then we were happy upon meat alone; until at least each one in his turn, both man and beast, were vomiting and fainting under the poisonous influence of some latent enemy that was floating in the air and threatening our destruction."

In another *Letter* written from the False Washita, the artist had more to say about the illness which had struck the dragoons with devastating effects:[86] "I have been detained here with the rest of the cavalcade from the extraordinary sickness which is affecting the regiment . . . nearly one-half of the command, including several officers, with General Leavenworth, have been thrown upon their backs with the epidemic, a slow and distressing bilious fever. The horses of the regiment are also sick, about an equal proportion . . . They are daily dying, and men falling sick, and General Leavenworth has ordered Colonel Dodge to select all the men and all the horses that are able to proceed, and be off tomorrow at 9 o'clock upon the march towards the Comanches, in hopes thereby to preserve the health of the men and make the most rapid advance towards the extreme point of destination . . . I am writing this under General Leavenworth's tent, where he has generously invited me . . . At the time I am writing the general lies pallid and emaciated before me on his couch, with a dragoon fanning him . . . although he is unwilling to admit that he is sick."

George Catlin and Joe accompanied the drastically reduced contingent that pushed on across the plains under Colonel Dodge. The merciless sun scorched the earth and everything upon it. There was an increasing scarcity of water, and often what they found was unfit for man or beast, and the chronic sickness continued to add casualties. Within a few more days little more than half the original number were able to travel in their own saddles. Although the artist's journal has little to say about his own health, the official report to the Adjutant General's Office makes the terse comment, in typical military fashion: "July 18 — Six litters (of sick) including Mr. Catlin."

Smithsonian Institution

PRAIRIE BLUFFS BURNING, UPPER MISSOURI

Smithsonian Institution

THE HILL OF DEATH, UPPER MISSOURI

Smithsonian Institution

BUFFALO CHASE, UPPER MISSOURI

16

Land of the Wild Comanches

Newberry Library, Chicago
COMANCHE WARRIOR

DAY AFTER DAY Colonel Dodge led his dragoons westward. For the time being there was an abundance of buffalo for meat and enough men able to tend the sick and keep the column moving on its way. The Indian scouts who roamed ahead began signaling back to interpreters who rode beside the commander that they were finding an increasing number of fresh tracks of Indian horsemen. Occasionally they reported the sighting of a smoke signal rising from a distant hilltop. It was known the dragoons were now in Comanche country and that the Indians were well aware of their presence, but there was no assurance that the Americans would be received in a friendly manner. The contrary was more to be expected, and there was little doubt that any sizeable attacking war-party would have much difficulty in cutting the badly incapacitated remnants of the regiment to pieces and would probably annihilate every man. At last, one day about noon, a large party of horsemen was sighted on a distant ridge, obviously showing themselves by intention. If Catlin was a litter-case at the time he certainly found enough strength to get onto his feet and observe everything that happened. Here is his own description of that critical incident:[87]

"From the glistening of the blades of their lances, which were blazing as they turned in the sun, it was at first thought they were Mexican cavalry, who might have been apprised of our approach into their country and had advanced to contest the point with us. On drawing a little closer, however, and scanning them with our spy-glasses, they were soon ascertained to be a war-party of Comanches. The regiment was called to a halt and the requisite preparations made and orders issued as we advanced in a direct line towards them . . . until they suddenly disappeared over the hill, and soon afterward showed themselves on another mound farther off in a different direction. The course of the regiment was changed and another advance towards them was commenced . . . After several such efforts had proved ineffectual, Col. Dodge ordered the command to halt, while he rode forward with a few of his staff, and an ensign carrying a white flag. I joined the advance, and the Indians stood their ground until we had come within half a mile of them . . . at which one of their party galloped out in advance of the war-party, on a milk-white horse, carrying a piece of white buffalo skin on the point of his long lance."

"This moment was the commencement of one of the most thrilling and beautiful scenes I ever witnessed," continues Catlin's journal. "On a beautiful and gently rolling prairie, he was reining and spurring and spurring his maddened horse, and gradually approaching us by tacking to the right and the left . . . He at length came prancing and leaping along till he met the flag of the regiment, when he leaned his spear for a moment against it, looking the bearer full in the face, then he wheeled his horse and dashed up to Col. Dodge [color plate page 181]. His hand was extended which was instantly grasped and shaken. We all had him by the hand in a moment, and the rest of the party seeing him received in this friendly manner, started under 'full whip' in a direct line towards us, and in a few moments were gathered around us! The regiment then moved up in regular order, and a general shake of the hand ensued, which was accomplished by each warrior riding along the ranks and shaking the hand of every one he passed."

The leader of this Comanche war-party "rode a fine and spirited horse . . . In his hand he tightly drew the reins upon a heavy Spanish bit; and at every jump he plunged into the animal's side, till they were in a gore of blood, a huge pair of spurs plundered no doubt from the Spaniards in their border wars . . ." The artist learned, when he painted the Indian's portrait (page 154), that his name was *His-oo-san-chees*, The Little Spaniard. Strangely enough, he was half-Spanish; and although the Comanches generally held half-breeds in contempt, this man was one of the most highly regarded warriors and leaders of the entire tribe — an Indian of particular glamour and distinction.

After the round of hand-shaking, both the red warriors and dragoons dismounted, the peace-pipe was lit, and a "talk" was held between the leaders, with the aid of a Spanish speaking interpreter and of some of the Comanches who had a little understanding of that language. Colonel Dodge explained the peaceful purpose of the expedition; and the Little Spaniard offered to escort the American visitors to their great village, where they might meet their chiefs and smoke the pipe with them. "We were again on the march in the afternoon of that day," wrote Catlin, "and from day to day they led us, over hill and dale, encamping by the side of us at night, and resuming the march in the morning."

There was an abundance of buffalo, and as both the dragoons and Indians subsisted principally on their meat, the red warriors pursued them almost constantly — not only out of necessity, but also because of the great pleasure the Indians took in displaying their skill and the mettle of their fine horses. On one occasion a large herd of stampeding buffalo came dashing directly through the column, upsetting horses and dragoons. Besides buffalo they saw numerous bands of wild horses — of all colors, and with profuse manes and tails that sometimes reached almost to the ground.

At the time of George Catlin's visit in 1834, the Comanches were enjoying the full bloom of their unspoiled primitive culture. They had already gained a wide reputation for their skills in horsemanship, and have since been recognized as among "the finest riders on earth." During the days when the Regiment traveled with the Little Spaniard's war-band the Indians bent every effort to put on a show of their riding skills — dashing at break-neck speed to sink an arrow into the heart of a buffalo, capturing and subduing the finest wild horses, and displaying their trickiest methods of the riding they did when engaged in mortal combat. This afforded Catlin a remarkable opportunity to observe them at their very best, and seriously ill though he was, the artist managed to take the fullest possible advantage of the situation. Although the pictures he made are not nearly as comprehensive as those of the tribes of the Upper Missouri, the notes of his journal are a great credit to his determination.

"When he starts for a wild horse," wrote the artist, "the Indian mounts one of the fleetest he can get, and coiling the *laso* on his arm he starts off under 'full whip' till he can enter the band and throw the noose over the neck of one of the number. Then he instantly dismounts . . . and runs as fast as he can, letting the *laso* pass out gradually through his hands, by which their speed is checked and they are 'choked-down' (page 149) until the wild horse falls for want of breath and lies helpless on the ground . . . When completely choked-down, the Indian advances closely towards the horse's head, keeping his *laso* tight upon its neck, until he fastens a pair of hobbles on the animal's two forefeet. Then the *laso* is loosened, giving the horse a chance to breathe. He puts a noose around its under jaw, by which he gets great power over the affrightened animal, which begins rearing and plunging when it gets breath. As he advances, hand over hand . . . the horse makes every possible effort to escape, until its power is exhausted and it becomes covered with foam, and at last yields to the power of man. He gradually advances, until able to place his hand on the animal's nose and over its eyes; and at length to breathe into its nostrils, when it soon becomes docile; so he has little else to do than remove the hobbles, and lead or ride it into camp . . . Great care is taken, however, in this and subsequent treatment, not to subdue the spirit of the animal, . . . although they use them with great severity, being cruel masters."

Among the most impressive feats of horsemanship practiced by the Comanches as well as by the Pawnees farther west, was their way of throwing themselves far down on the sides of their horses while riding at full speed in the heat of battle (page 151). This was practiced by other tribes, but nowhere with the perfection of these warriors. Some experts were able to shoot an arrow from under a horse's belly with deadly effect. "This is a strategem of war learned and practiced by every young man in the tribe," wrote Catlin. "He is able to drop his body upon the side of his horse at the instant of passing his enemy, effectually screened from their weapons, as he lays in a horizontal position behind the body of his horse, with his heel hanging over the horse's back, by which he has the power of throwing himself up again

The New York Historical Society

CAPTURING A WILD HORSE

and changing to the other side if necessary. In this wonderful condition he will hang while at fullest speed, carrying with him his bow and shield, and also his lance of fourteen feet in length, all of which he can wield upon his enemy as he passes . . . I had great curiosity to ascertain by what means their bodies could be suspended in this manner . . . until one day I coaxed a young fellow up close by offering him a few plugs of tobacco, and I found the explanation that a short hair halter was passed around under the neck of the horse and both ends tightly braided into the mane on the withers, leaving a loop to hang under the neck. This made a sling into which the rider's elbow falls, taking the weight of his body on the middle of the upper arm. Into this loop the rider drops suddenly and fearlessly, leaving his heel to hang over the horse's back to steady him and also to restore him when he wishes to regain his upright position on the horse's back . . . I am ready without hesitation to pronounce the Comanches the most extraordinary horsemen that I have seen and I doubt very much whether any people in the world can surpass them . . . A Comanche on his feet is out of his element and comparatively almost awkward . . . but the moment he lays hand upon his horse he gracefully flies away like an entirely different being."

The dragoons were finally brought to the top of a ridge from where they had their first view of the great Comanche village (page 153). It was situated in the beautiful valley of what is known today as Cache Creek, just east of the Wichita Mountains. There were some six hundred or more skin covered lodges, made of buffalo skins much in the manner of the northern Plains tribes. Thin wisps of gray smoke rose lazily above many of the tepees, and for a mile around the village the valley was speckled with an immense number of horses. The Little Spaniard requested the regiment to halt on the ridge until the war-party could ride in and inform their chiefs and all the people that friendly visitors were arriving. So the regimental bugler sounded "Halt — Dismount!" and the weary dragoons watched curiously from the ridge top while the Indians went racing down toward their village.

Very shortly after the war-party melted into the sprawling stand of brown skin lodges, the white men on the hill could see great activity among the Indians. Horses were being hurriedly rounded up and ridden into the village, and everywhere people were running excitedly about. After about an hour, several hundred mounted warriors and braves came racing out in a wild and disorganized dash, all yelling and screeching in an alarming manner. Colonel Dodge immediately ordered the bugler to sound the order to mount and the regiment was quickly drawn up in three compact columns. The commander and his staff with the most dependable of the Indian scouts took their position a little in front of the columns, and Catlin and Joe were mounted alongside. No one had any idea what was going to happen, but Colonel Dodge gave the order to parade slowly forward to meet the overwhelming number of wild Comanche riders — most of whom had never before seen an American soldier, and extremely few, if any, had seen white men. The dragoons paraded slowly forward while a lone standard bearer moved ahead holding the white flag, and every man tightened his grip on the rein and the weapon he carried.

As the horde of yelling Indian riders approached, they formed into a line, "dressed" like well-disciplined cavalry and one of their number advanced ahead of the rest, carrying their own "white flag." Riding directly to the dragoon standard-bearer, he planted his own emblem of albino buffalo skin beside the white flag of the American soldier. Then, as Catlin continues the description: "The two lines were drawn up, face to face, within thirty yards of each other . . and, to the everlasting credit of the Comanches, whom the world has always looked upon as murderous, they had come out *without a weapon of any kind*, to meet a war-party bristling with arms and trespassing in the middle of their country. They had every reason to look upon us as their natural enemy; and yet they had galloped out . . . to shake us by the hand, on the bare assertion of Colonel Dodge that we came to see them on a friendly visit . . . The head chief galloped up to Colonel Dodge, and having shaken him by the hand, he passed on to the officers in turn, and then rode alongside the different columns . . . and he was followed by his principal chiefs and warriors."

After the extended ceremonies of welcome, the dragoons were escorted to a camping place beside a clear stream, about half a mile from the village, where the regiment was soon comfortably bivouacked. Several of the officers rode in to pay an official visit to the village, and, although Catlin was suffering intensely with "fever and ague," he lost no time in getting out his artist's materials and going into the village to begin the work which had brought him there.

Although the Comanches were at this time one of the least known tribes of North American Indians, they had already gained an unsavory reputation among Mexicans and early Yankee adventurers who were pioneering the Santa Fe Trail, as well as among the other Indian tribes of the Great Plains. They were universally considered a wild and predatory people constantly in search of bloody conquests. Catlin estimated the total number of this tribe at somewhere between thirty thousand and forty thousand, and the "great village" which he visited in 1834 was their central rendezvous from which large war-parties roamed long distances in all directions. Like the other nomadic Plains tribes, they subsisted principally by hunting buffalo and other large game. The highest calling of every able bodied man was the warpath. In their leisure moments, the Comanche men indulged in much the same games and tests of strength and skill as the Sioux and other northern tribes, although in equestrian activities they "excelled all others."

Smithsonian Institution

COMANCHE FEATS OF HORSEMANSHIP

There is no doubt that George Catlin was a very sick man during the time he was in the great village of the Comanches. It is remarkable that he accomplished as much as he did. Among the portraits he managed to put on canvas is that of *Ta-wah-que-nah*, The Mountain of Rocks (page 157). The artist gives a graphic description of this unusual individual, who was at the time acting as head chief. His superior was away leading a large war-party on an exploit of conquest and plunder: "This huge monster is the largest and fattest Indian I ever saw. This enormous man whose flesh would undoubtedly weigh three hundred pounds or more . . . A perfect personification of Jack Falstaff (the fat and unscrupulous Shakesperian character) in size and in figure, with an African face and a beard on his chin of two or three inches in length. His name, he tells me, he got from having conducted a large party of Comanches through a secret and subterraneous passage, entirely through the mountain of granite rock which lies in back of the village; thereby saving their lives from a powerful enemy, who had 'cornered them up' in such a way there was no other possible escape . . . The mountain under which he conducted them is called '*ta-wah-que-nah*' (the mountain of rocks) and from this he has received his name, which would have been more appropriate if it had been *mountain of flesh*."

Catlin's remarkable faculty for winning the friendship and confidence of Indians served him particularly well among the Comanches, even though he was severely handicapped by the fact he was traveling with a heavily armed military force, which could only produce apprehension, in spite of his assurances of friendship. Furthermore, Colonel Dodge was reluctant to linger in any native village just to permit the leisurely painting of pictures or the delving into savage customs and culture. It is reasonable to suspect that the colonel wished he did not have responsibility for the sick civilian artist whom he had been obliged to take along. Having already buried such a large number of his troops along the route and with so many more being daily struck down by the same inescapable illness, and further weakening his command, the colonel wanted only to complete his mission as promptly as possible and get the remnants of the First Regiment of Dragoons back to Fort Gibson.

However the great Comanche village was not the end of the mission westward. The colonel's orders called for going to the headquarters of the Pawnee Picts, at the edge of the Rocky Mountains, and holding a council with their leaders. This he was still determined to do. Instead of carrying the litter-cases along, however, it was decided to leave behind all those who were not able to ride in their own saddles. A crude little fortification was hurriedly constructed at the camp-site, with a make-shift breastwork of timbers and brush, although this was a hopeless precaution in the face of the more than six thousand Comanche warriors, and those who were left behind would be entirely dependent on their continued hospitality. Some of the Comanches had offered to go along as guides, and preparations were rushed for the departure. About thirty of the dragoons were to be left behind, while an equal number of the more or less healthy were ordered to remain to care for them.

When the day and the hour to mount arrived, George Catlin could fight his illness no longer and was unable to put himself into the saddle which Joe Chadwick had cinched onto the back of "Charley." Struggle though Catlin did he was at the last moment unable even to stand any longer. Here is the comment made in his own journal:[88] "All hands (save those who were too sick) were on the start for the Pawnee village. Among those exceptions was I, before the hour of starting had arrived." Thus he was left behind, but he insisted that his companion Joe Chadwick go with the dragoons, and take along a sketch-book and notebook, to make such records as he could at the final goal.

Smithsonian Institution

COMANCHE VILLAGE IN TEXAS

Smithsonian Institution

HIS-OO-SAN-CHEES, The Little Spaniard
Famed Comanche Warrior

17

A Badge of Courage

Newberry Library, Chicago

THE IRON HORN

THE *ultima thule* of that first military expedition into what later became the southwestern part of the United States was reached under a forced march led by Colonel Dodge. He had with him less than one-fifth the number of dragoons originally intended to carry out the undertaking. These men were ragged and worn; they had left behind a trail of fresh graves and camps of the dying, and they were now open to annihilation by almost any organized attack from the red warriors in whose country they were trespassing. With the aid of their Comanche guides (friendly with the Pawnee Picts) the slender column of American soldiers went directly to the great village on the bank of the Red River in western "Texas."

The Pawnee Picts of the Southwest had no tribal connection whatever with the Pawnees of the Platte and Kansas river areas of the north. They are, incidentally, identifiable as the "people of Quivira" met by Coronado in 1541; and they became known to the early French traders from Louisiana as the "*Pane Piqué*," from which they had taken their name at the time of Catlin's journey in 1834. They have since become known as the "Wichitas."[89]

The rather brief notes which Catlin entered in his journal regarding these Indians were made by Joe Chadwick and are so credited by the artist.[90] The great village of the Pawnee Picts is described as being surrounded by "a stupendous range of mountains of reddish granite . . . some five or six hundred wigwams, all made of long prairie grass, thatched over poles fastened in the ground and bent in at the top; giving the appearance of straw beehives . . . We have found these people cultivating quite extensive fields of corn (maize), pumpkins, melons, beans, squashes." Joe also states that the dragoons encamped near the village and quickly became the subject of curious attention by the natives. Enroute from the Comanche village, the hunters had encountered unusual difficulty in finding game and the very last of the provisions had been consumed. Their condition was one of "almost literal starvation . . . and at the same time nearly half the number were too sick to have made a successful resistance if we were attacked." Seeing their pitiable condition, the head chief ordered the women of his village to supply the strangers with food from their lodges and fields. The squaws quickly appeared carrying "back-loads of dried buffalo meat and green corn, and threw it down amongst them." This "was like a providential deliverance" for the dragoons, who by this time had barely one hundred able-bodied men left to carry out the responsibilities and get the sick back to Fort Gibson.

Colonel Dodge completed his council meetings with the leaders of the Pawnee Picts as promptly as such ceremonies could be carried out, and then started the long journey homeward. The head chief and second chief of the tribe accompanied the dragoons to the great village of the Comanchees and then decided to continue on to visit Fort Gibson, together with a number of their tribesmen. During this time George Catlin found enough strength to paint their portraits. The head chief was a patriarch of great age named *Wee-ta-ra-sha-ro* (page 159) and the second chief was a fine looking man named *Sky-se-ro-ka* (page 159).

During Colonel Dodge's absence, additional men of his command had become litter-cases. No time was lost in getting the dragoons on the march again, towards home. It required six days of severe traveling to cover approximately one hundred miles to the Canadian River, where a brief stop was made to rest both men and horses. George Catlin, who was now among the critical litter-cases, found enough strength to make an occasional entry in his journal, and Joe Chadwick fortunately remained healthy and cared for him. "Many are carried on litters between two horses," wrote the artist. ". . . From the Comanche village to this place [the camp on the Canadian] the country has been entirely prairie . . . without water, for which we sometimes suffered very much. From day to day we have dragged along exposed to the burning sun . . . the grass scarcely affording a bite for our horses. The only water we could find was in stagnant pools, in which the buffaloes have been wallowing like hogs in a mud-puddle . . . From these dirty lavers we drove the wallowing buffaloes, and into which our almost dying horses irresistibly plunged their noses, sucking up the poisonous draught, until, in some instances, they fell dead in their tracks. The men also (and oftimes the writer of these lines) drank to almost fatal excess, and it filled our canteens . . . This poisonous water is the cause of the sickness of the horses and men . . . slow and distressing . . . which seems to terminate in a most frightful and fatal affection of the liver."

While the dragoons were making the brief stop on the Canadian River a messenger found them. He had been sent out from the encampment which the regiment had made at the mouth of the False Wichita on the outward journey. He brought to Colonel Dodge "the melancholy tidings of the death of General Leavenworth, Lieutenant McClure, and ten or fifteen of the men left at that place. This cast a gloom over our little encampment here, and seems to be received as a fatal foreboding by those who are sick with the same disease."

After leaving the camp on the upper Canadian River, Catlin became so ill that he was put in a baggage-wagon that was going back empty, along with several soldiers who were in an equally critical condition. In this rough conveyance he rode the rest of the way to Fort Gibson, most of the time delirious and clinging desperately to life, lying on the hard planks, jarred and jolted about until the skin was literally worn off his emaciated elbows and legs. When they finally reached the fort, the artist was put in a bed in the garrison hospital, under the care of Dr. Wright, an old friend.

Thus ended the United States Government's first military expedition into the far Southwest for the purpose of beginning friendly relations with the Indian tribes of that region and of laying plans for the acquisition of the area as part of the United States. About one-third of the men who started out gave up their lives, and a good many more succumbed after they were brought back.

"While at Fort Gibson, on my return from the Comanche country," wrote the artist when he was strong enough to take pencil in hand, "I was quartered in a room with my fellow companion in misery, Captain Wharton, of the dragoons, who had come in from the prairies in a condition very similar to mine, and laid in bed in the opposite corner of the room; where we laid for several weeks like two grim ghosts, rolling our staring eyeballs upon each other, when we were totally unable to hold converse . . . Many others were brought in

Smithsonian Institution

TA-WAH-QUE-NAH, The Mountain of Rocks
Comanche Chief

merely to die and get the privileges of a decent burial . . . Of those who are alive, there are not well ones enough to take care of the sick . . . and I hear the mournful sound of 'Roslin Castle,' with muffled drums, passing six or eight times a day under my window to the burying ground, which is but a little distance in front of my room."

As Catlin recuperated he began making plans to return to St. Louis and to rejoin his wife at Alton, Illinois, where she had been awaiting his return from the Southwest. It was a happy day when he was strong enough to have Joe Chadwick bring "Charley" up from the pasture where this beautiful horse had been waxing fat on leisure and good feed. The artist had become extremely fond of the spirited creature.

A good many years afterward Catlin wrote:[91] "I was anxious to take Charley to St. Louis, but to send him down the Arkansas 700 miles and then up the Mississippi 900, by steamer, would be a heavy expense, and I resolved that just as soon as I should be able to ride again, Charley and I would start for St. Louis by a shorter route, by crossing the intervening prairies, entirely wild and without roads; a distance in a straight line of about 540 miles. With a little compass in my pocket and plenty of ammunition, I felt no apprehension whatever for the result. So one morning in the beginning of September, feeling sufficiently strong to mount Charley with a little aid, and having prepared my little outfit, I was ready to be off. With a couple of buffalo robes for my bed, a small coffee-pot and tin cup tied to my saddle, and half a boiled ham and some salt, my pistols in my belt and my fowling-piece in my hand, I was ready to mount Charley . . . and take my leave of the officers of the post, and the chiefs, who had gathered to bid me good-bye. Charley and I mounted the grassy hills back of the fort, and soon disappeared. The country for 540 miles ahead of us — of meadows and grassy plains — with brooks and rivers, and oak, was vast and apparently tedious; but as my departure from the deadly atmosphere of Fort Gibson was a sort of escape, and myself in a state of convalescense, with the bracing air of autumn around me, I entered upon it with a pleasure that few can appreciate who have seen and felt but the monotonies of life."

There could hardly be a more modest statement, marking the end of a dramatic experience which was to become a page of history. There is no mention of the hardships and dangers of the past or of those of the future on a journey alone. Nor does he refer to the things that were undoubtedly very close to his heart, his wife and the sacrifice of family life. And yet this is the man whom some writers have accused of being sentimental and of exaggerating the scenes and situations he recorded on his travels.

"I was feeble," he continues, "having just risen from a bed of sickness, but I was every hour gaining strength. Every alternate day I had an ague chill and fever, and for these, as I felt them coming on, I dismounted and lay in the grass until they were over . . . With the exception of one night in twenty-five I managed to bivouac on the bank of some little stream or river, where there was water to make my coffee and wood to make a fire."

"My health improved daily from the time of my setting out at Fort Gibson," the original journal relates, "and I was now moving along cheerfully and in the hopes soon to reach the end of my toilsome journey . . ." The greatest obstacle on the trip was thus described: "The Osage River, which is a powerful stream, I struck at a place which seemed to stagger my courage very much. There had been heavy rains but a few days before and this furious stream was rolling along its wild waters with a freshet that spreads waters in many places over its banks . . . I stripped everything from Charley and tied him with his laso until I traveled the shore up and down for some distance and collected drift-wood enough for a small raft, which I constructed, to carry my clothes and saddle and other things safe over. This being completed, and my clothes taken off, and they and other things laid upon the raft, I took Charley to the bank and drove him in and across . . . and with all my possessions placed on the raft

Smithsonian Institution

WEE-TA-RA-SHA-RO, Chief of Pawnee Picts

Smithsonian Institution

SKY-SE-RO-KA, Second Chief Pawnee Picts

and the raft pushed into the stream I swam behind it and pushed it along before me until it reached the opposite shore at least half a mile below . . . Charley was caught and dressed and straddled, and I was on the way again."

Finally Catlin reached Booneville, on the western bank of the Missouri River, crossed to New Franklin, and finally reached Alton. There "under the roof of kind and hospitable friends, I found my dear wife, who had patiently waited to receive me back, a wreck . . . and who is to start in a few days with me to the coast of Florida, 1400 miles south of this, to spend the winter in patching up my health and fitting me for future campaigns."

Together Catlin and his wife sailed down the Mississippi on a steamboat in the fall of 1834 and spent the winter at New Orleans and on the Gulf of Mexico. But as soon as spring of 1835 was in the air he was ready to continue his work. As he stated:[92] "Having recruited my health during the last winter, in recreation and amusements on the Coast of Florida, like *a bird of passage* I started at the rallying notes of the swan and the wild goose, for the cool and freshness of the North." The artist and his wife traveled by river steamer to St. Louis; and Clara continued with him up the Mississippi River to the head of navigation. They spent some time together at Fort Snelling (page 162), just a few miles below the Falls of St. Anthony and a little way above the frontier trading post called "Pig's Eye," which was to become St. Paul, the capital of Minnesota. The great stone fortress on the high bluff overlooking the far reaches of the Father of Waters had been built in 1819 and had already become important as a frontier outpost for spreading Yankee control in the fabled *Land of the Dakota's*. Here, at the eastern edge of the vast domain of the Sioux (Dakota) tribe, a regiment or more of soldiers was kept constantly ready to make attempts to keep the peace between this powerful tribe and their neighbors the Chippewas (Ojibways), Sauks and Foxes, and other bordering tribes, as well as to protect the steadily increasing number of venturesome white settlers from the East who were filtering into that rich agricultural country.

The tribes that gathered around Fort Snelling provided another important part of George Catlin's documentation of the Indians of the West. After completing this part of his work, the artist planned to obtain a birch-bark canoe and make a leisurely journey down the Mississippi River to St. Louis, visiting the tribes along the way, just as he had done on the Missouri. This journey would also include the important council and treaty-making center of Prairie du Chien, and the tribal stronghold of the most famous of all the Indian leaders of the West, the colorful *Kee-o-kuk*, The Running Fox, ruler of the Sauks and Foxes.

Smithsonian Institution

OJIBWAY (CHIPPEWA) WOMAN AND BABY

Smithsonian Institution

WIFE OF *KEE-O-KUK*

Thomas Gilcrease Institute

FORT SNELLING ON THE UPPER MISSISSIPPI

Smithsonian Institution

AH-MOU-A, The Whale
Kee-O-Kuk Warrior

Smithsonian Institution

TAL-LEE, Noted Osage Warrior

Smithsonian Institution

MUK-A-TAH-MISH-O-KAH-KIAK, The Black Hawk
Leader in the Black Hawk War

Smithsonian Institution

WAH-PE-KEE-SUCK, The White Cloud
"Prophet" and Counselor to Black Hawk

18

Journey in a Birch-Bark Canoe

Newberry Library, Chicago

CHIPPEWA SAGE

WHILE Catlin was at Fort Snelling there was nearby the encampment of a large party of Chippewas (a popular adaptation of the name Ojibway), who had come down from the north to trade. The artist made almost daily visits to them, frequently accompanied by his wife. Unlike most of the Plains Tribes, these woodland people lived in lodges made of large sheets of birch-bark, covering a framework of slender poles stuck into the ground and bent over at the top. When the tribe moved, the coverings were rolled up so they could be transported. The attractive and well-dressed Mrs. Catlin was always a center of particular interest to the semi-civilized women of the tribe. On one such occasion, the artist relates: "I observed the women gathering around her, anxious to shake hands with her, and shew her their children, of which she took especial notice; and they literally filled her arms with *muk-kuks* of maple sugar which they manufacture and had brought in in great quantities to sell." One of these Chippewa women displayed her baby in an attractive native cradle, which Catlin painted (page 161). As in nearly all examples of infant cradles among these people, the picture shows the "*ni-ahkust-ahg*" (or umbilicus) elaborately decorated and hanging before the child's face, for its supernatural protection. The Chippewa woman's dress is mostly made of materials of civilized manufacture, but decorated according to Indian taste.

There were the usual tribal dances, which Catlin never failed to attend whenever the opportunity presented itself. One that was distinctive to the Chippewas and others of the northern tribes was *The Snow-Shoe Dance* (page 167). This was usually held at the falling of the first snow and the dancers wore snow-shoes on their feet. It was accompanied by their song of thanksgiving to the Great Spirit for sending the snow, when they could hunt on snow-shoes and more easily take the game.

The eastern Sioux who visited Fort Snelling were a part of the great tribal confederation with which Catlin had become familiar on the Upper Missouri. Their dominion extended westward from the Mississippi. Most of their customs were much the same everywhere. However, those who frequented Fort Snelling showed the effects of their much longer contact with the white man. "The Sioux in these parts," wrote Catlin[93] "who are out of the reach of the beavers and buffaloes, are poor and very meanly clad, compared to those on the Missouri where they are in the midst of those and other wild animals whose skins supply them with picturesque and comfortable dress. The same deterioration is seen in the morals and constitu-

Smithsonian Institution

DOWN THE MISSISSIPPI IN A BIRCH-BARK CANOE

tions of these . . . who live along the frontier in the vicinity of settlements where whiskey is sold to them and the small-pox and other diseases are introduced."

These eastern Sioux lived in the territory which began a few miles west of Fort Snelling and extended up the valley of the St. Peter's River to the fabled *Pipestone Quarry*, which was the sole source of the red, rock-like material from which the Indian tribes throughout North America made their smoking pipes. This was extremely sacred ground and, so far as is known, no white man had ever been permitted to set foot in the *Pipestone Quarry*. Chief Black Dog, whose Sioux name was *Wa-nah-de-tunk-ah*, and who was also known as The Big Eagle, visited Fort Snelling while Catlin was there and was persuaded to sit for his portrait (page 169). With him came the noted medicine man of the band, *Toh-to-wah-kon-da-pee*, otherwise known as The Blue Medicine, who was also painted (page 169). It was the religious duty of these Sioux to see that no infidel trespassers should set foot upon the hallowed pipe-stone ground, and it was well known that they thought little of murdering a white intruder. Why Catlin did not attempt to visit the Pipestone Quarry on this trip cannot be explained but he determined to return for that purpose.

Major Lawrence Taliaferro, who had been the Indian Agent of this area since Fort Snelling was built in 1819, assisted the artist in every possible way. The Fourth of July provided the excuse for a gala celebration with Indian games and dances, and word was sent out inviting as many of the tribesmen as would come and be guests at the fort, with the promise of an abundance of free food and presents. They responded in great numbers. As Catlin wrote:[94] "With the presence of several hundred of the wildest of the Chippewas and as many hundreds of the Sioux, we were prepared in abundance for the novel — for the wild and grotesque — as well as the grave and ludicrous. Major Taliaferro represented to them that I had witnessed the sports of a vast many Indians of different tribes, and had come to see whether the Sioux and Chippewas were equal in ball-play, etc., to their neighbors; and if they would come in on the fourth of July and give us a ball-play and some of their dances, in their best style, he would also have the *big gun* fired twenty-one times (the customary salute for that day), which they easily construed as a high compliment to themselves."

The ball-play of these eastern Sioux presented an interesting comparison with the same game of the southern Choctaws. The important variations were that the Sioux used only one ball-stick and the official dress was different. Catlin painted the portrait of the most distinguished of their players, *Ah-no-je-naje*, He Who Stands on Both Sides, who is shown at the extreme right in the color plate on page 181. In important games, among the Sioux, all the contestants of one team sometimes had their entire bodies painted white, as shown in the central figure of the same color plate. The game that Catlin witnessed at Fort Snelling was little more than a brief display. Soon all the red visitors assembled in front of the Indian Agent's Office, where they further entertained their white hosts with a series of dances, while they waited for and haggled over the gifts which had been promised for their theatricals.

What Catlin saw around Fort Snelling was hardly the sort of primitive Indian culture he was anxious to document, although it provided an interesting side light on the influence the white man was exerting upon the Indian race. "These two hostile foes (Sioux and Chippewas), who have, time out of mind, been continuously at war," he wrote; "are now camped here, on different sides of the Fort; and all difficulties have been arranged by the agent, in whose presence they have been making their speeches . . . indulging in every sort of amusement . . . and feasting and smoking together; only to raise the war-cry and the tomahawk again, when they get upon their hunting grounds."

In addition to making their lodges out of large strips of birch-bark, the Chippewas made excellent canoes of the same material. Tipsy and tricky for a novice to handle, they were wonderfully light, buoyant and swift. Naturally, George Catlin procured the very best of these, and mastered it as well as any Indian veteran.

"Having placed my wife on board the steamer, with a party of ladies, for Prairie du Chien," the artist's narration continues, "I embarked in a light bark canoe, on my home-

Smithsonian Institution

SNOW-SHOE DANCE OF THE CHIPPEWAS

ward course, with one companion, Corporal Allen, from the garrison; a young man having gained the indulgence of Major Bliss, the commanding officer, with permission to accompany me . . . to St. Louis, 900 miles . . . steering with my own paddle . . . and with sketch-book and colors prepared, we shoved off and swiftly glided away."

Shortly after leaving Fort Snelling the two travelers had an experience which indicates the changing character of the Sioux on the border of the white man's civilization. As the birch-bark canoe was passing a small group of lodges on the west bank of the river, the artist reports, "one of them ran into his lodge and coming out with his gun gave us a charge of buck-shot about our ears. One of them struck the canoe, passing through several folds of my coat which was folded and lying in front of my knees . . . There was no fun to this, and I ran my canoe to the shore as fast as possible. They all ran to the water's edge, meeting us with yells and laughter. As the canoe struck the shore I rose violently in my seat . . . thrusting my pistols in my belt and half a dozen bullets in my mouth, and with my double-barreled gun in my hand, I leaped ashore and chased the lot of them from the beach; putting myself between them and their wigwams, where I kept them for some time at a stand, with my barrels presented and threats that I would annihilate the whole lot of them in a minute . . . I slipped my sketch-book and pencil into my hand, and under the muzzle of my gun, each fellow stood for his likeness, which I made them understand, by signs, were to be sent to *Muzzabucksa* (Iron Cutter), the name they gave to Taliaferro, their agent at Saint Peters . . . I at length gradually drew off, but with a lingering eye upon the sneaking rascals, who stood in sullen silence . . . We seated ourselves in the canoe and quietly dipped our paddles again on our way. Some allowance must be made for this outrage . . . They have been for many years past made drunkards by the solicitations of white men, and then abused, and their families also; for which, when they are drunk (as in the present instance) they are often disposed to retaliate and return insult for injuries . . . We went on peaceably and pleasantly during the rest of our voyage, having ducks, deer, and bass for game and our food." When the wind was favorable, the corporal opened a large umbrella, which Catlin had brought along, and held it in the bow of the light canoe as a sail!

Prairie du Chien was about one-third of the distance to St. Louis. For Catlin it was a quiet, pleasant, but unrewarding jaunt. The corporal, however, had already had enough of such traveling and was ready to return to his barracks at Fort Snelling. Clara was waiting in the home of an old friend, but since there were very few Indians at the old treaty ground or around nearby Fort Crawford, the artist put his wife on the first river steamer bound downstream for Dubuque, Iowa; and he started off again. "I took my little bark canoe alone," he wrote, "which I paddled — cooking my own food and having my own fun as I passed along." While his interest in the semi-civilized Indians along the Mississippi River was diminishing, he clearly was and was strongly impressed with future possibilities of the country through which he was passing:[95] "During such a tour between the endless banks carpeted with green, with one of the richest countries in the world extending in every direction, the mind of a contemplative man is continually building for posterity splendid cities, towns, and villas; which a few years of rolling time will bring about . . . new states, and almost empires; for it would seem that this vast region of rich soil was almost enough for the world itself."

He met Clara at Dubuque. The artist's journey had by now become so cluttered with the rural dwellings of white settlers, and the Indian life there had become so prosaic, that Catlin loaded his canoe onto the next southbound river boat, and he and his wife together traveled the next two hundred miles or so to the mouth of the Des Moines River. Then they went up that stream another one hundred and fifty miles to Camp Des Moines, which was then a military post of dragoons under the command of Colonel Kearney. After a brief stop near the

Smithsonian Institution

WA-NAH-DE-TUNK-AH, The Black Dog
Eastern Sioux

Smithsonian Institution

TOH-TO-WAH-KON-DA-PEE, The Blue Medicine
Eastern Sioux

present capital of the State of Iowa, the artist put his wife on another river steamboat, this time bound for St. Louis, and he started overland up the bank of the Des Moines to the village headquarters of the great *Kee-o-kuk* the leader of the colorful Sauks and Foxes. This was one of the last strongholds of Indian authority in the region. Catlin was accompanied by General Joseph M. Street, Indian Agent of the area. Colonel Kearney gave them a corporal's command of eight men, with the necessary horses, and they made the sixty miles in two days.[96]

Kee-o-kuk was already an Indian with a long and interesting life. The Running Fox, as he was known, was then about sixty-seven years old. Though he was not a chief by birth, his exploits against the Osages before he was twenty had made him widely famous as a warrior and leader, and later both inter-tribal warfare and a friendly association with the white men had brought him into ever increasing prominence. His rivalry with Black Hawk had come to a climax with the signing of the treaty of July 15, 1830 at Prairie du Chien, by which the Sauks and Foxes had sold a great area of their tribal lands and agreed to move farther west. Black Hawk had bitterly opposed this and had led his followers into the Black Hawk War of 1830. *Kee-o-kuk* had kept about two-thirds of the warriors of the two tribes neutral, which was without doubt the cause of the prompt and successful termination of the war by the United States military forces. Black Hawk and his principal followers had ended up in balls and chains at Jefferson Barracks; and *Kee-o-kuk* had, through the influence of General Scott, been made the First Chief of the Sauks and Foxes with the approval of the tribal warriors.

"I found *Kee-o-kuk* to be a chief of fine and portly figure, with a great countenance, and great dignity and grace in his manners," wrote Catlin.[97] "General Street had some documents from Washington to read to him which he and his chiefs listened to with great patience; after which he placed before us good brandy and wine, and invited us to drink, and to lodge with him." When the artist proposed painting his portrait, the great chieftain responded with pleased vanity. Presenting himself accompanied by about twenty of his men to witness the procedure "he brought all his costly wardrobe, that I might select for his portrait such as suited me best; but at once named (of his own accord) the one that was purely Indian. In that he paraded for several days, and in it I painted him full length [color plate page 20, also see drawing on page 171]. He is a man of a great deal of pride, and makes truly a splendid appearance on his black horse. He owns the finest horse in the country, and is excessively vain of his appearance when mounted and arrayed in all their gear and trappings. He expressed a wish to see himself represented on horseback, and I painted him in that plight [color plate page 19]. He rode and nettled his prancing steed in front of my door, until its sides were a gore of blood. I succeeded to *his* satisfaction, his vanity increased by seeing himself immortalized in that way. After finishing him, I painted his favorite wife — the favored one of seven" [page 161 and in drawing on page 171].

Catlin also painted and sketched several other notables among *Kee-o-kuk*'s followers. Among these were *Ah-mou-a*, The Whale (color plate page 163); *Wah-pa-ko-las-kuk*, The Bear's Track (page 172); and *Pash-ee-pa-ho*, The Little Stabbing Chief (page 171). "After which," the artist concludes, "he and all his men shook hands with me . . . leaving as a token of regard, a beautiful string of wampum, which he took from his neck. Then they departed from their village in good spirits, to prepare for their fall hunt."

Catlin then returned to St. Louis to rejoin his wife, and renew old friendships in the city which he referred to as his "headquarters." Among the old friends was Joe Chadwick, who had served him so faithfully on the almost fatal journey into the far Southwest. A portrait was painted "to send to his mother." Shortly afterward Joe left to join General Houston in the Texas army, was taken prisoner in the first battle that was fought, and was among the four hundred prisoners who "were shot down in cold blood by the order of Santa Anna."

KEE-O-KUK'S WIFE; KEE-O-KUK; PASH-EE-PA-HO
The Little Stabbing Chief

Smithsonian Institution

WAH-PA-KO-LAS-KUK, The Bear's Track
Kee-o-kuk Warrior

19

A Garden of the Red Gods

Newberry Library, Chicago

THE PIPE SMOKER

A VISIT to the sacred Pipestone Quarry would be a fitting finale to George Catlin's documentation of the Indian tribes of the West. Everywhere the artist had gone in his travels, from the Mississippi to the Rocky Mountains, and from the Canadian border deep into Mexican territory, the smoking of the long-stemmed Indian pipe was an important ritual in practically every phase of peace and war. The pipe was smoked as a solemn sacrament in the contemplation of virtually every individual, family and tribal problem, and at the consummation of every ceremony or council meeting. Smoking was a custom of deep significance, which had originated among the American Indians many centuries before tobacco was first taken back to England and Sir Walter Raleigh introduced it as a pleasurable habit to his Queen and her people. The primitive Indians expended much time, labor and devotion in the making and decorating of their pipes — examples of which are to be seen in many of Catlin's portraits. Smoking the pipe had a significant function in most of the Indian's dances, and some of the tribes held special Pipe Dances for the consecration of the pipe (page 180) and the purification of young warriors. Among all the tribes that Catlin visited, the bowls of their pipes were invariably made of the same red claystone, which, as was noted before, came from that single quarry in the Sioux country west of Fort Snelling.

After Catlin had returned to St. Louis in the fall of 1835, he accompanied Clara back East to spend the following winter. The trip she had just made up the Mississippi to Fort Snelling was to be the last on which the artist's wife would either accompany him or await his return on the western frontier, for the following year they were expecting the happy arrival of their first child. Curiously enough, there is nothing whatever about this in any of his writings, nor is there even the date or place of the birth of this first, nor any of the other of his children.

Nor does Catlin anywhere mention the fact that he transported his collection of Indian portraits to Buffalo, New York, for what was probably his first serious public exhibition. This fact is substantiated, however, by several memoranda in his personal "receipt book" in the files of the Smithsonian Institution and which has previously been referred to. Among these are: "Buffalo, N.Y. July 6, 1836. To advertise Exhibition in *Daily Commercial Advertiser* for July 5 to July 9, and July 9 to August." A bill: "Buffalo, N.Y. August 1, 1836. Rent, August 1, 1836 of George Catlin Esq. for rent of House (formerly Baptist Church) for four weeks, due this day. [Signed] O. H. Dibble." Another bill is dated "Buffalo, January 3, 1837," and reads: "July 10, 1836. To printing 1000 show bills (Indian Portraits) — $10. The above is a small bill for printing which we done for you at the time of your Exhibition was in our city. The printing was done by order of your brother and by his request charged to you."

The artist's journal covering this particular period merely states:[98] "The reader . . . would follow me from St. Louis, and cross the Alleghany mountains to my own state, where I left my wife with my parents and wended my way to Buffalo on Lake Erie, where I deposited my collection, and from thence trace, as I did, the zigzag course of the lakes from Buffalo to Detroit, to the Sault St. Marie, to Mackinaw, to Green Bay; and thence the tortuous winding of the Fox and Ouisconsin (Wisconsin) rivers (600 miles) to the Fall of St. Anthony . . ." On this trip, which was one of no small consequence in 1836, Catlin added portraits of the semi-civilized Chippewas, Winnebagos and Menominees along the way. One of the latter is shown on page 187. This is a young Menominee boy by the name of *Tcha-kauks-o-ko-maugh*, The Great Chief, who lived in the present state of Wisconsin.

At Green Bay, on the northwestern shore of Lake Michigan, from where Catlin began his trip across Wisconsin, he recorded a side-light on the Indians of that region which is a significant comment on the period and well worth repeating here: "There have been two companies of U.S. Dragoons ordered and marched to Green Bay . . . in anticipation of difficulties; but in all probability without any real necessity; for the Winnebago chief answered the officer who asked him if they wanted to fight, 'that they (the Indians) could not, had they been so disposed, for we have no guns, no ammunition, nor anything to eat, and what is worst of all, one half of our men are dying from the small-pox. If you will give us guns and ammunition, and pork and flour and feed, and take care of our squaws and children, we will fight you; nevertheless we will try to fight you if you want us to, as it is.' "

The *Lawrence Taliaferro Papers*, the originals of which are in the handwriting of the Indian Agent, now are in the Reference Library of the Minnesota Historical Society, and give the following brief comment on Catlin's arrival at St. Peter's and his departure for the Pipestone Quarry:[99] "Wednesday, 17th August [1836]. Mr. Catlin and an English Gentleman arrive in company with the officers of the 1st Infantry. Col. Davenport and other officers expected from Prairie du Chien." Also: "Sunday. 21st August . . . Catlin the painter and Mr. Wood an Englishman go off this day to the Pipe Stone Quarry."

With his English companion, Robert Serrill Wood, the artist continued up the St. Peter's River as far as they could go in the birch-bark canoe. Then they obtained horses to travel overland for the balance of the one hundred seventy-five mile distance from Fort Snelling. They made a brief stop at the small trading post of a French-Canadian by the name of Le Blanc. At this place a large party of Sioux made a sudden appearance and announced in no uncertain terms that they had come to stop the two intruders from going any closer to the Sacred Pipestone Quarry. "These copper-visaged advocates of their country's rights had assembled about us," relates the artist,[100] "and filled up every avenue of the cabin . . . The son of the local chief opened the council meeting with a speech that was as though it was for the final disposition of the whole country. 'We have been told that you are going to the Pipe Stone Quarry. We come now to ask for what purpose you are going, and what business you have up there . . . We have seen always that the white people, when they see anything in our country that they want, send officers to value it, and then if they can't buy it, they will get it some other way . . . Brothers — I speak strong . . . the red pipe was given to the red men by the Great Spirit — it is part of our flesh, and it is great medicine . . . we know that no white man has ever been to the Pipe Stone Quarry, and our chiefs have often decided in council that no white man shall ever go to it. You have heard what I have to say, and you can go no farther, but you must turn about and go back.' After each statement that the spokesman made, all the others had vociferated approval with a loud '*How! how!*'"

With Le Blanc serving as interpreter, Catlin argued that he and his companion were merely "two poor men traveling to see the Sioux and shake hands with them, and examine what is interesting in their country . . ." But he was interrupted by another of the Indians "who shook his long shaggy locks as he rose, with his eyes fixed in direct hatred upon me, and his fists brandished within an inch of my face. 'Pale faces! You are our prisoners — our young men are about the house, and you must listen to what we have to say . . . no white man has been to the red pipe and none shall go!' ('*How! how!*')." Others made equally threatening speeches. But to all of this Catlin insisted: "We have started to go and see it; and we cannot think of being stopped." Later, Le Blanc warned the artist to go back, as these Sioux had ordered; but Catlin did not heed this advice.

"On our way again, we were notified at several villages which we passed, that we must go back; but we proceeded on, over a beautiful country of 100 miles or more, until our Indian guide brought us to the trading post of Monsieur La Tromboise . . . in the employe of the American Fur Company, near the base of the *Coteau des Prairies*, 40 or 50 miles from the pipe-stone quarry . . . where we rested from the fatigue of our journey and he very kindly joined us with fresh horses and piloted us to the pipe-stone quarry . . . a jolly and companionable man (part Indian) familiar with most of the traditions of this strange place."

Catlin and his companions reached the forbidden place without further adventure or interference. The quarry is located in what is today the southwest corner of the State of Minnesota, near the present town of Pipestone, county seat of Pipestone County. This "fountain of the red pipe" was situated on the high ground of a broad prairie pass, from which vicinity the rains of summer and the snows of winter drained eastward into the tributaries of the great Mississippi, and also westward into the tributaries of the great Missouri.

"This far have I strolled," related the artist;[101] "for the purpose of reaching the *classic ground*. Be not amazed if I have sought, in this distant realm, the Indian *Muse*, for here she dwells and here she must be invoked — nor be offended if my narratives from this moment should savor of poetry or appear like romance. If I can catch the inspiration, I may sing (or yell) a few epistles from this famed ground . . . This place is great, not in history, for there is none of it, but in traditions and stories . . . Here, according to their traditions, happened the mysterious birth of the red pipe, which has blown its fumes of peace and war to the remotest corners of the Continent . . .

"The Great Spirit, at an ancient period, here called the Indian nations together, and standing on the precipice of the red pipe stone rock, broke from its wall a piece, and made a huge pipe by turning it in his hand, which he smoked over them, to the North, the South, the East, and the West; and told them that this stone was red — that it was their flesh — that they must use it for their pipes of peace — that it belonged to them all, and that the war-club and scalping knife must not be raised on its ground. At the last whiff of his pipe his head went into a great cloud, and the whole surface of the rock for several miles was melted and glazed; two great ovens were opened beneath, and two women (guardian spirits of the place), entered them in a blaze of fire; and they are heard there yet (*Tso-mec-cos-tee* and *Tso-me-cos-te-won-dee*), answering to the invocations of the high-priests or medicine-men, who consult them when they are visitors to this sacred place.

"Near this spot, also, on a high mound, is the 'Thunderer's nest' (*nid-du-Tonnere*), where 'a very small bird sits upon her eggs during fair weather, and the skies are rent with bolts of thunder at the approach of a storm, which is occasioned by the hatching of her brood! This bird is eternal, and incapable of reproducing her own species. She has often been seen by the medicine-men, and is about as large as the end of the little finger. Her mate is a serpent, whose fiery tongue destroys the young ones as they are hatched, and the fiery noise darts through the skies.' Such are the stories of this famed land . . . a place renowned in Indian heraldry and tradition . . . With my excellent companion I am encamped on and writing from the very rock where 'the Great Spirit stood when he consecrated the *pipe of peace* . . . and smoked it over the congregated nations that were assembled about him . . .'

"The rock on which I sit to write, is the summit of a precipice thirty feet high, extending two miles in length [page 177] and much of the way polished, as if a liquid glazing had been poured on its surface. Not far from us, in the solid rock, are the deep impressed 'footsteps of the Great Spirit (in form of the tracks of a large bird), where he formerly stood when the blood of the buffaloes that he was devouring, ran into the rocks and turned them red.' A few yards from us leaps a beautiful little stream from the top of the precipice, into a deep blue basin below. Here, amid rocks of the loveliest hues but wildest contour, is seen the poor Indian performing ablution; and a little distance beyond, on the plain, at the base of five huge granite boulders, he is humbly propitiating the spirits of the place, by the sacrifice of tobacco, entreating for permission to take away a small piece of the red stone for a pipe. Farther along, and over the extended plain are seen, like gopher hills, their excavations, ancient and recent, and on the surface of the rocks, various marks and their sculptured hieroglyphics — their *wakons*, totems and medicines . . . graves, mounds, and ancient fortifications . . ."

Elsewhere the artist gives a further description of the quarry: "This beautiful wall is stratified in several distinct layers of light grey, and rose or flesh-colored quartz . . . the Indians procure the red stone for their pipes by digging through the soil and several slaty layers of the red stone . . . It would appear that this place has been for many centuries resorted to for the red stone . . . and also that it has been the resort of different tribes, who have made their regular pilgrimages here to renew their pipes."

The color of the pipe-stone varied from a pale greyish-red to a dark blood-red, and in some instances was attractively dappled red and gray. When freshly quarried it was sufficiently soft to be readily carved into such shapes as desired with stone knives and drilled with primitive hand drills. The structure of the pipe-stone varied from ten to twenty inches in thickness, the bands of pure, fine-grained material best-suited for the manufacture of pipes seldom measuring more than three or four inches in thickness. This stratum was embedded between massive layers of compact quartzite, which dipped slightly to the eastward. With the stone implements in common use in early times, the process of working the quarry was a very tedious one.[102] This particular quarry was not the only place where the pipe-stone was to be found, but it was the only location known to the Indians where it existed in appreciable quantity or was procured under religious sanction. As mentioned before, no important undertaking of any of the tribes was entered upon without deliberation and discussion in a solemn council at which the pipe was smoked by all present. Every individual engaged in war, hunting, fishing, or husbandry, and every clan and fraternity made supplication to the gods by smoking the pipe, which was believed to bring good and arrest evil, to give protection from enemies, to bring game or fish and allay storms. The calumet was employed by ambassadors and travelers as a passport on their journeys into enemy country; and in solemnizing the ceremonies designed to conclude treaties between hostile nations, which could not be violated without incurring the wrath of the red man's gods. The Indians in general chose not to and dared not to violate the faith attested to by the calumet, nor to make false use of it.[103]

George Catlin collected samples of the red pipe-stone, of which he shortly afterward made his own chemical analysis. Later, after his return to New York, the artist sent some of the samples to Dr. Charles Thomas Jackson, the eminent Boston mineralogist, who made his

Thomas Gilcrease Institute

THE SACRED RED PIPE—STONE QUARRY

own critical analysis and pronounced it "a new mineral compound." A comparison of these two findings is a credit to the artist, for their variance is remarkably slight. It was Dr. Jackson who gave the pipe-stone material the name by which it is commonly known today in the nomenclature of mineralogists and ethnologists: "*catlinite*" — a lasting honor to the first white man of record to visit the sacred quarry of the Indians, and who brought the material to the attention of the civilized world.

After satisfying his curiosity at the fountain of the red pipe, Catlin and Wood made their way on horseback across the country toward the St. Peter's River to return to Fort Snelling. "Whilst traversing this beautiful region," Catlin relates, "we passed the bands of Sioux who had made us so much trouble on our way to the Red Pipe Quarry, but we met with no further molestation. At the *Traverse de Sioux* (on the St. Peter's) our horses were left, and we committed our bodies and little traveling conveniences to the narrow compass of a modest canoe, that must have been dug from the *wrong side of a log* — that required us and everything in it to be exactly in the bottom, and then to look straight forward and speak from the *middle* of our *mouths*, or it was '*t'other side up*' in an instant. In this way we embarked . . . upon the bosom of the St. Peter's, for the Fall of St. Anthony . . . and *sans* accident we arrived at ten o'clock at night of the second day." The date of their return was recorded by Major Taliaferro in his *Daily Transactions* of the St. Peter's Indian Agency: "Monday. 5th September (1836). Mr. Catlin the artist and Mr. Wood an Englishman returned from their journey to the Pipe Stone Quarry beyond Blue River."[104] The major makes a further comment under the date of the following day: "Tuesday. 6th September. At Travers des Sioux and on Crooked River the Sioux are very much incensed at the determination of Messers Catlin and Wood to visit and inspect the 'Pipe Stone' Quarry."

Extremely anxious to get back East to his wife and the first-born child which might have arrived during his absence, the artist and his English companion refused to wait for the next river boat south and continued the journey in their dugout canoe. "Sans steamer, we were obliged to trust to our little tremulous craft to carry us through the windings of the mighty Mississippi and Lake Pipin, to Prairie du Chien, a distance of 400 miles, which I had traveled last summer in the same manner," the artist's journal explains;[105] "We at length arrived safe at Prairie du Chien, which was also *sans* steamer . . . and we dipped our paddles again." They determined not to delay further when they learned that the whole Sauk and Fox nation were gathered at Rock Island (Illinois), about two hundred seventy-five miles travel above St. Louis, for the signing of an important treaty with Colonel Dodge, who had just been made Governor, and Superintendent of Indian Affairs, of the newly created Territory of Wisconsin. Catlin and Wood arrived the day after the signing of the treaty, just in time to witness the Indian parades, dances, and imbibitions of that fateful celebration. The artist sketched and painted several of the dances; but there is deep irony in some of the other things he recorded, with typical restraint, in his journal:

"These people have sold so much of their land lately, that they have the luxuries of life to a considerable degree . . . consequently they look elated and happy, carrying themselves much above the humble manner of most of the semi-civilized tribes, whose heads are hanging in poverty and despair . . . The Sauks and Foxes are already drawing an annuity of $27,000 for thirty years to come; and by the present Treaty that amount will be enlarged to $37,000 per annum . . . for the purchase of a tract of land of 256,000 acres lying on the Ioway river [a reserve made at the end of the Black Hawk War] . . . The Treaty just made, by stipulation of the Government, to pay them $75 per acre . . . $62,000 of which was in payment of their debts and some little donations to widows and half-breed children . . . the American Fur Company being their principal creditor . . . The price for this tract . . . is a liberal one

. . . the usual price heretofore paid for Indian lands has been 1½ to 1¾¢ per acre!

"After the treaty was signed and witnessed, Governor Dodge requested (ordered) the chiefs and braves to move their families, and all their property from the tract, within one month, which time he would allow them, to make room for the whites . . .

"*Kee-o-kuk* was the principal speaker, being recognized as the head chief . . . The poor dethroned monarch, old Black Hawk [who had been released from his ball and chain, on a promise of good conduct], was present, and looked an object of pity. With an old frock coat and brown hat on, and a cane in his hand, he stood the whole time outside the group, in dumb and dismal silence, with his sons by his side, and also his *quondam* aide-de-camp, *Nah-pope*, and The Prophet. They were not allowed to speak, nor even to sign the Treaty. *Nah-pope* rose, however, and commenced a very earnest speech on the subject of temperance! but Governor Dodge ordered him to sit down."

The Black Hawk and his principal followers had been the pawns of a bit of further historic irony since Catlin had painted their portraits at Jefferson Barracks in October, 1832. Relieved of their prisoners' balls and chains, they had been taken East in the spring of 1833 for public exhibition in the white man's cities of civilization and culture. The side-show tour had been raised to its highest note of burlesque when the old patriarch of frontier wars had conferred upon him an honorary collegiate degree of Doctor of Literature. The ceremony was performed, in all baccalaureate seriousness, on July 5th, at the University of Meadville, with The Black Hawk garbed in cap-and-gown and the citation read in Latin.[106] It was not, however, until the following month that the old Indian was officially liberated, on probation, as a prisoner of war.

Catlin returned to St. Louis aboard a river steamer. Arriving late at night, he left his canoe on the deck, and his paintings and collected Indian treasures in his stateroom. Returning in the morning he found that both the canoe and a large bundle of the Indian materials had been stolen. Years later he commented on the incident:[107] "This accounted for the losses I had met with on former occasions of boxes and parcels sent back by steamer and other boats (to St. Louis), containing *one-third* at least of all the Indian manufacture I had ever procured . . . What a comment is this upon the glorious advantages of civilization!"

Gathering together all of his possessions which still remained stored in St. Louis, the artist took them to Albany. George Catlin was now ready to begin seriously the second phase of his life's work — an undertaking which was unfortunately destined to be far less successful than his experiences among the primitive Indian tribes of the wild and uncivilized West.

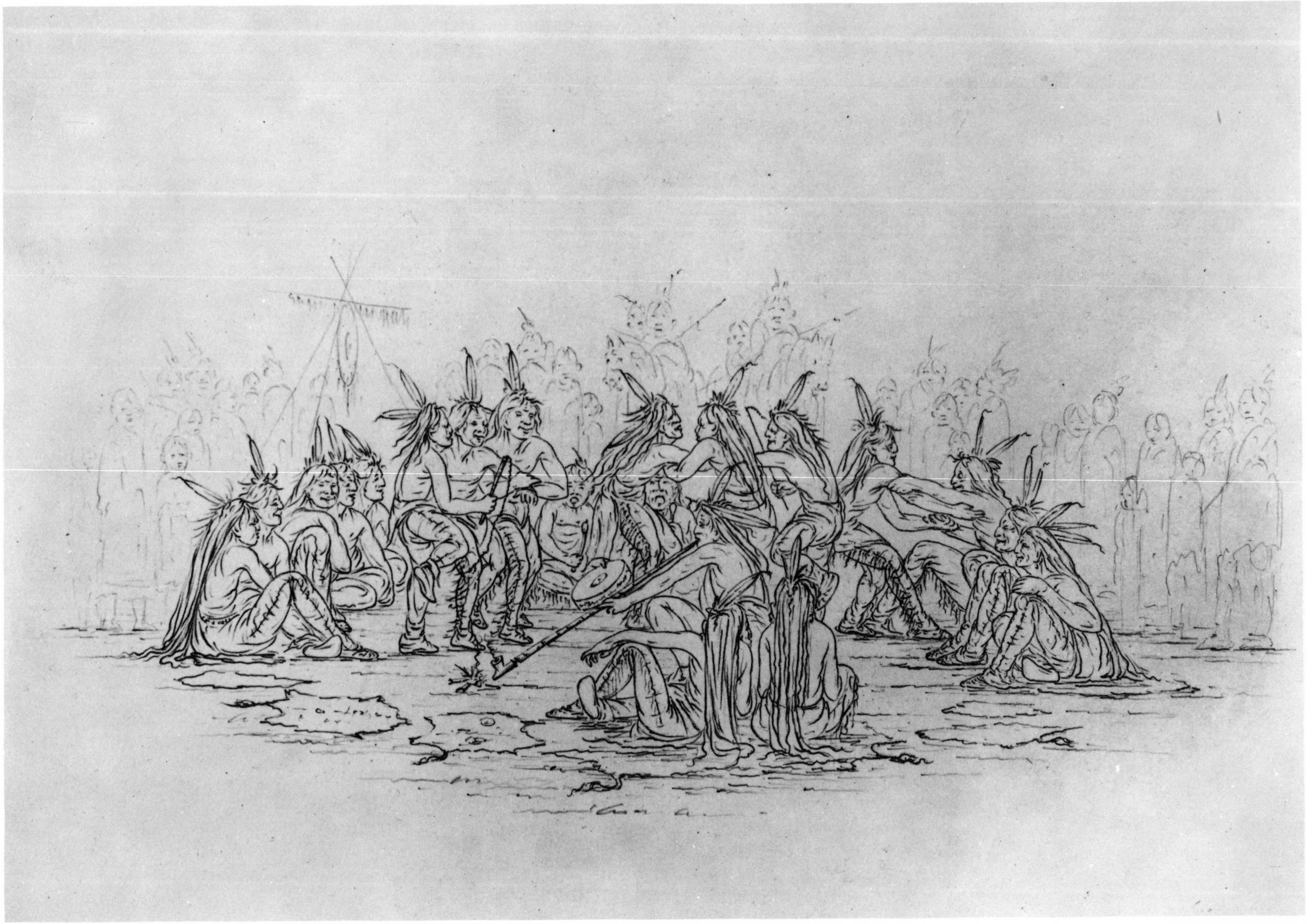

PIPE DANCE OF THE ASSINIBOINES

Smithsonian Institution

COMANCHE WAR PARTY MEETING DRAGOONS
On The Mexican Frontier, 1834

Lithograph

BALL PLAYERS—CHOCTAW AND SIOUX

American Museum of Natural History

SE-NON-TI-YAK, The Blistered Foot
Ioway Medicine Man

American Museum of Natural History

MEW-HEW-SHE-KAW, The White Cloud
Chief of the Ioways

20

A Lonely Crusade

Newberry Library, Chicago

THE VERY BRAVE CHIEF

CATLIN had now accomplished the making of a comprehensive pictorial record of the principal Indian tribes of the great American West—the area between the Mississippi River and the Rocky Mountains. He had gathered by far the most extensive and the finest collection of tribal costumes and other articles ever assembled. The collection of paintings and all the Indian materials he had collected would become the nucleus of a great National Museum, to be sponsored and financed by the United States Government. What he had done was as unique as it was extensive. Now he was ready to acquaint the civilized world with the true character of the Indians of the West, and champion their cause in the court of public opinion. He also wanted to promote his idea of a large National Park along the edge of the Rocky Mountains, a permanent sanctuary for the red men and native game animals of the West.

The writing of the few *Letters* which had been published in the New York *Commercial Advertiser* had gained some public attention, and Catlin intended to expand these into a book. He had tried out the exhibition of his "Indian Museum" of pictures and curiosities, with accompanying lectures, in Pittsburgh, Cincinnati and Buffalo. Now he pursued this course as a means of telling his story, as well as of gaining popular interest and support for his whole project. But the mere transportation of the vast and bulky materials would be expensive, as would be the renting of suitable halls—and he was a poor man, without sponsors. It would probably be very difficult to change the attitude the civilized world held toward the "savage red-skins," who had all come to be looked upon only as perpetrators of bloody massacres and torturers of innocent women and captive children. George Catlin was well aware of the difficulties that lay ahead, but his faith, his confidence, and his courage were strong. As in the past, he planned methodically. First he would put on his exhibitions and lectures in New York and other big cities in the East, and then, with all the publicity and popular support that he could muster to aid the project, he would take his Indian Gallery to Washington, D.C. and present the plan to Congress.

He returned to his home in Albany and, after assembling everything there in the late fall of 1836, he spent the winter putting finishing touches on many of the paintings that had not already been completed and creating additional ones from field sketches. Most of the oil paintings had been made in a uniform size of 28″ x 23″, which made them more convenient to pack and transport.

Before launching his one-man crusade in New York City, he decided on a few more try-outs in less important places. He began in Albany, where the local newspaper, *The Argus*, in the issue of May 15th, 1837, carried the first of a series of paid advertisements announcing the opening. The results were not particularly successful and his difficulties were further aggravated by a recurrence of ill-health. The situation in which Catlin found himself is indicated in a letter which is addressed at Albany, to an unknown person, dated 10th June 1837, and reads in part: "Dear Sir—I arrived in Albany some 4 weeks ago and after having made the preparations for my Exhibition, and having commenced it for a few evenings and just got the public attention attracted to it, I was *smitten* with a sudden attack of fever and infection of the lungs, which has laid me upon my back for at least two weeks. . . . I am now free of fever and all ailing except that of weakness and exhaustion. . . . In these times I almost flinch at the thought of entering New York with my paintings. . . . [Signed] Geo. Catlin."

An advertisement in the Albany *Argus* on June 17th announced the re-opening of the exhibition. This was followed by another try-out in Troy, New York, which was advertised in the *Daily Whig* for July 6th to 20th. After this, Catlin returned to Albany to make further preparations for the fateful invasion of sophisticated Manhattan.

The New York *Commercial Advertiser* of September 23, 1837 carried the following advertisement in that newspaper's Amusement notices: "CATLIN'S INDIAN GALLERY. Opens for exhibition on Monday Evening, the 25th instant and will be continued each evening. . . . In the lecture room of Clinton Hall. There will be several hundred Portraits exhibited, as well as Splendid Costumes—Paintings of their villages—Dances—Buffalo Hunts—Religious Ceremonies, etc. Collected by himself, among the wildest tribes of America, during an absence from this city of seven years. Mr. Catlin will be present at all of these exhibitions, giving illustrations and explanations in the form of a Lecture. . . . Each admission 50 cents."

Thus George Catlin became the first person to present a *Wild West* exhibition for the entertainment of the American public. His Indian Gallery and lectures in old Clinton Hall marked the beginning of one of the longest surviving of all the popular interests our country has experienced. Curiosity brought New Yorkers to see what Catlin had brought back and hear what he had to say about the little-known wilderness of the Far West. They crowded into the gallery to gaze at the pictures. In the formal lectures, as he put each picture upon an easel, he gave a rather pastoral dissertation on the subject, supplemented by his displaying the actual garments in which the chief or medicine man was shown, or the weapons or other paraphernalia. What he said about the Indians was quite different from what had been expected, although the deep sincerity with which Catlin told his story went a long way to captivate his audiences. And when he showed the Mandan torture scenes, there was enough excitement to satisfy even the most sensational taste.

Much of Catlin's account was so different from what was generally believed or so new that it was doubted or denied, even by some so-called experts in the field. It was almost impossible to believe that this mild-mannered artist could have wandered alone through such remarkable experiences, among so many different tribes, enjoying their hospitality, without being tortured or scalped. The pedants were quite sure his story of the *O-kee-pe* of the Mandans was nothing more than the preposterous creation of an exhibitionist's imagination, and they could not even conceive of any Indian showing such a civilized trait as religious behavior. Furthermore, Catlin spoke entirely too vehemently about the practices of the powerful fur companies, the agents of which ruled like pagan czars over great areas of the West, peddling cheap whiskey at exorbitant rates, debauching the character of the Indians, teaching them by example to cheat and steal and be immoral, and building among all the red men a universal hatred against all white men. Catlin also spoke too frankly for his own good about the sins of our Government and its policy of signing "treaties" with the various tribes for the acquisition of vast areas of land—treaties for which the red men had consistently shown far more respect than those who had so ardently promoted the bargain.

"It is astonishing," he stated, "that under all the invasions, the frauds and deceptions, as well as force, that have been practiced upon the American Indians, to push them from their lands, and step by step towards the setting sun, these abused people have exercised so little cruelty as they have; that whiskey and small-pox, of the white man's importation amongst them, have been submitted to; and border warfare, until they are reduced, tribe by tribe, to mere remnants, and still pushed again and again to the west.

"All history on the subject goes to prove, that when first visited by civilized people, the American Indians have been found friendly and hospitable—from the days of Christopher Columbus to the Lewis and Clark Expedition. . . . And so also have a great many other travelers, including *myself*. Nowhere, to my knowledge, have they stolen a six-pence worth of my property, though in their countries there are no laws to punish for theft. I have visited forty-eight different tribes, and I feel authorized to say that the North American Indian *in his native state* is honest, hospitable; faithful, warlike, brave, cruel, relentless—and an honorable and religious human being."

Along with a compassionate plea for understanding and fair treatment for the Indians, Catlin expounded his plans for a National Museum and his hope that the Government would acquire his entire Indian Gallery as the beginning of such an institution.

The exhibition in Clinton Hall closed October 6, 1837; and re-opened on October 9th in larger quarters at Stuyvesant Institute, on Broadway at Bond Street. Encouraged by the public's interest and support, the artist promoted his lectures with even greater determination. He distributed thousands of hand-bills to promote attendance; prepared a rather elaborate *Catalogue*[108] and began working hard on a book.

On the evening of November 1, 1837, some special guests were in attendance at the evening lecture at Stuyvesant Hall, who had an intimate connection with the artist, his pictures, and some of the statements he had been making. *Kee-o-kuk*, the famous chief of the Sauks and Foxes, with his wife and a group of twenty notable members of his tribe, were in New York City on a visit, and they had accepted Catlin's invitation to attend his lecture. The special event was properly advertised, and 1500 customers paid the increased admission of $1 to attend. The Indians were seated on an elevated platform in view of the audience and where they would have an unobstructed view of the paintings and the lecturer. When Catlin displayed the picture of *Kee-o-kuk* on his war-horse, (color plate page 19) all of the Indians suddenly sprang to their feet with a spontaneous burst of jabbering and yelling. They made such a commotion that the dignified old *Kee-o-kuk* rose to his feet and after quieting his compatriots made a public apology to the audience, which was translated by LeClare, the interpreter who was accompanying them. "My friends," he said[109] "I hope you will pardon my men for making so much noise, as they were very much excited by seeing me on my favorite war-horse, which they all recognized in a moment." This was followed by Catlin's assertion that "many persons had questioned the correctness of the picture of the horse . . . that no Indian on the frontier rode so fine an animal." When this was explained to *Kee-o-kuk*, he became quite indignant and again rose to address the audience, asking, "why *Kee-o-kuk* could not ride as good a horse as any white man?" Then LeClare, the interpreter spoke for himself, explaining that he too had immediately recognized the horse, for it was he who had sold the animal to *Kee-o-kuk*—for three hundred dollars—and that it was known to be the finest horse on the frontier that belonged to either red or white man. To all of this the audience responded with loud applause. Catlin also addressed to the Indians some other questions, which had arisen from doubts or denials by certain querulous visitors to his lecture room, and the artist was gratified by complete support by the natives from the West.

Catlin's Indian Gallery continued to attract large public audiences, in spite of the fact that the newspapers had been reluctant to commit themselves one way or another regarding this unusual exhibition. The scholarly aspects of the artist's story began attracting the attention of an increasing number of scientists and intellectuals, and although he was plagued by ill-health, the project continued to prosper, financially at least. The success continued until late in December, when the newspapers carried some stories which caused Catlin to close his exhibition abruptly and leave the city. These accounts related to the long and bitter Indian war in Florida. But now *Os-ce-o-la*, The Black Drink, the leader of the recalcitrant Seminoles, along with a large group of his followers, had been taken prisoner and brought north to Fort Moultrie, at Charleston, North Carolina. The capture had not been the result of any distinguished military accomplishment on the part of the Army. Quite the contrary—*Os-ce-o-la* and his stalwarts had been seized while responding to a peace conference with General Jessup, "*under a flag of truce*!"[110] This high-level treachery in dealing with the Indians so fired George Catlin's indignation that he closed his exhibition in New York and went direct to Fort Moultrie, to get the facts and to paint the portrait of *Os-ce-o-la* and others of the group.

Bitter as the half-breed Seminole leader was—he was supposed to be the son of a white man by the name of Powell and a Creek woman—the old warrior quickly became very friendly to the artist and willingly posed for his picture (page 190). "This gallant fellow," wrote Catlin[111] "is grieving with a broken spirit, and ready to die, cursing the white man, no doubt to the end of his breath. The surgeon of the post, Dr. Weedon . . . has told me from day to day, that he will not live many weeks."

Catlin stayed at Fort Moultrie, painting and waiting to be with *Os-ce-o-la* during his last hour; but the artist finally left for New York City on January 29, 1838. *Os-ce-o-la* died the following day.[112] Catlin did, however, record the old warrior's last moments, the details of which were sent to him by Dr. Weedon:[113] "About half an hour before he died . . . he signaled by signs that he wished me to send for the chiefs and the officers of the post, whom I called. He made signs to his two wives and also two fine children, to go and bring his full dress, which he wore in times of war; which having been brought in, he rose up in his bed, which was on the floor, and put on his shirt, leggings, and moccasins—girded on his war-belt—his bullet-pouch and powder-horn, and laid his knife on the floor. He then called for his red paint, and his looking glass, which was held before him, when he deliberately painted one-half of his face, his neck and throat—his wrists—the backs of his hands, and the handle of his knife, red with vermillion; a custom practiced when the irrevocable oath of war is taken. His knife he then placed in its sheath, under his belt; and he carefully arranged his turban on his head, and his ostrich plumes. Being thus prepared in full dress, he laid down a few minutes to recover sufficient strength, when he rose up as before, and with most benignant and pleasing smiles, extended his hand to me and to all the officers and chiefs who were about him; and shook hands with all of us in dead silence; and also with his wives and children; he then made a signal for them to lower him down upon his bed, which was done, and he then slowly drew from his war-belt his scalping knife, which he firmly grasped in his right hand, laying it across the other, on his breast, and in a moment smiled away his last breath, without a struggle or a groan."

Shortly afterward Catlin made a large engraving on stone (19 13/16″ x 26 7/8″) for a handsome printed-in-black lithograph of his full length portrait of *Os-ce-o-la* (page 187). A print of this was filed for copyright and dated February 27, 1838. Another smaller one was also made (7 1/2″ x 8 3/4″) at about the same time.

Kennedy Galleries, New York

OSCEOLA, of Florida

Smithsonian Institution

TCHA-KAUKS-O-KO-MAUGH, The Great Chief
Menominee Boy

In the 1837–1838 session of the United States Congress, a resolution was introduced in the House of Representatives, on the purchase of the "Catlin Collection of Indian Portraits & curiosities" for the purpose of preserving this material. This was referred to the Committee on Indian Affairs and a report on the matter was prepared by the Chairman, but, "owing to the near approach of the close of the session, was not considered."[114] It might have been said, more truthfully, that George Catlin, by his frankness, had stepped on too many toes in high places.

Catlin was, however, greatly encouraged by the public reponse to his exhibitions and by the mere fact that Congress had seriously considered the purchase of his entire collection, and decided to take the Gallery to the national capitol. There he could invite influential people to visit the exhibitions and lectures, and thus better enlist support to accomplish his ultimate purpose. The vast amount of material was packed into boxes and crates and bundles, and shipped to Washington, D.C. The Indian Gallery was installed in the Old Theatre, and the opening took place on April 9th, 1838.

That Catlin put every effort into this fateful presentation of his Indian Gallery is indicated by the receipts covering payment of moneys, which are today in the files of the Smithsonian Institution. These cover the printing of 2,500 new and somewhat enlarged catalogues and of 10,850 show-bills, advertisements in the Washington *Globe*, reprints of advertisements, and other expenditures. Most of these receipts are dated during April.

In his earlier days as a miniaturist and portrait painter, before he went West, Catlin had made a good many friends of importance in Washington. He now renewed these old friendships and added many new ones. His personality and brilliance always made a strong and favorable impression upon men of intellect, whether or not they agreed with all of his ideas. His admirers now included Henry Clay, Daniel Webster, William H. Seward, and many more. All of these became strong supporters of Catlin's plan for the establishment of a National Museum. But politics often have a strange effect on matters which reflect even vaguely upon national policies—particularly when those policies may be vulnerable to public question or criticism. Official Washington already had a guilty conscience regarding the treatment of the Indians, and George Catlin had strongly established himself on the wrong side. While he made many friends and won much praise for his artistic accomplishments as well as for his humanitarian attitude, he got nowhere with either the purchase of his collection or the establishment of a National Museum.

Discouraged but not dismayed, Catlin moved the Indian Gallery to Baltimore. On July 2nd the Baltimore and Ohio Railroad transported "one car load of Merchandise, for G. Catlin;" and on July 4th the Baltimore newspapers *The Sun* and *The Commercial Transcript* each carried advertisements of the opening of the exhibition in that city. All his expenses and the support of his growing family had to be financed entirely from admission fees paid by the public, and when returns fell below outlay, Catlin had no alternative but to move to a new location. On July 23rd, everything was again shipped—this time to Philadelphia.

The newspapers and other periodicals had remained surprisingly apathetic to the public exhibitions of Catlin's Indian Gallery, although the reviewer for the *Philadelphia Saturday Courier* had the following to say: "There is not in our land, nor in any part of Europe . . . anything of the kind more extraordinary or more interesting. The galleries illustrative of national character and antiquities which are to be found in London, Paris, Florence and other cities, have been collected by the power of great kings; and the outlay of immense treasure, and the apparatus of negotiations, and special ministers, and agents innumerable . . . This is the work of a single individual, a man without fortune and without patronage, who created it with his own mind and hand, without aid and even against countenance . . .

He may point to his magnificent collection which now receives the admiration of every eye, and say with honest pride, Alone I did it!"

Nevertheless, the Indian Gallery had to be moved on — this time to Boston. There, on August 16th, it opened in Amory Hall; and after a month was moved for an additional period in Faneuil Hall. Then back to storage in New York City.

Since he was still getting nowhere in Washington, D.C. inspite of continual correspondence and trips to the national capitol, Catlin decided upon a desperate strategy. Early in the summer of 1838 he had announced that the entire collection would be taken to Europe, where it might be disposed of to a foreign government. He requested his good friend Henry Clay to write a letter of introduction to Lord Selkirk. That letter, dated July 7, 1838, has already been quoted on page 16.

That the idea was in large part a subterfuge is borne out by the numerous letters which the artist wrote to his friends and the plea which he addressed as a last resort to the Secretary of War. He even re-opened his exhibition in New York City, and from the lecture platform and in the newspaper advertisements declared his intention of taking everything to Europe. The reaction to this was prompt.

"No artist in this country possesses a more graphic pencil," stated an editorial in *The United States Gazette;* "perhaps no one, since Hogarth, has had so high a degree of faculty in seizing the true impression of a scene before his eyes and transferring it to canvas . . . Mr. Catlin has accomplished a work which will forever associate his name in the highest rank of honor, with a subject that will interest the civilized world every year more and more through all time to come. We have learned with great regret that he will certainly take his museum to England in the course of a few weeks." *The American Sentinel* had this to say: "Mr. Catlin's extraordinary exhibition of Indian curiosities and paintings will be closed in the course of a few days . . . as it will be taken to England at once and there disposed of . . . No citizen should suffer it to leave this country." And the *New York Evening Star* editoralized: "Catlin's Indian Gallery . . . will be closed after the lapse of a single week and will never again be exhibited in America . . . It is one of the most remarkable and interesting works that the genius and labor of an individual has created in this age and country . . . Nothing could redound more to the patriotism, national pride, and honor of our country, than the purchase by Congress of this collection of Aboriginal Curiosities, to enrich a National Museum at Washington."

But Catlin could not turn back now. He had done everything within his power to accomplish the aim toward which he had striven and sacrificed. Furthermore, the commercial possibilities of his Indian Gallery had been practically exhausted in the large cities of the United States, and he did not have the means to go on without the receipt of admission fees. He could have abandoned the whole thing and returned to the old routine as a portrait painter of wealthy Americans, but this was entirely unthinkable. London, and maybe Paris and other European cities offered new fields of remuneration — and there was still his undying hope that Congress might act favorably and call him home.

Smithsonian Institution

OSCEOLA, The Black Drink
Great Seminole Warrior

21

A Reluctant Exile

TABLEAUX VIVANS

IN THE FALL of 1839 [November 25th]," wrote George Catlin,[115] "I embarked at New York on board the packet-ship *Roscius*, for Liverpool, with my Indian Collection . . . eight tons of freight, consisting of 600 portraits and other paintings . . . and several thousands of Indian costumes, weapons, etc." There is no bitterness in what he wrote about that departure from his native land — no mention of the faded but not abandoned dream — no mention, either, of the wife and daughter, and the second child that was expected soon. But one can easily surmise, without presumption, that his heart was very heavy as the little packet-ship moved out into the stormy Atlantic at that Thanksgiving Time.

It is a long story from that unhappy departure to George Catlin's return. It is a saga of remarkable triumphs — and bitter sorrows. The first part of that reluctant exile is well detailed in the artist's two volume publication, *Notes on Eight Years Travel and Residence In Europe* (1848); but much of the remainder of that long exile will probably never be written.

Arriving in London with his Indian Gallery, Catlin lost no time in getting to the purpose of his visit. On December 30, 1839, he signed an agreement for the rental of three large gallery rooms in Egyptian Hall, Piccadilly, at £ 550 per year, beginning on that date.[116] In the making of this and other arrangements he had the friendly help of C. A. Murray, Master of Her Majesty's Household, with whom Catlin had travelled on the Mississippi River, when that gentleman was enjoying a bit of adventure on the American frontier.

The main gallery in Egyptian Hall was one hundred six feet long and provided excellent space for the display of the collection of paintings and other materials. This would be an exhibition the likes of which Europe had never seen before; and the preview opening was well-calculated to attract public attention. "My friend the Hon. C. A. Murray," Catlin described it,[117] "with several others, had now announced my collection open to their numerous friends, during the first three days when it was submitted to their private view . . . Amongst the most conspicuous of these were H.R.H. the Duke of Cambridge, the Duke and Duchess of Sutherland . . . Duke of Wellington, Bishop of London . . . and many others of nobility, with most of the press . . . and scientific gentlemen." Thus was Catlin's Gallery of North American Indians launched upon its European tour. "I opened it for the inspection of the public on the first day of February, 1840," the artist states.[118] The admission was one shilling, and from morning to evening he was in the exhibition rooms, answering questions.

In the evenings he gave the formal lecture. English periodicals gave it a large amount of space and praise, and the undertaking quickly became a tremendous success. George Catlin also became a celebrity, much sought after as the honored guest in the most exclusive homes.

Catlin now turned seriously to the completion of the writing of his *Letters and Notes* on his travels among the Indians. Unable to find a publisher for such an elaborately illustrated work as he had in mind he set about making the line drawings from his paintings. Unable to find a private sponsor for the undertaking, he determined to have the project privately printed.[119] This took time, although meanwhile the exhibition continued to gain success. In October, 1841, Catlin had the first copies of *Letters and Notes of the Manners, Customs, and Condition of the North American Indians . . . In Two volumes, with Four Hundred Illustrations . . . Published by the Author, At Egyptian Hall, Piccadilly.* Heading a long list of distinguished subscribers were Her Majesty Queen Victoria and H.R.H. Prince Albert, and many other members of royalty and the gentry. The English newspapers and literary periodicals were most generous with space and praise. The important *London Literary Gazette* printed three notices, totaling twenty-six columns of comments and quotes. The *United States Gazette*, London edition, summarized the growing opinion of the author: "Mr. Catlin is one of the most remarkable men of the age." The two volumes became the most widely praised and most successful work of its kind that had ever been published.[120] Catlin also became sought after as the special speaker at important gatherings of scientific and literary men. Among the learned groups which he was invited to address were the Royal Institute and the Royal Geographical and Historical societies. In every instance his theme was the American Indian, and a somewhat broadened proposal for a Museum of Mankind.

At this moment of greatest triumph, his wife and two little daughters arrived on the ship *British Queen* from New York. "The advent of my dear Clara, with her two babies," the artist wrote several years afterward,[121] "was like the coming of the warm and gentle breeze of spring — she who, though delicate and tender, had been, during the last three years of my rambles in the Indian wilds, my indefatiguable companion . . . who had blessed her husband in the richness of gift with two children, was once more by his side, to cheer him with the familiar sounds in which he never knew guile . . . which filled (at that moment at least) the cup of our mutual enjoyment." The little family was established in an attractive little home, appropriately known as "Rose Cottage," at Walham Green, a suburb of London.

Never content with a goal achieved, Catlin devised a plan for adding greater interest and effectiveness to his exhibitions. This was the introduction of a *tableaux vivans*, in which a group of carefully selected actors were trained to perform Indian dances, ceremonies and scenes of warfare, all properly garbed in costumes from his collection, with their bodies and faces appropriately painted, and instructed in the red man's songs and yells and warwhoops. This added even greater success at Egyptian Hall (page 197).

The weeks passed into months, but by the time the third year in Egyptian Hall neared its close, attendance began to dwindle. Throughout this period Catlin had kept up a continuous correspondence with his friends in America, pleading and hoping that Congress would purchase his collection and establish the National Museum which would call him home again. Now that he had just about "done London" he was compelled to seek new fields, and so he decided to take his show on a brief tour of other British cities and then ship everything back to the United States. This plan began with modified exhibitions at Liverpool, Manchester, Edinburgh and other places. He announced his departure, but in the midst of his preparations, a group of nine Ojibway Indians unexpectedly arrived at Liverpool on a tour of England. They had been brought over on speculation by Arthur Rankin, who immediately sought out George Catlin and suggested that they join his exhibition. The possibilities of this fired the artist's enthusiasm — and back to London they all went. Egyptian Hall was again leased, with "real live American Indians" as a new attraction, replacing mere actors in the *tableaux*. All the Ojibways were taken to Buckingham Palace to make a "command appearance" before Her Majesty Queen Victoria and her royal consort, in the presence of a large gathering of royal guests in the spacious elegance of Waterloo Gallery (page 195). The public and the press were duly impressed, although the Indian Gallery was something of an old story, and there were some whose comments regarding the "noble savages" were not conducive to continued success. No less a personage than Charles Dickens was particularly derogatory after visiting the exhibition. He described Catlin as "an energetic, earnest man," and then the great English journalist referred to the Indians as "squatting and spitting on the table before him . . . mere animals and wretched creatures; and their dances no better than the chorus of an Italian Opera in England."[122] Catlin also became the victim in further unfavorable publicity, when the English-speaking Indian, *Cadotte*, The Strong Wind, got amorously involved with an English woman, and an ill-advised marriage resulted. This event was capitalized upon by Rankin, who induced the entire group of Indians to leave Catlin, and set up his own "side show" in competition. The newspapers severely condemned the whole affair — although it was Catlin who suffered the most. It was an ironic turning point in the artist's destiny.

Encumbered with an unexpired lease of Egyptian Hall, and unable to attract audiences merely to see his pictures and hear him repeat his lectures, Catlin turned to the preparation of another publication, a large portfolio of colored reproductions of some of his most interesting pictures. According to the subscription blank, Catlin's *North American Indian* PORTFOLIO *of Hunting Scenes and Amusements* contained twenty-five views, 18 by 25 inches. There was a regular edition "in printed tints, at Five Guineas." ($25.00) and a deluxe edition "in printed tints and coloured, at Eight Guineas." ($40.00). The portfolio was published by the artist early in 1844. Six additional prints were soon added and apparently no less than five editions were issued during the first year. According to a now-rare broadside that was placed in the early editions, Catlin planned three additional volumes of the same size, to be issued quarterly.[123] Unfortunately this plan did not materialize.

"My large work now published in London," wrote Catlin [124], "and like my former one kindly noticed and highly approved by the press, I felt as if my labors in England were coming near to a close; and, having a little leisure, I was drawing my little children (of whom I now had four) nearer to me than ever." There were three girls — Elizabeth, Clara and Victoria. The third of these, born in England, was named after the Queen. The last child was a son, George Catlin, Jr., who was the pride and joy of his father's life. They looked forward eagerly to their return to their native land together — although that happy occasion was never to be realized.

The departure was first delayed as a result of Catlin's becoming involved in one of his inventions — a "floating quarter-deck for sea-going vessels," intended to save the lives of passengers and crewmen at time of disaster at sea. After spending considerable time and expense on this project, he found the idea had already been patented by someone else. Immediately following this experience, fourteen Ioway Indians unexpectedly arrived in London and appealed to Catlin for aid and cooperation. Their interpreter, and the promoter of their trip, was a man named Melody, who was an old acquaintance of the artist. Also, *Mew-hew-she-kaw*, The White Cloud, first chief of the Ioways (color plate page 182) was the son of an old friend of earlier days in the Indian country. George Catlin could not resist their importunities and the next thing he knew they were all together in a re-opened exhibition in Egyptian Hall. It was summer; and in an effort to add something new to the old story, Catlin staged an out-door display against the beautiful background of London's Vauxhall Gardens. He hired horses, and had whooping and yelling Indians riding wildly around the improvised tents.

Their success was only moderate, however, and soon expenses began to exceed returns. This ate into what little money Catlin had saved from the previous exhibitions and his publications. At the expiration of the lease on Egyptian Hall, he took the Ioways on a tour of other cities of the British Isles, where, unable to stand the damp English climate, several of the Indians contracted serious colds. One of the infants, known as "Corsair," the son of Little Wolf, developed pneumonia and died in the father's arms. Shortly afterward, *No-ho-mun-ya,* The Roman Nose, had to be put in a hospital in Liverpool and soon passed away. The show went on, but the situation steadily worsened. In a desperate effort to recoup his losses, Catlin decided to take his exhibition and troupe of Ioways to Paris. All England had now been "done out," but maybe France would offer new possibilities for the enterprise. Even the language barrier did not discourage him, for being a natural linguist, he could quickly learn to lecture in French.

The artist went to Paris in April, 1845, to make the necessary advance arrangements. Since he intended to go direct from France to the United States, he took his wife and four small children along, and they found living quarters for themselves and the Indians at the Victoria Hotel. Catlin leased the large hall of the Salle Valentino in Rue St. Honore, and shortly afterward the Ioways arrived, along with the eight tons of Indian collection and paintings. While the gallery was being made ready, Catlin set about attracting public attention to his exhibitions and lectures. He had become quite adept at this and was well aware of the value of publicity. Among other things, he laid plans to introduce the Ioways to the King of France, who would have more than a casual curiosity in them. For not only had Louis Philippe been a subscriber to Catlin's recent *Portfolio,* but the king had himself been in the Indian country during his exile in 1797 to 1800, having floated down the Ohio and Mississippi in a small boat.

The morning after the Ioways arrived they were all taken to pay their respects at the American Embassy. In a hired omnibus drawn by four horses they were driven through the streets of Paris, by a roundabout route — all painted and dressed in their most elaborate manner. Nothing like them had ever been seen before on the boulevards, and they caused considerable excitement among the Parisians who saw them. Arriving at the Embassy, they were received with warm hospitality by Mr. King, the United States Minister to France, who invited them all to stay for lunch and expressed a keen interest to assist Catlin. After lunch they were taken to be officially presented to the Prefect de Police. Crowds gathered wherever they stopped, and that was sufficient to bring newsmen around for stories.

The King of France promptly granted an audience, and at the appointed time Catlin and his Indians arrived by omnibus at the Palace of Tuileries. They were received by Louis Philippe and his Queen, along with the Duchess of Orleans and Count de Paris, Princess Adelaide, the Prince and Princess de Joinville, and other royal guests. (page 203) "Tell these good fellows I am glad to see them," the King told Jeffery, their interpreter;[125] "that I have been in many of the wigwams of the Indians in America, when I was a young man, and they treated me everywhere kindly . . . Tell them, Jeffery, that this is the Queen . . . these lads are my grandsons; this one, if he lives, will be King of the Belgians, and that one King of the French." After the introductions, they all moved into the elegant Salle du Ball, where the Indians entertained the royal party with a dance or two and George Catlin gave an impromptu explanation of the procedures.

The public exhibition and lectures opened on June 3rd, 1845, and enjoyed a popularity similar to that accorded during Catlin's first days in London. The large audiences and leading journals pronounced it one of the most interesting and extraordinary presentations ever seen in Paris. It also attracted a long list of distinguished visitors, among whom were Victor Hugo, Madame George Sand, Baron de Humboldt, and many more. In spite of the success, the Ioways were becoming very homesick, and, to add to their unhappy state, more of them had become ill with "consumption of the lungs." Then, quite suddenly, another died. This was the wife of Little Wolf, who had previously lost his little son, and it caused the rest of the Indians to decide they were immediately going home to their own villages and native prairies. They embarked from Havre for New York in July, 1845.

Weary, discouraged, and in poor health himself, George Catlin once again decided to return to the United States with his family and gallery. With what little money he had left, he could just about pay the transportation to New York. But he still had an unexpired lease on the Salle Valentino, as well as some unfinished paintings he had contracted to do. Before he could straighten out these matters, his wife was abruptly confined to her bed with a severe cold, and in a few days pneumonia developed. Clara had always been handicapped with a delicate constitution. On the 28th of July, 1845, she passed away.

"To those who have felt pangs like mine which followed, I need but merely mention them," wrote Catlin in his restrained manner;[126] "and to those who have never felt them, it would be in vain to describe. Her feeble form wasted away; and in her dying moments, with Christian hope, she was in the midst of happiness, blessing her dear little children as she committed them to my care and protection. Thus suddenly closed forever the smiles and cheer of an affectionate wife and a devoted mother, whose remains were sent back to her native land." Clara Gregory Catlin was only thirty-seven years and ten months of age at the time of her death. Neither relative nor friend accompanied the body on its long trip across the Atlantic. She was buried on December 6th, 1845, in the Gregory family plot, on a beautiful wooded knoll of Green-Wood Cemetery, Gowanus Heights, Brooklyn, New York.

Clara's death left George Catlin numbed and bewildered. He had adored her, and she

THE OJIBWAYS MEET QUEEN VICTORIA

fairly worshipped him. He must have felt the terrible guilt of suddenly realizing the great sacrifice which he had exacted from his wife, and which she had so willingly accepted as her contribution to his career — her death probably the price of her unfailing devotion. She had often pleaded with him to go home to America with his family — that he was an artist and should not waste his talents, soul and body, in pursuit of a futile ideal in which the world had only a curious and superficial interest. But now it was too late. In an effort to fight off the growing bitterness, he turned with intense devotion to his four small, motherless children — aged ten, eight, six and three — quite alone in a foreign land.

In the midst of Catlin's dilemma over which way to turn, another party of American Indians arrived in Paris. They had just finished a brief and unsuccessful attempt at a public exhibition in London, and having learned that the Ioways had gone home, they hurried to Paris to join the famous American artist and his Indian gallery. As the new lease on the Salle Valentino still had some time to run, Catlin entered into an agreement with the group of eleven Ojibways, and once again began advertising the exhibitions. But public interest in Paris had faded and the new venture failed.

It was at this time that the King and Queen of Belgium came to Paris to visit the King and Queen of France. As part of the entertainment for the visiting monarchs, Louis Philippe invited George Catlin to attend a royal breakfast at the Palace of St. Cloud. Half a century before, the Belgian king had visited America — had been a guest of George Washington at Mount Vernon, and had been present at the general's Farewell Address in Philadelphia. The king was very interested in the American artist and his Indians. During this royal party, Louis Philippe requested Catlin to set up his Gallery, with its Ojibways, in one of the large halls of the Louvre, for a private showing to the Royal Family and their special guests. There was also a suggestion that the entire collection might be purchased by the French Government. Catlin accepted the invitation, and everything was promptly moved into the Salle de Seance in the world famous Louvre.

Louis Philippe first came alone to see the Gallery and the Indian dances, and to listen to Catlin's lecture. Approving of what he saw and heard, he brought his Queen, his family and other royal guests for a repeat performance. On this occasion Catlin was requested to have his four small children on hand, along with their nurse, to make a social bow to the Queen (page 198). But there was no further mention of purchasing the Gallery, although Philippe did order copies of fifteen of the Indian pictures to be hung in his Palace of Versailles.

During Catlin's conversation with the King of Belgium, the artist had been invited to bring his Indians to Brussels. With the Ojibways now an idle expense and with the Gallery completely tied up in the Louvre, Catlin left the children in the care of their nurse and the troupe traveled to Belgium. Just as the impromptu exhibition opened in Brussels, however, one of the Indians became sick with small-pox and was confined to a hospital. A day or two later others were stricken with the same disease and had to be hospitalized — at Catlin's expense. Within a very short time, three of them died, and for nearly two months the artist was tied body and pocketbook to his Ojibways. Finally he got the survivors on a boat from Antwerp to the United States, paying their fares and giving them each a little money for expenses after their arrival in New York. Then he hurried back to Paris. According to his own notes, this was in mid-January of 1846 and he was poorer by £ 350 ($1750).

He was extended the courtesy of studio space in the Louvre to paint the pictures ordered by the King. But the Gallery was soon packed up and put in storage and Catlin returned to his apartment to continue his work where he might better take care of the children.

In the meantime he had put on a new and intensive campaign of writing letters to his most influential friends in America, imploring them to use every effort to induce the United

CATLIN'S INDIANS IN EGYPTIAN HALL

States Government to purchase his Indian Gallery — although never had this possibility seemed so far from realization. He was hardly in a state of mind to sit at an easel trying to paint pictures for the King of France, with four small children begging for his undivided attention. Furthermore, his funds were steadily running out. In desperation he wrote to his English friend, Sir Thomas Phillipps. The letter was dated February 17, 1846, at his living quarters at 21 Place Madeleine, Paris; and in it he begged the baronet to aid him in the sale of the Indian Gallery to "the British Museum or some English Nobleman or Gentleman." A price of £ 7,000 ($35,000) was suggested as an acceptable price. That Catlin was not optimistic even about the commission from Louis Philippe to paint the fifteen pictures for him, is indicated in this same letter: "The compliment has been a very high one, but what the emolument will be I don't yet know: probably, like the *honour*, it will be a costly article."[127]

Catlin also prepared a lengthy "memorial" which was addressed "To the honorable the Senate and House of Representatives of the United States," praying Congress to purchase his collection of Indian portraits and curiosities. This was dated April 2, 1846, and forwarded through proper channels.[128] It was further supported by a voluntary petition to Congress by an imposing list of artists who were at the time members of the American art colony in Paris.

Throughout these intensive efforts and other more immediate problems, Catlin stayed persistently at the easel in his apartment. "My house, though there was a gloom about it, had a melancholy charm from its associations," the artist later wrote;[129] "whilst its halls were enlivened by the notes of my little innocents . . . My dear little namesake, George, and my only boy, then three and a half years old, was my youngest, and being the only one of my little flock to perpetuate my name, had adopted my painting room as his constant play-house, and cronies as we had become there, our mutual enjoyment was, as our happiness was, in the

CATLIN'S INDIAN GALLERY IN THE LOUVRE
The Artist's Four Children at Right

dependence I was placing on him for the society of my future days. His first passion had been for the drum . . . with drum-sticks in hand, he made my *atelier* and appartment ring, and never was I more happy or proud than when we addressed him as 'Tambour Major', by which name he familiarly went . . . Besides the company of this dear little fellow, I had the sweet society of my three little girls . . . I counted myself in the enjoyment of life that I would have been unwilling for any consideration to part with. I thus painted on . . . resolving and re-resolving to devote the remainder of my life to my art . . . to illustrate the early history of my country in its various dealings with the Indian tribes of America."

But the ebb tide in the life of George Catlin had begun to run, carrying with it the things which he had held closest to his heart. One by one the children stopped their playing and were put to bed with the same illness that had so recently taken their mother. Throughout the days and the long nights their father stayed at their bedsides, with no time for or interest in sitting at the easel — until the hand of Fate pointed its finger at another. And once again "a broken heart . . . My Tambour Major . . . Little George, who had lived in the sweetness of his innocence, to gladden and then break the heart of his doting parent . . . now the only one to mourn for him. The remains of this dear little fellow were sent to New York, as a lovely flower to be planted by the grave of his mother."[130]

American Museum of Natural History

EXCAVATING A CANOE, BRITISH COLUMBIA

Lithograph, Kennedy Galleries

FIRING COLT'S RIFLE IN SOUTH AMERICA

American Museum of Natural History

THE HANDSOME DANCE, VENEZUELA, SOUTH AMERICA

American Museum of Natural History

URUGUAY MEDICINE MAN, SOUTH AMERICA

22

End of a Long Trail

Newberry Library, Chicago

FLATHEAD WOMAN

AT THIS TIME of Catlin's deep despondency and mounting difficulties, his sense of devotion and responsibility to three motherless girls, kept him close to the apartment on the Place Madeleine where he continued to apply paint to the canvases set on his easel. The girls had inherited the lovely image and delicate grace of their mother, whose benevolent care was not easily replaced by a father who had spent so many years among primitive Indians and rough fur men beyond the American frontier. Now past fifty years, he was still very young in spirit, and he worked diligently if not too well. The old days when he could easily turn out a picture in such a remarkably short time seemed to have slipped beyond his grasp.

Ironically, in 1846 a bill was passed by the United States Congress establishing a National Museum, to be known as the Smithsonian Institution, under the terms of the will of an Englishman, the late James Smithson. Included in the bill was an authorization for a gallery of art, although there was no mention or reference to George Catlin, the reluctant exile, who was at the time struggling for survival in Paris.

On July 24th the Congressional Joint Committee on the Library made a report and recommendation in relation to the purchase of Catlin's Indian Gallery. The report said that "The Bill which has recently passed the House for the establishment of the Smithsonian Institution provides there shall be a gallery of art . . . That such works should be principally American is the obvious dictate of patriotism. No productions, your committee believes, at present exist, more appropriate to this gallery, than those of Mr. Catlin, or of equal importance." However, owing to the sudden outbreak of the Mexican War, no further action was taken on the recommended purchase.[131]

Late that summer Catlin made a brief trip to London to see his friend Sir Thomas Phillipps about the sale of the Indian Gallery or to try and raise money in some other way. He also met with Henry Rowe Schoolcraft, an American ethnologist and writer who was working on a plan to get authorization and financial subsidy from the United States Congress for the publication of an elaborate encyclopedia on the Indian Tribes of America. Schoolcraft had made the trip to Europe principally to obtain the use of Catlin's pictures. He brought with him a letter of introduction written by Catlin's old friend General Lewis Cass, then a senator from Michigan. Catlin promptly and emphatically turned down the proposal. That Schoolcraft was not only disappointed but deeply angered by this rebuff was well demonstrated by his actions. Returning to the United States, he procured the services of another artist, Seth Eastman, to help illustrate the proposed works; and on March 3, 1847 Schoolcraft managed to obtain the passage of an Act of Congress, by which he was appointed to "collect and digest such statistics and materials as may illustrate the history, present condition, and future prospects of the Indian tribes of the United States." Thus the better politician gained for himself what amounted to a complete subsidy for an almost unlimited period of time and insured the publication of what developed into the six monstrous volumes entitled *Historical and Statistical Information Respecting The History, Condition, and Prospects of the Indian Tribes of the United States.* These volumes were not "privately printed by the author," but entirely paid for by the Government of the United States.

Back in Paris, Catlin hurried through the completion of the paintings for Louis Philippe, and the King was so pleased with these that he ordered another group of twenty-nine originals depicting the story of the illustrious seventeenth century French explorer, Rouen Robert Cavalier, better known as La Salle. An ardent admirer of the early explorer, the King went over the planning of the series with Catlin. Based both upon research and on the artist's imagination, they were splashed with color rather than keeping to the realism of his other work. It took nearly a year to finish the series — although the task would have been accomplished in a fraction of the time in Catlin's earlier days on the Indian frontier. The La Salle pictures were finally delivered along with an urgent request for the payment of little more than $100 apiece which had been agreed upon. Catlin never received one franc. How he managed to live is difficult to understand.

This was the winter of 1847–'48, and Italy, Germany, Poland and Greece were in political turmoil. The urge to overthrow royalty struck France with violent force. On the morning of February 22nd the populace of Paris crowded the Place Madeleine, where Catlin lived, and beneath his windows rose the wild chant of "*Vive la Reforme!*" mingled with the garbled singing of the *Marseillaise.* The militant throng quickly developed into a revolutionary mob. Louis Philippe and his Queen were secretly spirited away to England. Catlin's association with the King was too well known for his own good. His apartment was invaded by the mob, and some of the paintings in his studio were destroyed with bayonets. He managed to escape with his three little girls, and even to get his entire Indian Gallery out of Paris and across the Channel to England. Otherwise he was pretty well wiped out.

Haunted by earlier successes in London, and desperately in need of money, he rented rooms at 6 Waterloo Place, Pall Mall, which provided living quarters and studio space, as well as a showroom into which he could crowd enough Indian paintings and other materials to lure some paying admissions. When not occupied with answering visitors' questions at a shilling a person, he could work at copying the best of his paintings to be sold to old acquaintances. He was, however, beginning to suffer another difficulty. He had developed a deafness, which in time became so serious that it caused considerable embarrassment when he was talking to strangers. Now there were not many shillings to be collected at the door of the exhibition room, and the wealthy acquaintances who had once begged to purchase Indian paintings had mostly lost interest. According to the personal papers of Sir Thomas Phillipps, on the 25th of August, 1848, that baronet purchased one copy of an original which had hung in the Gallery and returned a sympathetic rejection to Catlin's urgent request for a loan of £ 600 as a mortgage on the entire collection. Later Sir Phillipps loaned him £ 100, for which twenty of the original paintings were delivered as security.[132]

Catlin turned to the writing of another book. After the showroom was locked and the three girls tucked into their beds, he would sit late into the night and work intensively at setting down the story of his *Eight Years' Travel and Residence in Europe* with his *North American*

Indian Collection. This developed into another two-volume work, with a few sketchy illustrations and photographic reproductions, and was "Published by the Author" late in 1848. This account of his experiences with the Gallery and the three groups of Indians, was marred by the inclusion of all the incidental hobnobbing with European royalty and gentry, and other rambling chit-chat which quite obscured what little material of importance the book contained.

Weeks dragged into months. With uncompromising determination George Catlin held to his singular theme, but more and more the once distinguished celebrity faded to little more than an artistic and intellectual eccentric, who now drew only pictures of American savages and hovered about three pretty daughters in dusty rooms crowded with strange mementoes of the American Wild West.

In April, 1851 Catlin made an agreement with Sir Thomas Phillipps to paint fifty-five copies of his original pictures at the lowly rate of £ 2 ($10) each — with an extra two shillings for frames! It was also during that same year that he did the series of 167 beautifully executed pencil drawings entitled "*Souvenir of the North American Indians,*" which is today in the New York Public Library. Selections from that series are reproduced in this book. At least two more of these penciled "*Souvenirs*" were done the following year. One collection of 217 drawings, now in the Newberry Library, Chicago, has also furnished illustrations for this book. A third series of 216 drawings is in the Yale Library of Western Americana. Catlin also did several smaller collections of water color copies of his pictures, which were assembled under the rather misleading titles of "*Album Unique.*"

In the 1852–'53 session of Congress, the Bill for the proposed purchase of the George Catlin Indian Gallery finally came to a fateful vote. Henry R. Schoolcraft had been very aggressively engaged in a campaign against the Bill, although it had some distinguished supporters. Daniel Webster made an ardent plea on its behalf on the floor of the Senate, describ-

THE IOWAYS MEET THE KING OF FRANCE

ing the Catlin Indian Gallery as "more important than all the other drawings and representations on the face of the earth;" and saying that its purchase and preservation would be an "important public act." Among the others who eulogized the artist and his work, was Jefferson Davis, then a member of the Senate, from Kentucky, who had himself been with Catlin through the ill-fated expedition of the First Dragoons in the Southwest in 1834, and had sat by the artist and watched him paint some of the pictures that were under consideration by the Congress. In ending his speech, however, the gentleman from Kentucky announced that, because of his political party's principle (he was a Southern Democrat and the party was anti-Indian) "he was bound to vote *against* the Bill." Ironically, when the vote was taken, it was defeated by *one vote* — the vote of Jefferson Davis, of Kentucky.[133]

Catlin had been so confident that his Bill would pass, that he had borrowed as heavily as he could against the Indian Gallery. But now, with all hope for its purchase gone beyond recall, he faced inescapable disaster. His creditors abruptly closed in like prairie wolves upon an aged buffalo bull. They began haggling over the Indian Gallery, and small lots were put up for auction. The bids were so small that this procedure was promptly abandoned and other means of satisfaction were sought. Catlin stood by helplessly.

Among the many creditors was one Joseph Harrison, a wealthy American who was head of the Harrison Boiler Works in Philadelphia — at the time the largest locomotive building concern in the world. Harrison had just arrived in London after completing an extremely remunerative railroad building contract in Russia. He paid off the principle debts against the Indian Gallery, and, to keep it from being tied up by unknown claim-holders, had it hurriedly crated and put aboard the first ship bound for Philadelphia. Other creditors did appear on the scene, and with the rooms at 6 Waterloo Place stripped of all the paintings and Indian things, these late comers levied bailiff's attachments against the furnishings with which the artist had made a home for his children and himself.

Rumors that George Catlin's castle was crumbling had reached the ears of his Gregory in-laws in America, and they had hurried across the Atlantic to get first hand information. Uncle Dudley Gregory had become extremely wealthy, and he could easily have paid off Catlin's debts and even built a museum in which to house the collection. But Clara's husband was now looked down on by his late wife's family, as little more than an eccentric and when his world collapsed, it provided them a valid excuse for taking possession of the three little girls. Quickly and quietly, they were taken aboard a ship bound for New York. Too numbed to realize what was happening, George Catlin was left with little more than the clothes upon his back. With a few drawings and sketches which he managed to snatch from under the eyes of the bailiffs, he slipped away into the darkness of incognito escape.

He returned to Paris, where he found a cheap room in the Hotel des Etrangers, on the Rue Tronchet, from which address on January 23, 1853 he wrote to Sir Thomas Phillipps. The letter apologized for the fact that the fifty-five copies of his paintings which had been promised in settlement of previous obligations, and which had been practically finished, had inadvertently been taken by Joseph Harrison along with everything else shipped to America, but that an effort was being made to have them returned. Catlin offered to sell the baronet seventy additional water colors which he had managed to salvage from the catastrophy, at the small price of three dollars each — money, which the artist emphasized, he sorely needed. The fifty-five paintings were gotten back from Philadelphia and sent from Paris on October 26, 1853, and their safe arrival was acknowledged in a letter dated November 7, 1853.[134] In all, Sir Thomas acquired at least one hundred and twenty-eight Catlin pictures, most of them now in the museum of the Thomas Gilcrease Institute in Tulsa, Oklahoma.

Through that unhappy winter Catlin wandered blindly about the by-ways and boulevards of Paris. He was now past fifty-six years old — destitute, despondent and deaf, but still without bitterness. "In this dilemma I was lost," he wrote[135] "but *my collection* was saved to my country by an American gentleman . . . My occupation gone, and with no other means on earth than my hands and my brushes, and less than half a life, at best, before me . . . my thoughts turned towards Dame Fortune, to know if there was anything yet in store for me."

One of the places in Paris where Catlin whiled away his time was the reading room of the Biblotheque Imperial — a favorite haunt of intellectuals and scholarly researchers. There he became acquainted with another *habitue*, who related the result of his delving into old Spanish volumes. It had to do with some ancient gold mines of fabulous richness, in the Crystal Mountains of northern Brazil, the exact location of which had never been learned by civilized man. Catlin became fascinated. He loved the lore of the Indians — and he had always wanted to visit South America, anyhow. So, with an enthusiasm undiminished by his age, and with a hope that had never known limitations, he set out for the jungle-shrouded mountains of Brazil. At this point there begins a new and quite different volume in the story of George Catlin. It is a saga of high adventure in wilderness areas, as extraordinary as anything experienced by any man of his period. To tell that story does not come within the purpose of this book for it is a whole book in itself. To pass it over entirely would be unpardonable. It must, however, be told with great brevity.

Catlin slipped away from Paris like a fugitive. "I obtained a British passport for Brazil, and an incognito cognomen, as kings and emperors sometimes do," he later related.[136] He went to Venezuela, up the Orinoco, ascended the Essequibo, and then crossed the remote Crystal (Tumucache) Mountains in a desperate but futile search for the "lost gold mines." Finally abandoning the phantom quest, he turned again to painting and set out to document the primitive Indian tribes of South America as he had the tribes of North America. Through the amazing painting expeditions which followed, Catlin traveled with a lone companion — a husky six foot, two-inch Negro maroon by the name of "Caesar Bolla," who had escaped from slavery in Havana. It was Caesar who carried the artist's painting materials and whose back became an easel when there were pictures to be made along the jungle trails they followed together. This strange pair wandered through thousands of square miles of wilderness far more difficult and hazardous than anything to be found in North America. They visited scores of primitive tribes, many of whom had never seen a white man before.

Between 1853 and 1858 Catlin and Caesar made three extensive trips, following their lonely course like a pair of wandering vagabonds, traveling mostly by foot and native canoe. They crossed the entire jungle interior of Brazil, and then went up the great Amazon to its source and on over the high Andes to the Pacific coast of Peru. They crossed the pampas of Argentina and the formidable Matto Grosso — went to Terra del Fuego at the southern end of the continent, and completely around the cost of South America in a small sailing packet. Everywhere Catlin's purpose was to paint the most primitive Indians that could be found. All this was more than a hundred years ago, and they were without the aid of modern drugs, equipment, or financial assistance. All together Catlin covered more little-or-unknown territory and visited more of South America's primitive tribes than any other white man of record, either before or since. It is a story which far exceeds the fictional one of Robinson Crusoe and his Man Friday. Still not content, Catlin and Caesar later traveled up the Pacific Coast along the entire West Coast of North America, to the Aleutian Islands and across Bering Sea to Siberia. On the way back to South America they crossed the Rocky Mountains from Southern California to the Gulf of Mexico. They went by boat to Yucatan, where, at Sisal, the artist and ex-slave parted company after five adventurous and extraordinary years together. Here is Catlin's account of that farewell, written as he went on to Europe for the last time:[137] "Caesar was impatient to unfold to Sally Bool, a beautiful mulatto girl who sells oranges at the head of the quay, [at Para, at the mouth of the Amazon, where Catlin had first met him], the wonders of his voyages — going to see his old sweetheart, and I going to my old friend Baron de Humboldt [in Germany]. We shook hands three times, and at the end of each shake, he exclaimed, 'Oh de lord preserb you, good Massa Catlin!' I never will forget it."

George Catlin was approaching sixty-two years of age when he returned to Paris from this last and most strenuous of all his trips. While he was painting primitive natives in the jungles of South America, the Aleutian Islands, Siberia and deserts of our Southwest, the first three volumes of Schoolcraft's work were being printed. Catlin had heard about this in a letter that reached him in Uruguay, written June 9th, 1856, from Potsdam by his good friend Baron Alexander Humboldt. The world famous traveler and historian had this to say:[138] "An immense *Scrap-book* on the North American Indians, written by Schoolcraft . . . has been sent me as a present; and I find that he denies the truth of the *Mandan Religious Ceremonies*, distinctly saying that they are contrary to facts; and the works of your imagination, etc. Now, my dear and esteemed friend, this charge, made by such a man as Schoolcraft and *under the authority of the Government of the United States*, to stand in the libraries of the scientific Institutions of the whole civilized world, to which they are being sent as presents from your Government, is calculated, not only to injure your hard-earned good name, but to destroy the value of your precious works . . . I have often conversed with our illustrious traveler in America, Prince Maximilian of Neuwied, who spent a winter with the Mandans . . . entirely corroborating your descriptions . . . [signed] Your sincere friend, A. Humboldt." Schoolcraft's reference to George Catlin was challenged and refuted by men of renown. Unfounded and incorrect though Schoolcraft's information regarding the Mandans was, thousands of copies of the six volumes were sent as gifts throughout the world, and they still stand on the shelves of many libraries, a misleading reference on the subject. Thus by a pebble from the sling of a pigmy, carrying the stamp of approval of the United States Government, was one giant of American ethnology felled! Catlin made an attempt to correct this injustice, but the books were in print and distributed, and that was that.

After returning from his third trip to South America, Catlin retired to a little studio in Brussels. There he set about the long task of finishing his collection of paintings of the Indians of the Latin American countries and the North Pacific coast regions. He also undertook to repaint copies of most of the pictures in the original Gallery of North American subjects which were not ignominiously packed away in a warehouse of the Harrison Boiler Works in Philadelphia. He called these new pictures "cartoons" — using the word not in the sense that we think of it today, but to describe outline pen drawings on heavy art-cardboard, brushed over by hand with pale, lightly applied oil color, with a few done on canvas. Some of the popular subjects which had been in the original gallery were repeatedly duplicated for sale to whoever might be induced to purchase them. These were produced by making a pencil drawing, probably from the engravings published in his *Letters and Notes*, and transferring the drawing by tracing to cardboard. Some of these "tracing" masters, outlined with heavy pencil on the reverse side of the paper, are today preserved in the Library of Congress and elsewhere.

General A. L. Chetlain, of Chicago, who was the United States Consul at Brussels at the time when Catlin was there, gives the following account of the artist:[139] "Mr. Catlin was then in good health and quite robust and active for one of his advanced years . . . His hearing was so impaired it was with great difficulty one could talk to him . . . His studio was in an obscure street near the Antwerp railroad station . . . a large front room, in which he exhibited his paintings and did his work; the other, a rear and smaller room, used as a sleeping and store room. Both were scantily furnished. He lived in a frugal way. His expenses were light, not exceeding . . . over five francs per day. He seemed to have few acquaintances . . . He talked to me often about his collections of paintings and sketches, and expressed a hope that all his works might be brought together and placed in the hands of the Government of the United States . . . He evidently felt more anxiety for the future of his life long work than to execute orders . . . and always took pride in calling himself the 'friend of the Indian' . . . His life in Brussels was almost that of a recluse . . . He never alluded to his family or family affairs, and gave no reason for the singular life he chose to live in Brussels."

During this time he wrote some additional books, principal of which is *O-Kee-Pa* (1867) — with an appendix containing some irrefutable certifications regarding the authenticity of the writer's descriptions of the controversial Mandan religious ceremonies. Unfortunately, this volume is today a scarce collector's item. The other books included *Life Amongst the Indians* (1861) and *Last Rambles Amongst the Indians* (1868).

In 1870 George Catlin finally returned to New York — after an absence of thirty-one years — at the venerable age of seventy-four. He had long looked forward to a reunion with his daughters, who had lived in affluent comfort with their late mother's family in Jersey City. Although wrinkled and deaf, Catlin stood as straight and proud as a professional soldier on his last parade, for Manhattan had a lot of memories for the artist. He brought with him another and new collection of paintings of primitive Indians. He had duplicated nearly all the pictures which had been in the original gallery, and in addition he had the La Salle paintings which he had recovered in France, as well as more than 150 portrayals of the native tribes of South America. He called all of these "Catlin's Indian Cartoons;" and while they lacked the brilliance of inspiration which had marked the original gallery, they had the same unmistakable stamp of genius. He wanted his countrymen to see and appreciate his new Indian paintings and with the hope that had never faded through the years, he opened an exhibition at the Sommerville Gallery, at Fifth Avenue and 14th Street, starting all over again on a program to interest the Government or some big museum in the purchase of the new gallery. He also wished for the resurrection of the old gallery from its grave in the Harrison Boiler Works, and for the permanent display of all his life's work. But the exhibition at the Sommerville Gallery did not go too well, and early in the fall all the paintings were packed up and put in storage.

Then a bit of new sunshine broke through the dark clouds. He was invited to hang his exhibition in the Smithsonian Institution in Washington. The invitation came from its Secretary and Director, Joseph Henry, an old friend of the early days in Albany, when they had both been young and beginning their careers. For this final plea before Congress, the artist prepared a ninety-nine-page *Catalogue Descriptive and Instructive of Catlin's Indian Cartoons*, which he had printed in New York early in 1871. Shortly afterward all the paintings were at last hung in the National Museum, which was his life's most cherished dream.

The Annual Report of the Smithsonian Institution for the year 1871 (pages 40–41) includes the following memorandum: "At present a portion of the large room in the second floor is used for the exhibition of the cartoons or original sketches made by the celebrated Indian traveler and explorer Mr. George Catlin. The object of this exhibition is to induce the Government to purchase the whole collection . . . which comprises about 1200 paintings and sketches . . . Whatever may be thought of the paintings from an artistic point of view, they are certainly of great value as faithful reproductions of the person, features, manners, customs, implements, festivals, superstitions, and everything which relates to the ethnological characteristics of the primitive inhabitants of our country . . . and we trust that Congress will not fail at the next session to act in accordance with this feeling. It is the only general collection of the kind in existence. [signed] Joseph Henry. January, 1872."

Time dragged wearily on. There was pleasant talk by important members of the Congress, both in and out of the chambers of the House and the Senate — but nothing was done. Why didn't the old man leave his pictures where they hung, as a *gift* to the Smithsonian Institution? Why should he worry about leaving an estate to his three beautiful daughters, who were well provided for by the wealthy Gregory family? Catlin had been given the use of some rooms in the front tower of the Smithsonian building, previously used as the director's office, where the artist continued to do some painting and where there was an improvised bed to lie down on when he became too weak and weary to sit at his easel or to talk to visitors in the exhibition room on the floor below. But time was rapidly running out for George Catlin and realizing that he had failed again, his courage and his stamina quickly disintegrated.

On October 29, 1872, Joseph Henry wrote an urgent letter to Dudley S. Gregory in Jersey City: "Mr. Catlin, although very ill is not confined to his bed . . . his physician has no hope for his recovery . . . Mr. Catlin is not fully aware of the hopelessness . . . and the Doctor has thought it best to allow him to continue painting as far as his strength will permit." Two days later another letter followed: "He has packed up his pictures (to ship them to his daughters in Jersey City) . . . has stopped work . . . He is, although somewhat despondent, not in an unhappy state of mind. His life on the whole has been a successful one. He has succeeded in identifying his name with the history of the early inhabitants of this country, and is frequently referred to in foreign works as the celebrated American ethnologist, and in the line of this branch of knowledge is esteemed above anyone that has given attention to this subject. [signed] Joseph Henry."[140]

Immediately thereafter Catlin went to Jersey City, to be close to his daughters. "His agony was intense, but he bore it like an Indian," wrote Thomas Donaldson.[141] "He would sit for hours, his profile turned to the faithful daughter who was with him, bearing the pain like a stoic. When he first realized his helplessness, he sprang from his chair and walked the floor until his strength gave out, saying 'Oh, if I was down in the valley of the Amazon I could walk off this weakness' . . . While in his last sickness his anxiety was to know what would happen to his gallery. He constantly referred to it, and almost the last words he spoke were, 'What will happen to my gallery?' "

The end of the long trail for George Catlin came at 5:30 on the morning of December 23, 1872, at his rooms in the Darcy Building in Jersey City, New Jersey. He was well into the seventy-seventh year of life.

For some unknown reason George Catlin was not immediately buried beside his wife and infant son in the Gregory plot in Green-Wood Cemetery, Brooklyn. It was a full year later, on December 9, 1873, that his body was laid to final rest beside Clara and George Junior, on the beautifully wooded knoll in Gowanus Heights. On an adjoining knoll stands a heroic bronze statue of De Witt Clinton, with large bronze plaques on its base, commemorating his great achievements. Also near by are the graves and imposing monuments of Samuel F. B. Morse, Henry Ward Beecher, Horace Greeley (*Go West Young Man!*), and many other familiar names. Not so much as a simple headstone marks the grave of George Catlin — there is only a small yellow card in the cemetery's mortuary record file. But George Catlin left a monument which time will never crumble or efface.

The original *Catlin Indian Gallery* finally went to the Smithsonian Institution, not by any act of the Congress of the United States, but as a gift to the nation by the heirs of Joseph Harrison. Unfortunately, during the many years of improper storage in the Boiler Works, most of the fine Indian costumes and other vulnerable material had been ruined by moths, mice, fire and water; and many of the paintings were seriously damaged. On the 19th of

Smithsonian Institution

GEORGE CATLIN AT 72

May, 1879, however, the collection was turned over to Thomas Donaldson, who officially received it on behalf of the Smithsonian. The restored paintings are today the proud possession of that great scientific institution — as custodian for the American people. The *Catlin Cartoon Collection* remained in the possession of George Catlin's daughters until 1909, when the aging Miss Elizabeth Catlin loaned the collection to The American Museum of National History in New York, on an option to purchase — which was exercised three years later.

The paintings and drawings of George Catlin have been a guiding inspiration for practically every artist who has followed his footsteps into the field of Western Americana art. They have furnished illustrations for literally thousands of publications on the Indians and the Old West of America. They have been copied, modified and plagiarized, but they still remain identifiable as his work. Catlin's writings have been drawn upon by hundreds of ethnologists and thousands of writers. The theatre, Wild West shows, movies and television have all found inspiration from his work. It can be said with justice and justification that no other artist or writer in the field of the North American Indian and the Old West has had as long and broad an influence as George Catlin.

References and Notes

CHAPTER 1

1. Thomas Donaldson, *The George Catlin Indian Gallery.* Annual Report . . . Smithsonian Institution . . . for 1885. Washington. 1886. Part II. p. 740 (Hereinafter referred to as "Donaldson") A quote from *Report of Engagements With Hostile Indians* . . . from 1868 to 1882
2. George Catlin, *Last Rambles Amongst the Indians of the Rocky Mountains and the Andes.* London 1868. pp. 354–355. (Hereinafter referred to as "Last Rambles")
3. Donaldson. p. 505

CHAPTER 2

4. *ibid.* pp. 701–703
5. *ibid.* p. 706
6. Original letter in archival file of the Smithsonian Institution
7. *ibid.*
8. George Catlin, *Letters and Notes on the Manners, Customs, and Conditions of the North American Indians . . . In Two Volumes* . . . London. Published by the Author, at Egyptian Hall, Piccadilly. 1841. (Hereinafter referred to as "Letters and Notes") Vol. II pp. 2–3
9. William L. Stone, *Narrative of the Festivities in Honor of the Completion of the Grand Erie Canal.* New York. 1825. Contains full-page portrait of Governor De Witt Clinton, with notation: "Drawn from nature and lithographed by Geo. Catlin Esq. . . . Painted at Albany, December 1824. Engraved by J. B. Longacre from a miniature by G. Catlin."
10. *ibid.* Catlin's "Views of the Erie Canal" reproduced in this publication
11. Letter to Harold McCracken, July 3, 1958, from Vernon C. Porter, Director, National Academy of Design
12. West Point prints: one of parade ground and another a view of the Hudson. "Drawn by G. Catlin. Engraved, Printed and Colored by J. Hill. Published May 15, 1828 by G. Catlin, New York."
13. Donaldson. p. 708
14. Original letter in Newberry Library, Chicago
15. Donaldson. p. 708
16. The originals of these are in The New York Historical Society

CHAPTER 3

17. George Catlin, *Life Amongst the Indians.* London. 1861. (Hereinafter referred to as "Life Amongst the Indians") pp. 134–136
18. *Handbook of American Indians,* Bureau of American Ethnology. Washington. 1912. (Hereinafter referred to as "Handbook") Vol. II, p. 16
19. Donaldson. *Footnote,* p. 22
20. *Letters and Notes.* Vol. I, p. 23
21. Loyd Haberly. *Pursuit of the Horizon.* New York. 1948. (Hereinafter referred to as "Haberly"). p. 46 *et seq.*
22. John C. Ewers, *George Catlin: Painter of Indians of the West.* Reprinted from Annual Report of Smithsonian Institution for 1955. (Hereinafter referred to as "Ewers"). pp. 483–528

CHAPTER 4

23. *Letters and Notes.* Vol. II, p. 17
24. *ibid.* Vol. I, p. 212
25. *ibid.* Vol. I, p. 217

CHAPTER 5

26. *ibid.* p. 208
27. *ibid.* p. 208
28. *ibid.* pp. 226–227
29. *ibid.* p. 241
30. *ibid.* pp. 232–237

CHAPTER 6

31. *ibid.* Vol. II, pp. 90–91; also pp. 186–194
32. *ibid.* Vol. I, p. 247 *et seq.*
33. *ibid.* p. 56 *et seq.*

CHAPTER 7

34. *ibid.* pp. 59–61
35. *ibid.* pp. 51–52
36. *ibid.* pp. 29–43
37. *ibid.* pp. 38–40

CHAPTER 8

38. *ibid.* p. 32
39. *ibid.* pp. 261–262
40. *ibid.* p. 49 *et seq.*
41. *Life Amongst the Indians.* p. 115

CHAPTER 9

42. *Letters and Notes.* Vol. I, p. 79
43. Donaldson. p. 438
44. *Letters and Notes.* Vol. I, p. 80 *et seq.*

45. *ibid.* pp. 93–95
46. *ibid.* pp. 87–88
47. *ibid.* pp. 112–113
48. *ibid.* pp. 120–121
49. *ibid.* p. 96

CHAPTER 10

50. *ibid.* pp. 110–111
51. *ibid.* pp. 114–117
52. *ibid.* pp. 89–91

CHAPTER 11

53. *ibid.* pp. 133–134
54. *ibid.* p. 105
55. The account is given in full in George Catlin's book *O-Kee-Pa: A Religious Ceremony . . . of the Mandans.* London (and Philadelphia) 1867. (Hereinafter referred to as *O-Kee-Pa*); also *Letters and Notes.* Vol. I, pp. 155–184

CHAPTER 12

56. *Letters and Notes.* Vol. I, pp. 203–204
57. *ibid.* p. 185
58. *ibid.* p. 205
59. *Life Amongst the Indians.* pp. 140–141
60. *Letters and Notes.* Vol. II, pp. 257–259
61. *ibid.* Vol. I, p. 184

CHAPTER 13

62. *ibid.* Vol. II, pp. 12–14
63. *ibid.* p. 23 *et seq.*
64. Ewers. p. 493
65. *Letters and Notes.* Vol. II, pp. 29–30
66. *New York Commercial Advertiser*, Sept. 22, 1832. p. 2
67. Donaldson. p. 25
68. Same as #66
69. *Letters and Notes.* Vol. II, p. 111

CHAPTER 14

70. *Catalogue . . . of Catlin's Indian Cartoons* . . . New York. 1871. p. 90
71. Donaldson. p. 475
72. *ibid.* p. 68
73. *Letters and Notes.* Vol. II, p. 31
74. *History of the Indian Tribes of North America*, by Thomas L. McKenney and James Hall. 3 vol. folio. Philadelphia, 1837
75. *Letters and Notes.* Vol. II, pp. 32–35
76. *Journal of the Campaign of the Regiment of Dragoons . . . Fort Gibson to the Rocky Mountains*, by Lt. Thomas B. Wheelock. Public Doc. of the U.S. Senate, 2nd Session of 23rd Congress. Vol. I. Washington. 1834

CHAPTER 15

77. *Letters and Notes.* Vol. II, p. 80
78. *ibid.* pp. 41–42
79. *ibid.* p. 122
80. *ibid.* p. 37
81. *Life Amongst the Indians.* pp. 175–176
82. *Letters and Notes.* Vol. II, p. 38
83. Donaldson. p. 479
84. *Letters and Notes.* Vol. II, pp. 45–49
85. *ibid.* pp. 84–85
86. *ibid.* pp. 49–52

CHAPTER 16

87. *ibid.* p. 53 *et seq.*
88. *ibid.* p. 70

CHAPTER 17

89. *Handbook.* Part II, p. 947
90. *Letters and Notes.* Vol. II, p. 70
91. *Life Amongst the Indians.* p. 198
92. *Letters and Notes.* Vol. II, p. 129

CHAPTER 18

93. *ibid.* p. 129 *et seq.*
94. *ibid.* p. 135
95. *ibid.* pp. 147–148
96. *ibid.* p. 149
97. *ibid.* pp. 149–150

CHAPTER 19

98. *ibid.* p. 160
99. Lawrence Taliaferro Journals, 1836. 10th Volume. *Daily Transactions and other Matters on Indian Affairs. St. Peters Agency.* pp. 152–153. (Original in Minnesota Historical Society)
100. *Letters and Notes.* Vol. II, pp. 172–177
101. *ibid.* p. 163
102. *Handbook.* Part I, p. 192
103. *ibid.* p. 192 and 217
104. *Taliaferro Journals.* 10th Volume. p. 156
105. *Letters and Notes.* Vol. II, p. 208
106. *New York Commercial Advertiser.* July 15, 1833. p. 2, col. 1
107. *Life Amongst the Indians.* pp. 171–172

CHAPTER 20

108. *Catalogue of Catlin's Indian Gallery* . . . New York. 1837 (& 1838)
109. *Letters and Notes.* Vol. II, Footnote, pp. 212–213
110. *Handbook.* Part II, p. 159
111. *Letters and Notes.* Vol. II, pp. 218–222
112. Donaldson. p. 218
113. *Letters and Notes.* Vol. II, Footnote, pp. 221–222
114. *Memorial of R. R. Gurley.* U.S. Senate, 30th Congress, 1st Session. Misc. Papers. No. 152. July 10, 1848

CHAPTER 21

115. *Catlin's Notes on Eight Years' Travel in Europe* . . . In Two Volumes . . . Published by the Author. London. (and New York). 1848. (Hereinafter referred to as "Catlin in Europe"). p. 1
116. The original agreement is in the Smithsonian Institution
117. *Catlin in Europe.* Vol. I, pp. 34–35
118. *ibid.* p. 38
119. *Phillipps Studies No. 4*, by A.N.L. Mumby, Librarian of Kings' College, Cambridge. London. 1956. Chapt. III *George Catlin*—pp. 49–64
120. *Donaldson.* pp. 525–526
121. *Catlin in Europe.* Vol. I, p. 65
122. *Phillipps Studies No. 4* (*Reprinted Pieces*, Gadskill ed., 1899. p. 121). Footnote pp. 53–54
123. Archival files in Smithsonian Institution
124. *Catlin in Europe.* Vol. I, p. 197
125. *ibid.* Vol. II, pp. 211–212
126. *ibid.* p. 276
127. *Phillipps Studies No. 4*, pp. 53–54
128. U.S. Senate, Misc. No. 152, Washington, 1848. pp. 3–4
129. *Catlin in Europe.* Vol. II, pp. 211–212
130. *ibid.* p. 323

CHAPTER 22

131. *R. R. Gurley Memorial*, pp. 6–7
132. *Phillipps Studies No. 4* pp. 56–58
133. *Last Rambles.* pp. 47–51
134. *Phillipps Studies No. 4*
135. *Last Rambles.* p. 51
136. *ibid.* p. 54
137. *ibid.* p. 209
138. Archival files of the Smithsonian Institution
139. Donaldson. p. 715. Letter dated at Chicago, June 22, 1886
140. Originals of these two letters in archival files in the Smithsonian Institution
141. Donaldson, pp. 716–717

Bibliographical Check List

Publications by and about George Catlin

1825

1. *Views of the Erie Canal:* in *Narrative of the Festivities Observed in Honor of the Completion of the Grand Erie Canal,* by William L. Stone and others. New York. 1825. Contains six pictures "Drawn from nature and lithographed by Geo. Catlin, Esq.". Also portrait "De Witt Clinton, Painted at Albany, December 1824. Engraved by J. B. Longacre from a miniature by G. Catlin".

1828

2. *Views of West Point:* Two (or more) art prints—one of parade ground and one a view of the Hudson River. (11⅞" x 18¼"). "Drawn by G. Catlin". "Engraved, Printed & Colored by J. Hill. Published May 15, 1828 by G. Catlin".

c. 1831

3. *Views of Niagara:* "Drawn on stone and colored from nature, by George Catlin". 1 1., 6 colored plates, 2 maps. n.p.,n.d. (c. 1831) 29 cm.

1832

4. *Letters* in the *New York Commercial Advertiser* (newspaper): The first of these (unsigned) appears in the issue of July 24, 1832. Between that date and September 30, 1837 a total of fifteen appeared. These were later elaborated into George Catlin's two volume work *Letters and Notes on the Manners, Customs, and Condition of the North American Indians* (1844).

1837

5. *Catalogue: Catalogue of Catlin's Indian Gallery of Portraits, Landscapes, Manners and Customs, Costumes* etc. etc. Collected during Seven Years' Travel Amongst Thirty-eight Different Tribes . . . New York. Piercy & Read . . . 1837. Paper bound, 36 p., 18½ cm . . . Lists 494 pictures.

5A. *SAME.* 1838. 40 p., 17 cm.

1838

6. *Osceola* (art print): "Osceola of Florida. Drawn on stone by George Catlin from his Original Portrait. New York. 1838". (Filed print in Library of Congress dated February 27, 1838). Litho. printed in black, 26⅜" x 19 13/16".

6A. *SAME.* "Engraved by I. Sartain. Printed by I. Sartain. New York. 1838. 8¾" x 7½".

1840

7. *Catalogue: A Descriptive Catalogue of Catlin's Indian Gallery: containing Portraits, Landscapes, Costumes,* etc. . . Exhibited at the Egyptian Hall, Piccadilly, London . . . C. Adlard, 1840. 47 p., 21 x 16½ cm. Complete re-arrangement and re-numbering of paintings, re-printed several times.

1841

8. *Letters and Notes on the Manners, Customs, and Condition of the North American Indians,* by Geo. Catlin. Written during eight years' travel amongst the wildest tribes of Indians in North America in 1832 . . . and '39. In Two Volumes, with four hundred illustrations, carefully engraved from his original paintings . . . Published by the Author, at the Egyptian Hall, Piccadilly. Printed by Tosswill and Myers 24 Budge Row. 1841. Vol. I: front illus. untitled; errata slip; iii–viii; folded map; and p. 1–264; individual black-line illus. only numbered; plates signed "G. Catlin" (left) and "Tosswill & Myers, sc" (right). Vol. II, iii–viii; map; p. 1–256; Appendix p. 257–266. 25½ cm.

8A. *SAME:* New York: Wiley and Putnam, 161 Broadway, 1841. "Copyrighted—District of Massachusetts . . . 17th May 1841. Royal Octavo, with 400 Illustrations". 25½ cm. (First American edition).

This is Catlin's most important work. There are numerous reprints and subsequent editions. Some subsequent editions bear the original title page and date 1841. To establish a correct and definitive bibliography is extremely difficult if not impossible. Some of the most important editions are listed hereafter:

8B. 1841. *SAME:* Published for the Author by David Bogue, Fleet Street. (London).

8C. 1841. *SAME:* Title: *Illustrations of the Manners, Customs and Condition of the North American Indians . . .* London: Henry G. Bohn, York Street, Covent Garden (London) 1841. 26 cm.

8D. 1841. *SAME:* Published by Chatto & Windus, London. Colored front and colored plates.

Index